Ndè Sìì Wet'aʔà

Ndè Sìì Wet'aɂà[1]

Northern Indigenous Voices on Land, Life, and Art

Edited by Kyla LeSage, Thumlee Drybones-Foliot, & Leanne Betasamosake Simpson

Dechinta Centre for Research and Learning
Yellowknife, NWT

ARP Books | Winnipeg

1   The Land is very important.

ARP Books (Arbeiter Ring Publishing)
205-70 Arthur Street
Winnipeg, Manitoba
Treaty 1 Territory and Historic Métis Nation Homeland
Canada R3B 1G7
arpbooks.org

Cover artwork by Lianne Marie Leda Charlie.
Cover design by Bret Parenteau and interior layout by Relish New Brand Experience.
Printed and bound in Canada by Imprimerie Gauvin.

ARP Books acknowledges the generous support of the Manitoba Arts Council and the
Canada Council for the Arts for our publishing program. We acknowledge the financial
support of the Government of Canada and the Province of Manitoba through the
Book Publishing Tax Credit and the Book Publisher Marketing Assistance Program of
Manitoba Culture, Heritage, and Tourism.

Library and Archives Canada Cataloguing in Publication

Title: Ndè sìi wet'aʔà : northern Indigenous voices on land, life, and art / edited by Kyla
    LeSage, Thumlee Drybones-Foliot, & Leanne Betasamosake Simpson.
Other titles: Land is very important
Names: LeSage, Kyla, editor. | Drybones-Foliot, Thumlee, editor. | Simpson, Leanne
    Betasamosake, 1971- editor.
Identifiers: Canadiana (print) 20220149232 | Canadiana (ebook) 20220149356 | ISBN
    9781927886625 (softcover) | ISBN 9781927886632 (ebook)
Subjects: CSH: Indigenous literature (English)—Canada, Northern. | CSH: Indigenous
    artists—Canada, Northern—Interviews.| LCSH: Indigenous authors—Canada,
    Northern—Interviews. | LCSH: Indigenous peoples—Canada, Northern—
    Interviews. | LCSH: Indigenous peoples—Canada, Northern. | LCSH: Indigenous
    peoples—Canada, Northern—Social life and customs. | LCGFT: Literature. |
    LCGFT: Interviews.
Classification: LCC PS8235.I6 N34 2022 | DDC C810.8/08970719—dc23

To James Sangris, our beloved bush professor. For all of your stories, your teachings, your kindness and for gently passing along your love of the land to us. You always saw how hard we tried. Mahsì Cho. We miss you.

Contents

Mahsì Cho!

Mahsì | Mársı | Máhsı | Hą̀į' | Quana | ᖁᔭᓈᒥᒃ (Qujannamiik) | Quyanainni | Kinanāskomitin| Miigwech

The editorial team would like to thank the very amazing executive director of the Dechinta Centre for Research and Learning, Kelsey Wrightson, for her endless support and encouragement throughout the project. Mahsì Cho to Mary Rose Sundberg for help with the title, various translations and her editorial contributions. We would also like to thank Morgan Tsetta for filming some of the interviews and Sydney Krill for transcription of the interviews. Thank you to *Briarpatch Magazine* and *Up Here Magazine* for previously publishing pieces by Chloe Dragon Smith and Robert Grandjambe, Leela Gilday, and Katłįà Lafferty and for giving their permission to reprint here. Thank you to *Canadian Art* for previously publishing the piece by Tiffany Ayalik and Niillas Holmberg. Thank you to The Centre for Expanded Poetics and Anteism Books for the reprint of Tanya Lukin Linklater's poems, excerpted from her book *Slow Scrape*. "Caribou People" by Siku Allooloo was originally published in the *Malahat Review*'s Indigenous Perspectives Issue (2018), and in *Shapes of Native Nonfiction: Collected Essays by Contemporary Writers* (University of Washington Press, 2019). A special thanks to Lianne Marie Leda Charlie who created the perfect visual representation of the book in her cover art. Mahsì Cho to all the first-time writers that attended our writing workshops and trusted us with your work, and mahsì to the amazing musicians, artists, storytellers, Elders, alumni, and language speakers that supported us throughout this project. Mahsì Cho to all of our friends at ARP Books, especially Irene Bindi who supported us every step of the way. Thanks to Rena Mainville for proofreading.

Ndè Sìì Wet'aʔà

Kyla LeSage, Thumlee Drybones-Foliot,
and Leanne Betasamosake Simpson

For the past decade, the Dechinta Centre for Research and Learning has engaged in land-based community-led Indigenous arts and educational programming in the Northwest Territories and Yukon. Our programs are grown from relationships with community land-based practitioners and Elders and we strive to centre the voices, knowledge, expertise, and perspective of Indigenous Peoples in the North. In our post-secondary, university accredited programming, we've often pulled together reading packages from books, websites, magazines, blogs, and journals to provide our students with relevant course material centring the voices and experiences of Indigenous northerners. But we wanted to do more. We wanted to bring the immense beauty and rigour of northern Indigenous storytellers, writers, practitioners, artists, academics, and thinkers, not only to our students, but to a wider audience. To this end, Kyla LeSage, Thumlee Drybones-Foliot, and Leanne Betasamosake Simpson came together as part of a larger Dechinta community to edit this anthology. Kyla is Vuntut Gwitchin and Anishinaabe from Garden River, Ontario. She is a past Dechinta alumni and the current Land Based Academic Coordinator and Regional Outreach Coordinator. Thumlee is Dënesųłiné from Yellowknives Dene First Nation and is also a Dechinta alumni. Leanne is Nishnaabe, a long-time instructor in our land-based programming and a member of our board.

As an editorial collective—educators, land-based practitioners, and of course readers—we are deeply appreciative of the Elders, language speakers, and oral storytellers that have given so much to our peoples and our students. We are also grateful to the northern Indigenous writers we've used in our past courses—George Blondin, Morris Neyelle,

Siku Allooloo, Phoebe Nahanni, T'áncháy Redvers, Richard Van Camp, Katłįà Lafferty, Glen Coulthard, Lianne Marie Leda Charlie, Sheila Watt-Cloutier, Reneltta Arluk, and Tanya Tagaq, to name just a few. We are also grateful to the many storytellers and oral historians that have shared their wisdom with our students through story and practice—Fred Sangris, Mary Rose Sundberg, Paul McKenzie, Madeline Judas, Alice Wifladt, Frederick Andrew, Sam Gargan, Norman Sterriah and Grady Sterriah, again to name just a few. It has been an honour to witness northern Indigenous students connecting to these storytellers and practitioners and seeing their own lives and experiences reflected back to them on the page. In many ways, this work has uplifted our students and inspired them to find their own voices, and we are so very proud to include over ten Dechinta alumni in this book project.

We were also committed to reaching out beyond our Dechinta community in this project to include pieces from emerging Indigenous writers from across the Yukon, Northwest Territories, Nunavut, Nunavik, Alaska, Northern British Columbia, and Alberta. We wanted to hold up the voices of Indigenous women and Two-Spirit and Queer writers. We wanted to curate a choir of voices reflecting a deep love of Indigenous cultures, languages, homelands, and the North. We wanted to include oral historians, language experts, and land-based practitioners. We wanted readers to be transformed by the power of Inuit women writing, singing, creating and challenging.

To this end, we posted an open call for submissions on social media, and we were generously met with a wealth of Dene (Gwich'in, Sahtú, Dehcho, Tłįchǫ, Sayisi, Kaska, Dënesųłiné, Wıìlıìdeh) Inuit, Alutiiq, Inuvialuit, Métis, Nêhiyawak (Cree), Northern Tutchone, and Tanana Athabascan creative brilliance. We reached out to artists, musicians, language experts, and knowledge holders in the form of interviews and conversations to bring as many stories as possible into the book.

Some very strong themes quickly emerged from reading the submissions. Writers wrote passionately about family, land, culture, community, and language. Language expert and contributor Mary Rose (Maro) Sundberg encouraged us to include as many northern languages as we could, and because of the oral nature of these languages, we have left spellings up to individual authors. Writers like Antoine Mountain, Katłįà Lafferty, Angela Code, and Joshua Barichello, along with Maro's song writing in "Dene Laws" with Leela Gilday which is the first piece in the book, brought this richness to the text.

We then commissioned a series of pieces from northern Indigenous artists—singer-songwriter Leela Gilday teaches us about Dene music in her piece "The Song We All Should Be Listening To." Randy Baillargeon tells the phenomenal story of how he became lead singer for the Wı̀ı̀lı̀ı̀deh Drummers. Inuit sisters, songwriters, and throat singers Tiffany Ayalik and Inuksuk Mackay of PIQSIQ, brought the power of Inuit women through their interview and discussion of performance, artistic practice, and resistance in Canada and beyond. Two-Spirit Vuntut Gwitchin visual artist Jeneen Frei Njootli talks snowmobiles, frequency, mosquitoes, and their community-immersed artistic practice. Inuk singer-songwriter and documentary filmmaker Elisapie discusses the work her films, videos, and albums do in the North and beyond, and singer-songwriter Beatrice Deer discusses the northern Inuit roots of her song writing. In "ᐅᐸᒡ/ūdzi," Angela Code takes us inside Dene hand games to reveal the cultural work these gatherings do in the North. Visual artist and academic Camille Georgeson-Usher writes about connection and belonging in a letter to our damaged earth.

In addition to pieces by poets Tanya Lukin Linklater and Dian Million, poet T'áncháy Redvers's prose are in constant conversation with the land in "Re-membering, re-naming and re-connecting." Their sibling Juniper, tells us a story of a solo winter journey back to their ancestral homeland. Chloe Dragon Smith has an intimate conversation with her Mom Brenda Dragon about parenting, and with Robert Grandjambe in "To Wood Buffalo National Park with Love" the pair write back against the legacy of power and control of Parks Canada yields towards lands and peoples once again living within the Park in deep reciprocity. Land-based practitioner and educator Noel-Leigh Cockney shares with us his family's deep connection to their Inuvialuit homeland on the Arctic Ocean. In "Golǫdhé," Kristen Tanche tells us her precious story of tanning her first moose hide. It is a story of love, connection, and beautiful Dehcho Dene resistance. Siku Allooloo's poem "Star Path" is set partially in Nío Nę P'ęnę́, where we held the 2019 Dechinta Summer Semester, and grounded in the healing gifted from both that land and her home community in Denendeh.

One part of the book we hold very dear to our hearts are the pieces by Dechinta alumni and emerging writers. Our students and staff come from incredibly rich oral storytelling and artistic cultures rooted in land-based practice. As a result, we had the honour of reading first-time writers express their love of land, culture, and language in our assignments. We are grateful so many of them participated in our writer's workshops and submitted pieces to this book. The brilliance of northern Indigenous young writers dances off these pages with love letters to water, land, grandparents, and siblings. These are stories of adventures on the land, persistence, connection, and a beautiful sense of belonging. We are grateful for your trust in us as editors, Coleen, Jasmine, Jessica, Taylor, Tyra, and Rachel, and we can't wait to read more.

The process of making this book has been one of profound listening. When we began the project, we were unsure if anyone would submit to the project and our backup plan was to gather previously published work as a more robust reading package to use in our courses. Thumlee and Kyla reached out to so many young writers on social media, encouraging them and supporting them in getting their pieces in. Leanne reached out to established writers and artists to figure out ways of including a diverse set of voices in book form. The writers themselves, through the topics and experiences they chose to focus on and share, defined the thematic scope of the book, and our job became one of holding space, encouraging, and curating rather than directing. In that sense, this book was built from the ground up. It was a communal affair. It was a northern affair, born out of thousands of years of storytelling with the aim of nourishing thousands of more years of northern Indigenous storytelling. Our hope is that these words nurture these writers and their families and their communities. Our hope is that this anthology is not an ending, but the beginning of a listening across geographies, cultures, and time. Our hope is that these writers feed our collective fires.

Gonàowo

Mary Rose Sundberg & Leela Gilday

Gonàowo, Gonàowo, Gonàowo

Ełeghàts'edı, Ełets'àts'edì

Ełeghǫnets'etǫ, Ełeghǫnets'etǫ

Gonàowo, Gonàowo, Gonàowo

Goʔǫhdaà/Ǫhndaà wenaets'eet'ı̨ Ełenàts'eèt'ı̨

Dzę̀ę̀ eghàlats'eda toò ts'eteè

Gonàowo, Gonàowo, Gonàowo

Ełek'ech'à gots'ede-le

Dǫzhìa t'eka nezı̨ edek'egendì

Gonàowo, Gonàowo, Gonàowo

Ełeghàłets'etǫ

Ats'ǫ naxınà/ats'ǫ sègòet'ı̨ı̨

Gonàowo, Gonàowo, Gonàowo

Caribou People[2]

Siku Allooloo

Tuktu glow

It was Christmas break in Yellowknife, and we were celebrating. We were three Inuit women of three generations: my cousin, whose family had been relocated from our home community of Pond Inlet by the Royal Canadian Mounted Police (RCMP), was one of the last to attend a Residential School; her friend, like my Father, was one of the last to be born and raised on the land; and me, one of the first raised outside of Nunavut and not in Residential School. Like others, our lives were each threaded with an array of colonial trauma, though that evening all of this was furthest from our minds. For this brief, unexpected moment we transcended everything.

My cousin had lovingly roasted a large, beautiful piece of caribou just for us, so we sat around it with great joy. We cut pieces off with a knife and brought it to our mouths with our fingers. Tuktu was getting harder to come by and this was my first in a long time. I chewed and the meat felt insatiably delicious in my teeth. They clenched and grinded each bite with pleasure as the flavour I was raised on dilated my every cell and brought my whole being forward to intoxicating focus. In a breath of sudden self-consciousness, I looked up at the other two women and saw they were already in deep, their eyes downturned and far away as they savoured each mouthful. Without hesitating, I took another large bite. The pull carried us to an innate world. Somewhere primal, dark. Endless. Like a full moon in winter, eternity blowing in the wind across the blackness of the night. An ancient existence. A womb.

2   "Caribou People" was originally published in the *Malahat Review's* Indigenous Perspectives Issue (2018). It was republished in *Shapes of Native Nonfiction: Collected Essays by Contemporary Writers* (University of Washington Press, 2019).

When we came back into the room, forty-five minutes had passed. Not a word had been spoken. The meat was all gone. We looked at each other.

"Holy fuck," my cousin finally said, and we all broke into laughter. "Look at us, three Inuit women, eating tuktu! What our people have eaten for thousands of years. It's so deep in our dna that it just took us back."

We were still glowing.

"They were so incredibly tough.... To survive out there on their own. In the freezing cold, with only animal skins and snow houses. Travelling in the dark, no sun for months. Giving birth. Hunting for days, sometimes coming back with nothing.... And her, she was raised like that!" my cousin said, pointing to her friend beside me. "When all the children were being taken away, her grandmother packed her in a qamutiik and took her out into the cold. She built them an igloo and they lived there together for as long as they could, until eventually they had to go back.... Isn't that amazing?"

Memory of stars

The enormous Bathurst caribou herd used to pass by my hometown of Yellowknife in the early winter when I was growing up. I remember my Mom taking my little brother and me out to see them in 1992, just after she and our Father split up. I was six years old; my little brother was not yet four. She was a newly single Mother of four and our rock. It seemed at that time our world would be forever cast in grey, punctuated by incomprehensible heartache and confusion. *How was it possible to lose half of ourselves?* Something inside I wasn't aware of before felt exposed in its brokenness. The form I had been, that contained me, now a mess of shattered pieces. I wondered how it was possible to exist. *Was this really our life now, forever?*

She told us we were going to see something amazing as she drove out along the Ingraham Trail, a road we knew well and were fond of, as it was the way to our cabin. Halfway there, we came upon several vehicles parked along the side of the road, at Pontoon Lake. She pulled over into an open spot and turned off the ignition. We stepped out onto the ground, a bit bewildered. We had never stopped here before or seen so many people along this quiet dirt road. Rifles fired in the distance, the sharp cracks slightly dulled and resounding across the treetops below us. The air was charged with excitement, glimmering on the faces of people buzzing by.

The three of us walked down from the road into the bush, through fresh fallen snow. We kept forward through the pines, birch, and willows. Not too long and we could see through the trees a few caribou on the edge of the clearing. Like magic. We continued on and our eyes filled with even wider amazement as we made our way to the shore. We nestled beneath the trees and watched in awe as hundreds of thousands of caribou crossed the frozen lake, just metres before us. A multitude of brown, grey, and white walking steadily ahead, their breath hanging in the air in frozen clouds, just like ours. I remember the snow on the lake, padded down by millions of hoof prints, and how special it felt to be so close to them, the three of us, like some miraculous dream. They remained calm and unhurried despite the presence of all who had come to see or hunt them. To this day, I have never seen anything so majestic.

They say the Bathurst herd was at least 350,000 strong that year. Difficult to imagine now, twenty-four years on, when they are down to a mere 15,000 (or less).

My Dad faded out of our lives in a similarly drastic fashion at that time, like a mirrored disappearance. We barely saw him. We would often come home to find fresh tuktu stashed outside, though—in the deep freeze or the shed—that he had dropped by for us, always while we were away. Like so many other families, we carried the fallout of all that colonial atrocity right through to our bones. But despite all the hard truths that can be said about my Dad and the impacts of colonial violence that ripple through our family, he always provided us with meat. In this way, he loved us and fulfilled part of his role the best way he knew how.

Years later, after our Mother's death, my little brother and I were adopted into an extended Dene family. I learned that the Dené Sųłıné word for barrenland caribou (of which the Bathurst is one herd) is etthën. It is the same word for 'star,' and as my stepfather put it, "perhaps because there were so many..." Exactly how it was that day, like watching a million ancient beings in the snow, their light spanning across an unfathomable distance.

Or, like two hind quarters appearing in the shed—a distant reminder of love, of family connection. A speck of light that made it through and kept us nourished.

"We sew it up"

People often speak of the North as a place of extremes and harsh realities: long, frozen winters, endless summer daylight, constant winter darkness, vast and all but uninhabited wilderness. As a northerner rooted in both Inuit and Dene cultures, the harshest extreme to me is how rapidly and far-reaching colonialism has set into our world.

Within the span of two lifetimes, my parents' and grandparents' generations have seen drastic changes both in our ways of life and our homelands. My Inuit grandparents went from freely travelling the land as our ancestors had always done to living in a permanent community. The RCMP forced Inuit into settlements in the 1950s in order to bring us under government control. They slaughtered our sled dogs so we were immobile and also split entire family groups apart, scattering us across different communities.

My Father was born in a sod house in 1949 and was raised to travel the land and provide for his family from a very young age. He can navigate using constellations and landmarks, make traditional tools, build shelter in any season, attend to injuries, and his intimate knowledge of our world makes him a very skilled hunter on both the land and the sea. At the age of eight years old, he was able to go out for the day alone and come back with a seal to feed the family. At eight years old is also when he was taken from his parents and sent to Residential School thousands of kilometres away, which he was lucky to have survived.

He was one of tens of thousands of children stolen from every Indigenous nation across the country by the Canadian government and forced into assimilation schools. They knew our entire societies stem from the land, which meant we would never give it up and that we would always protect it. So, for 150 years Canada stole all of our children—our heart, indeed our future—and sought to break them of our ways and collapse our societies in the process. Many of these children suffered unthinkable atrocities during their time at these schools, and thousands never made it home to our families. It is a devastating and recent history, with the last schools finally closing in 1996, and Indigenous Peoples throughout the country are still working through the debilitating repercussions that persist in our lives.

The desire to dominate and exploit peoples and lands in order to create wealth—this is the driving force of colonialism and also the lifeblood of this country. If there is any hope of recuperating a sense of humanity, or of surviving the climate crisis that is rapidly intensifying throughout the world, we need to engage the reality of everything we are up against. The stakes are too high.

It is no exaggeration to say that Canada is built on racism, genocide, violence, and theft. The founding and daily maintenance of this colony depends expressly on the domination of Indigenous Peoples through the illegal seizure and occupation of our territories, colonial laws and policies, police brutality, excessive incarceration, economic marginalization, gender violence, child apprehension, and the suppression of our governance systems, spiritual practices, and ancestral ways of life—all of which remain deeply rooted in our lands.

Canada is sustained by a resource-based economy—if there is any doubt as to the racism and brutality this necessitates every day, just consider: where do the resources come from and how are they obtained—are they not violently torn from the earth? And are those sites of extraction not integral parts of Indigenous homelands or crucial to animal and plant life? Why is it that most Indigenous Peoples are living in extremely impoverished conditions on reserves, in remote communities, and in urban centres, whereas the resources stripped from our lands generate massive amounts of wealth for governments and corporations? Is this country not home to the tar sands, one of the biggest and most destructive industrial operations on the planet?[3] How many of our territories and water systems have been contaminated by hydroelectric dams, oil, gas, and toxic waste and how many lives are being lost to new cancers as a result every year? How many community members have been harmed or arrested for protecting their homelands from pipelines and mining operations? What recourse do we have to the distinct rise in gender violence and narcotics that come with intensified mining in our communities?

Treaties 8 and 11 grant permission for settlers to coexist on our lands and were contingent upon certain terms, including mutual autonomy, self-governance, and the provision of health care—but how many of our men, women, Elders and youth continually suffer violence at the hands of police officers or are denied adequate care by health providers?

3   Christopher Hatch and Matt Price, *Canada's Toxic Tar Sands: The Most Destructive Project on Earth*, February 2008, https://environmentaldefence.ca/report/report-canadas-toxic-tar-sands-the-most-destructive-project-on-earth/.

These treaties were also meant to ensure that Indigenous ways of life would continue despite the presence of settlers—meaning that all of the elements that sustain life on the land would remain protected—so that our people could continue to live according to our ancestral ways forever.

Due to ongoing colonial policies, industrial exploitation, and now climate change, places where we used to be able to harvest food or medicines, drink the water, and inhabit alongside other forms of life are being turned into wastelands.

My hometown of Yellowknife was built for gold mining in 1934 and became home to one of the richest gold mines in Canadian history. Giant Mine sits on the shore of Great Slave Lake, one of the largest fresh water sources on the planet. Though the mine closed in 2004 its toxic repercussions will last forever: the deteriorating site rests upon 237,000 tonnes of arsenic trioxide,[4] a lethal byproduct of gold mining that is impossible to remediate or prevent from leaking into the surrounding lakes and atmosphere, which it is doing at a disturbing rate. A study released in April 2016 showed mercury and arsenic levels to be dangerously high in lakes within a twenty-five–kilometre radius of Giant Mine: in some cases, over thirteen times the limit for drinking water and twenty-seven times the level deemed adequate for aquatic life.[5]

Canadians tend to romanticize the northern town for its remnants of a frontier history forged by sweat and gold as well as for its supposed "untouched, pristine wilderness"—but the truth is we can no longer drink the water or eat the fish in that area and now have to travel long distances to harvest foods and medicines. They say Giant Mine rests upon enough arsenic to kill the entire planet twice over—and though there have been several attempts over the years to contain the toxic waste, there has never been an adequate plan to protect the environment from contamination. For me, this is the clearest indication of Western society's single-minded focus on obtaining wealth at any expense. There is no contingency plan or thought of the future or respect for any form of

---

4   *Shadow of a Giant*, directed by Clark Ferguson, produced by Lesley Johnson and Clark Ferguson with Western Arctic Moving Pictures, written by Clark Ferguson and Lesley Johnson, 2015, https://vimeo.com/126623856.

5   Ivan Semeniuk, "Lakes near Yellowknife contaminated with arsenic, mercury years after mine closing," *The Globe and Mail*, April 6, 2016, https://www.theglobeandmail.com/news/national/yellowknife-lake-has-high-levels-of-arsenic-mercury-years-after-mine-closure/article29544969/.

life. The only drive is money—and this is true of any mining operation in the country, whether diamonds or oil and gas or gold.

Today, the beautiful, vast, wild landscape of Denendeh is riddled with large-scale mining operations that have destroyed numerous lakes and river ecosystems, as well as the migration and calving grounds of caribou—an essential source of sustenance for both Inuit and Dene alike since time immemorial. We are caribou people, and the widespread decline of this ancestral relation is a source of deepening loss across the North.

There are many stories of their generosity and benevolence, how they offer themselves in times of need. Dene and Inuit would not exist without the caribou: its hide has given us warmth and protection from the cold, its meat our main source of nourishment, its bones and antlers our tools, its skin stretched on drums that carry our songs and spiritual connection. It was the caribou who taught us how to honour our kinship and practice ways that sustain us both. A growing anxiety throughout our communities is: *What happens when there are no more caribou? Are we still caribou people? If we can no longer practise our culture in all of the ways that depend on the caribou, are we still Dene or Inuit?*

Protecting the caribou was once a major rallying point for northerners. It's what galvanized us to stand strong against the Mackenzie Valley Pipeline and assimilative government policies in the 1970s and also work toward self-determination. Since then both the caribou population and our anticolonial nerve have been in steep decline. We have veered quite far from the unified vision we once fought hard for to ensure that our homelands would remain grounded in Indigenous principles, values, and ways of life well into the future.

Last spring, I spent some time with a very knowledgeable and beloved Elder, Ethel Lamothe. We were at the Dechinta Centre for Research and Learning—a northern organization based outside of Yellowknife that delivers Indigenous education on the land and one of the saving graces in my own educational journey. I was helping her scrape her moose hide in preparation for tanning, and as our hands worked we talked about womanhood, spirituality, and bush medicines. She told me about the work she and others did in previous decades to advance decolonization, social transformation, and healing in Denendeh, and also shared insight about the challenges. I had been troubled lately about the gap between Elders and young people, the cultural inheritance being lost, the growing alienation I see in current generations, and the complexity of overcoming all these challenges when we are starting from such fragmentation. At one point Ethel stopped and said: "Our society is full of holes now, like the ones in this hide. So we have to sew them up. Where there's a hole there instead of a Mother or a Father, an aunty or grandparent steps in to raise the kids. We have holes in our spirituality and culture, how we relate to each other and deal with things, so we have to find ways to relearn that. You know, we lost some of our own ceremonies and ways of praying but we can learn from other cultures who still have it. You don't have any grandmothers to teach what you need to know as a woman so you adopt a new grandmother who can teach you. So we do it like that. We sew it up."

The Elders kept heart
In 2015, I led a project with Elders and youth on the land near Fort Smith to study how climate change impacts ancestral foods and ways of life. The changes are drastic: massive declines in animal and plant populations, erratic weather, disrupted seasonal patterns, diminishing quality of snow and ice, disappearing sources of fresh water. The land is growing more dangerous to travel. People are having to go farther to search for food, medicine, and materials, and everything is less abundant. Etthën, for example, have not passed through this territory in over fifty years.

It is very difficult to face the extent of these changes, to realize how much everything our cultures depend on is bearing the brunt of climate change and industrial development, the same way we as Indigenous Peoples are bearing the brunt of colonialism in our everyday lives. It was especially difficult for the youth, whose entry point to their culture and territory came with the disappointment of realizing how much is being lost. The Elders kept heart. They stressed the importance of survival skills, encouraging us to become self-sufficient and adaptive on the land—the same way our peoples have always had to be. They said that though we are unable to stop the changes, we must continue on and not be afraid.

Beautiful; wise Ethel also taught me to cut upwards when harvesting plants for medicine. "Because life goes *up*!" The same way my brothers honour their kill by setting its ears in the direction it was headed so its spirit can go forward. Everything is done with respect to the natural flow and continuation of life, even when taking life, because we exist as a continuum. The essence that we come from will always carry through us and beyond us.

Though the birds no longer black out the sky as they migrate and the fish no longer teem and the river no longer breaks up in a thunderous crash of six-foot-thick sheets of ice, the Elders remain in close connection to the land as it is now; they continue to live in our ways despite unprecedented changes and endlessly destructive forces. They lead us younger ones to fortify from within, from the richness our cultures, from the sources that strengthen, connect, heal, and affirm. An understanding of how potent our lifeways remain begins to emerge—lifeways meaning ways of life we belong to and also ways that give life. Those old ones knew it was always about both.

So when we experience something that breaks through the haze, like eating caribou meat or spending time on the land, we meet a profound and undeniable truth: that our ancestral connection is alive, embodied, and easily reawakened.

Re-membering, re-claiming, re-connecting

T'áncháy Redvers

Disconnection

As a child I was lucky enough to be raised in the North, among the birch trees that sheltered our family cabin along the river, within the bushes of cranberries and raspberries that populated my Mother's First Nation, and beside fires that roasted the wild game and fish my Father would harvest. As a Dene and Métis girl I was a child of the land. Even though I didn't recognize it at the time, I was taught the beauty of connection, and the reciprocal power of my relationship with the physical world. Through picking wild mint and watching my Dad clean trout, I learned to only take from the land what I needed and to return to it what I didn't. I learned that in giving love, offerings, and thanks to the land, I would receive love and offerings in return. The land and I held each other as I rolled up in blankets on cold winter nights in order to draw shapes in the stars and sat quietly in the willows in order to listen to the sounds of beavers working or geese flying above. I had so much respect for the stories the land told and love it gave.

The land is inherent to Dene culture. In fact, there is no culture without the land. When I think of my ancestors, I think of grandmas sitting by lake's edge weaving sinew through birch bark baskets with their tanned hands as children splash, laughing out loud in the water and aunties and uncles hang dryfish above the fire, enjoying each other's company. One uncle would make fun of the other uncle about how poorly he filleted the whitefish, auntie would be telling her niece about the good-looking trapper a camp over, and grandbaby would be sitting in grandma's lap as grandma, with her arms hugged around, would show her how to thread the sinew. Everyone was connected to each other—physically, emotionally, mentally, spiritually—and grounded and rooted in the love and respect of the land.

land loves

unconditionally,

wholly,

offering truth and awareness

of one's own self

and breeding reciprocal

connection

I was lucky enough to be raised in the North and build connection to my ancestral land. However, there was a large thread of disconnection that, as I grew older, began to weave itself stronger and stronger into my life. Unlike my ancestors—who were wholly and unconditionally rooted in and connected to cultural being through language, traditional practices, ceremonies, and kinship structures—my family was not. My grandmother was raised in a Residential School, my Mother attended Residential School, and therefore I am an intergenerational Residential School survivor. As a result of this, I did not learn my language and my spiritual understanding was often confused with Roman Catholicism. In fact, time on the land growing up was solace—a safe haven away from the day-to-day reality of homelife in town, which was often instable, chaotic, and at times pretty scary. The reciprocal and unconditional love, respect, and connection I learned from the land was not always reflected in my family life. Instead, I was receiving, learning, and internalizing shame, trauma, and emotional abuse. And because connection is reciprocal, these were things that began to be reciprocated.

Life away from the land was full of teachings that collided with the ones the land offered, and in moving to the city from my hometown, I no longer had the safe haven reminder of unconditional love, respect, and connection. I become almost utterly disconnected from the land and instead caught up in the whirlwind of colonial reality. Through bullying, abusive relationships, family trauma, and alcohol, I became lost and jaded. I succumbed to colonial expectations of self-worth, appeasement, and success, and before I knew it, I wanted nothing more than to run away from the North, the place that had once offered me so much. So that is exactly what I did.

In losing connection to the stories, teachings, and beauty of the land, I lost connection to myself and my body. I carried trauma in my blood, shame in my heart, and the abuse I had experienced on my back. I suffered severe self-esteem and self-worth issues, I reciprocated the unhealthy behaviours I had learned in various relationships, and I desperately searched and searched for validation in others in what became a vicious cycle of giving myself to others in hopes I would find something in return.

this body

is a shell

empty, lost, broken

i can give you what

you want

if that's what it takes

to feel whole

Belonging

The first time I attended a women's drum circle, the moment my stick hit the drum in unison with the others, I started to cry. In that one beat, I felt like I had come home—I was wandering aimlessly through the dark night only to stumble across a warm cabin on the river. I felt the skin of the animal stretched over the wooden rim and thought about how it had gifted itself so that others could beat it, singing proud. I was told that the beat of the drum was the heartbeat of Mother Earth, beating in unison with my own heartbeat, as if we were one. I felt the connection to my homelands, even though I was thousands of kilometres away in a big city.

The first time I did a burlesque class, the moment the music started and we were motioned to touch our neck, hips, thighs, I felt uncomfortable and I felt joy—I felt an uncomfortable joy. Everything in my head was telling me that it was wrong and that I should not be doing this, let alone enjoying this. Unlike the first time I had hit the drum and felt at home, the welcome of home when I touched my own body was less obvious, less welcoming, but nonetheless present.

The trauma, shame, abuse, and ultimately disconnection I felt throughout my adolescence had implanted itself into my bones and skin. As a young Dene woman, I was entrenched in a world that normalized the disconnection to myself. The same world that displaced me from the land I had grown up on, had enforced a belief that I was not worthy and that I was powerless. My growth into womanhood was intertwined with the toxic narratives that surrounded me. Indigenous women were dispensable and weak. They were stereotyped and wrongly sexualized—costumes to be worn on Halloween; addicts and unfit mothers who couldn't raise their own children; objects to be abused, raped, and assaulted. There were constant nameless headlines; they were missing and murdered—never worthy of being found nor their murderers brought to justice. They were always less than—ploys of the colonizer used to enforce paternalistic gendered roles. They were never beautiful or good enough to be on TV or in magazines. They were victims. So, to explore my sexuality and sensuality on my own terms, to feel joy in my own skin, to feel beautiful and in control, felt strange. Much like women drummers are seen as unwelcome in many communities and not tradition (as a result of religious and state-led colonization), the autonomy of our own bodies and being is unwelcome.

Over time, the experience of feeling and beating the skin of that drum became the same as enjoying the touch of my own. It reconnected me to my own homelands that are also being exploited, disrespected, used, and abused. Colonization and Residential Schools stole the respect of Indigenous land and women while demonizing self and community love, pleasure, and joy. As a Dene woman, I am the land. In pursuing burlesque as a performer, I am re-membering my connection to myself, and thus the land. I am conjuring up the teachings of respect and reciprocity I once learned. I am re-learning unconditional love for the wounds and imperfections that stretch their way across my body, my home beyond my homelands. For me, re-claiming, re-membering, and re-connecting to my body is just as cultural as re-claiming, re-membering, and re-connecting with the land. It is ceremonial.

Before traders and missionaries came to my homelands of Denendeh, the Dene had strong medicine power. Their medicine gifts came from the land—the animals, plant life, natural elements—and with them they survived, healed, and received songs and teachings. Strong medicine people would also use their medicine to ward off and rid of bad medicine that threatened to harm, weaken, or kill them and their kin. I have come to believe burlesque to be a medicine power—a reclamation and remembrance of the power that once was. As Midnight Wolverine—a strong, Indigenous, Two-Spirit being—my medicine is to ward off and rid of the bad medicine: the colonial patriarchy that continues to silence, abuse, and murder Indigenous land, women, and Two-Spirit beings. By actively taking the control of my own body back, I am recreating the narrative that Indigenous women are powerful. By practising the same unconditional love, respect, and reciprocity with myself as I do with the land, I am restoring these traditional and cultural values. In celebrating myself in front of others, I am resisting and challenging the theft of pleasure and joy. I am bringing community together, re-instilling the collective belief that Indigenous women are beautiful and worthy beings to be loved, respected, and celebrated.

my hand caresses

skin, worked and stretched

making sounds

connection

with her, Earth

she is beauty, power, love

resistance to all that

doubt her,

attempt to destroy her

i will never be made to feel

shame for her, again

she offers me so much.

Journeying home across Tu Nedhé

Juniper Redvers

At some point, my grandmother, she talked a lot. She told lots of stories about the Land, the life of the Land. She spoke to me one time; I might have been about thirteen, I guess, and she'd talk about how we were from the Land. We were the Land, not from it, but we were the Land. That I was the earth, and I was the fire, and I was the water, and I was the air, right, and all of them were things that contributed to give me life. And so, without any one of them I would not be able to exist. And she spoke to me, she said once that, "A long time ago everybody used to speak the same language." And at the time I thought she meant English, right. Later in my life I realized it wasn't a spoken language, it was a spirit language really that she was talking about. And when she said 'everybody' she meant every living thing. And one of the things she said was, "We are the only ones who don't know the language anymore." That we didn't speak it, but everything else still did speak it.

And so, it kind of stuck with me that. And I always had a relationship with the Land pre-camp days; I would, I understood it, I know that I didn't really fully remember. I believe that is a cellular thing that is going on; I am my grandmother's breath. It is in my DNA and in my bloodline. I always had this idea. Even just sitting somewhere in Vancouver, downtown Vancouver, the little sparrow that hops around underneath your feet at Starbucks, I always made connections with it, with the

plants and with the animals. I certainly attribute lots of that
to my grandmother's life, lots of it. It was inside of me already.

Phillip Gatensby, Tlingit Peacemaker[6]

I was six when my grandmother Judith Sanderson passed over into Spirit world. There she would rejoin her parents Johnny Benaya, who was Denesųłıne and a member of Yellowknives Dene, and Sophie Kits'indla, who is thought to be Tłįchǫ, as my ancestors. It wasn't until I was older that I learned more about my grandmother's life in the context of the confusing world in which I grew up. I remember her as strong, kind, and bush savvy. She was a skilled moccasin maker, always keeping my Dene feet warm as I grew. I remember the smell of singed duck before putting my spoon into a warm bowl of her famous duck soup and crunching into her delicious dry meat smeared with hunks of greasy lard. Her first language was Denesųłıne, which she and my grandpa still spoke when I was young. My first felt memory is being rocked by her in a Dene cradle swing. She was born a Benaya at her family's fish camp on Benaya Island, just southeast from what we now call Yellowknife. It was close to Cabin Island where our family lived in a small traditional settlement with other families from the Yellowknives Dene Nation, similar to other settlements spread right across the north shore of Tu Nedhé (the 'large lake,' also called Great Slave Lake).[7]

During a particularly dark and personally challenging Yellowknife winter, I worked as a health researcher on a project looking at suicide prevention within the context of the circumpolar north[8]. During this time, I found myself fighting chronic illness and struggling for answers about my own history and sense of identity. I realized that Cabin Island

6   Phillip Gatensby's Tlingit name is [oral only]. He is from the Kùkhhittàn clan, which is the Raven Clan, and is the grandchild of the Yen yèdí which is the grizzly bear people. He is an advocate, a Father, a holder of ceremony and traditional teachings, and a cultural counsellor and teacher. I interviewed him in a truck stop café on the Klondike Highway. Quote from J.M. Redvers, "Land-based Practice for Indigenous Health and Wellness in the Yukon, Nunavut, and the Northwest Territories" (unpublished master's thesis, University of Calgary, 2016), 64, http://theses.ucalgary.ca/handle/11023/2996.

7   Fred Sangris, Personal Communication, March 15, 2017.

8   Jennifer Redvers, Peter Bjerregaard, Heidi Eriksen, Sahar Fanian, Gwen Healey, Vanessa Hiratsuka, Michael Jong, Christina Viskum Lytken Larsen, Janice Linton, Nathaniel Pollock, Anne Silviken, Petter Stoor, and Susan Chatwood, "A scoping review of Indigenous suicide prevention in circumpolar regions," *International Journal of Circumpolar Health*, 74:1 (2015), https://doi.org/10.3402/ijch.v74.27509.

represented a dramatic turning point in my family's relationship to a life deeply connected to land, family, community, and language. Influenza had spread rapidly through the North in 1928 and both my great grandparents died, leaving six children of varying ages orphaned along the shore of Tu Nedhé. My grandma was only five years old when her and three of her sisters were consequently sent to the Catholic mission Residential School in Fort Resolution (home of the Deninu Kų́ę First Nation, which I am now a member of). This is where she would remain until age sixteen, in the "care" of priests and nuns full time. Eventually she was married off by the nuns to my dear Denesųłıne-Métis bushman grandpa George. It was at the mission school where the darkness crept in from the missionaries. I am told by my parents that my grandma would not talk about her years at this "school."

When reading the section in the Final Report of the Truth and Reconciliation Commission titled "Resistance,"[9] I was very inspired by the following quote about this school, showing that despite the horror and external control forced upon us, our people had never given up resisting this darkness:

> One of the more unusual protests was mounted by First Nations people (Dene) in the Northwest Territories, who, in 1937, refused to accept their Treaty payments in protest of conditions at the Fort Resolution school. Their children, they said, were "living in hell."[10]

Feeling full of anger and sadness within the conflicted context of my own life and the intergenerational and life traumas that held onto me like a lead weight, I felt threatened with suffocation at any moment in the city. I found solace on my daily cross-country skis around Yellowknife as I studied our current suicide crisis among our youth. After reading too many infuriating archaic academic articles from Western researcher's perspectives on suicide, I remember finally finding some more recent

---

9   "Resistance: "I am the Father of this child." Parents and children developed a variety of strategies to resist residential schooling. Parents might refuse to enrol students, refuse to return runaways, or they might refuse to return students to school at the end of the summer holidays." Quote from The Truth and Reconciliation Commission of Canada, *Honouring the Truth, Reconciling for the Future: Summary of the Final Report of the Truth and Reconciliation Commission of Canada* (2015), p.114.

10   The Truth and Reconciliation Commission of Canada, *Honouring the Truth, Reconciling for the Future: Summary of the Final Report of the Truth and Reconciliation Commission of Canada* (2015), p.117.

articles on resilience, and Indigenous resilience in particular, which shifted my perspective and hope.[11]

Resilience, in ecology, refers to the ability of a forest or other natural system to *transform* and *adapt to catastrophe or drastic change.*[12] In psychology, resilience is the characteristics that allow a person to mentally, physically, and spiritually *thrive despite immense challenge and adversity.*[13] Indigenous conceptions include the land as a relational part of resilience in a holistic philosophy of health and well-being.[14]

It was in a state of being triggered by intergenerational trauma from the project I was leading, and struggling with my undiagnosed pain condition, that I was desperately seeking answers. I had to get out of the city. And in April of 2013 I decided I would journey to the island where my grandmother was born. With my drum and tobacco in hand, I planned to travel solo to the place where the land and language connection was disrupted in my family. In the early morning, I asked my Dad to drop me off with my skis in Yellowknife Bay, close to the start of the ice road to T'è?ehdaà (Dettah). I had borrowed a fancy Norwegian pulk from a friend and organized all of my camping gear the night before: axe, food, snowshoes, tarp, extra clothes, minus-thirty sleeping bag, GPS, first aid kit, and tent, along with other personal and cultural items. I loaded the pulk, slipped on the waist harness, and strapped on my worn cross-country skis. It was expected to be minus seven during the days, which was comfortable skiing weather. I soon pushed off into the April sunshine, skiing along the icy lake filled with frost heaves.

Hour after hour, I criss-crossed the melting ice road, slick and shiny. I followed Ski-Doo trails where possible, accompanied by melodic

11   Kirmayer, L., Sehdev, M., Whitley, R., Dandeneau, S. F., and Isaac, C., "Community Resilience: Models, Metaphors and Measures," *International Journal of Indigenous Health,* 5:1 (2009), 62-117, https://jps.library.utoronto.ca/index.php/ijih/article/view/28978/23910; M. Tousignant and N. Sioui, "Resilience & Aboriginal Communities In Crisis: Theory and Interventions," *International Journal of Indigenous Health,* 5:1 (2009), 43-61, https://jps.library.utoronto.ca/index.php/ijih/article/view/28977/23907.

12   B. Walker, C.S. Holling, S.R. Carpenter, and A. Kinzig, "Resilience, Adapability and Transformability in Social-ecological Systems," *Ecology and Society,* 9:2 (2004), 5-13, https://doi.org/10.5751/ES-00650-090205

13   L. Kirmayer, S.F. Dandeneau, E. Marshall, M.K. Phillips, K.J. and Williamson, K. J., "Rethinking Resilience from Indigenous Perspectives", *Canadian Journal of Psychiatry,* 56:2 (2011), 84-91, https://doi.org/10.1177/070674371105600203.

14   J.M. Redvers, "'The land is a healer': Perspectives on land-based healing from Indigenous practitioners in northern Canada," *International Journal of Indigenous Health,* 15:1(2020), 90-107, https://doi.org/10.32799/ijih.v15i1.34046.

ravens overhead. Pretty soon, the Ski-Doo tracks petered out and I was on my own, out of the narrow portion of Yellowknife Bay, well past T'èʔehdaà. I continued to slide further out toward the main part of the lake. The spring sun shone bright during the afternoon, and I stripped down layer by layer to a t-shirt as I pulled sixty to seventy pounds of gear behind me. I constantly slip-slided up the slightly softened peaks and zoomed down the icy crests of the bumpy lake ice as the pulk would catch up with me and push me from behind. One last snowmobile drove by, echoing its engine in the distance, and even the ravens had stayed closer to shore. At that point, it was just me and my thoughts. Me and my trauma, my troubled feelings, and my scattered, unclear memories of childhood that felt split apart like pieces of glass. I felt like I could never put the pieces of myself back together as I drifted across the endless, white, icy lake.

At the end of the first day, as the sun started to set and the cool winter air drifted in, I stopped on a little windswept island with a small group of spruce trees. I remember cooling off quickly as I stopped moving and unwrapped the tarp covering my sled to grab the tent I had loaded into my Dad's truck earlier that morning. But I could only find the poles. I had a moment of panic, realizing I had forgotten my tent in the rush to get going!

I quickly and purposefully reminded myself of my Dene ancestry and all the experience I had already amassed in the outdoors as a Park Warden, as a biology student in Patagonia, and as a remote canoe guide on northern rivers. I composed myself and got to work setting up a place to sleep for the night in a way I would like to think made my ancestors proud. I put my winter gear on, including my mukluks, made a fire, dug a tunnel in the snow for a bed, and started collecting as many spruce boughs as I could to lay under my body. It was hard work cutting and hauling the boughs. Then I continued with other camp tasks like boiling snow for water and chopping wood for the night and early morning. I never stopped moving even once as the temperature dropped quickly and the night set in. I ate some curried whitefish with rice and heated up Nalgene bottles with hot water to throw into my sleeping bag with me. I then got into my sleeping bag with the bottles, wrapped myself in a tarp like a burrito in my snow tunnel, and duct taped myself in, with a little crack for the moisture of my breath to escape and to see the stars.

As I looked up into the clear night sky, through my toque and crinkly tarp, I felt warm, capable, and at peace. The weariness of my muscles, tired from the many kilometres of skiing across uneven ice and setting up camp, and the smell of campfire smoke and spruce needles lulled me into a deep sleep. Despite the minus-twenty temperatures on the vast Tu Nedhé, my sleep was only interrupted by a few vivid dreams.

The next morning, I melted grip wax on the fire and applied it to the entire bottom of my old skis. Happy with the newfound grip, I elegantly skied ten hours farther and farther out onto the big lake. I finally reached the little windswept Benaya Island with great joy, greeted by two large eagles atop a patch of spruce trees. I said many prayers and set up another camp while revelling in the connection there. At night under the directions of an Elder, I placed tobacco on my drum and set it up in a tree overnight to bless it under the moonlight. Here on the island, I experienced many magical moments that helped bring the land alive within me. The next day, I felt cared for, connected, and at peace. I continued on my journey, filled with resilience as I looked onward to Cabin Island, angling back to shore travelling farther east.

It was on this third day, as I left the island in high spirits filled with the magic language of the land, that I eventually skied back toward the main shore in Drybones Bay. As I glided closer and closer to the main shore, I suddenly became aware of a feeling of the latent anguish of those who had died and were orphaned so many years ago. It was through sensations in my body that I became aware of the scale of the gravesites along this part of the lake, which had never dawned on me. As this sunk in, I saw what looked like a building in the distance. As I got closer to shore, I realized I had skied up to a parked truck at an exploration drilling camp on shore, in the same area I was now sure our ancestors had been buried. The gravity of its existence hit me like a brick in my stomach after only seeing snow and ice for three days. It was clear from the unhealthy energy here that they were drilling in a place that should not be drilled.[15]

15   I was not aware of this development before I left Yellowknife and I have included some references here to show the strength of the Yellowknives Dene leadership in fighting this exploration drilling from the beginning, in a deeply troubling environmental assessment process. They held the sacredness of this area in their hearts, and after years of appeals, ultimately prevented this development from going any further: https://www.cbc.ca/news/canada/north/ice-road-truckers-star-s-mining-proposal-opposed-1.1041871;

This pain in my stomach led me to discontinue my journey to Cabin Island. Instead, I laid some tobacco in honour of the losses that had occurred so many years ago that were not being respected by the people in charge of this camp. Quickly turning around, trying to outski the sickness permeating my belly, I cruised back northwest staying closer to the shoreline. As I left that bay, I could feel a sense of deep connection with the land, and also a validation of the anger constantly present inside of me. I spent two more days and nights solo out under the stars and northern lights, making four in total. In the late afternoon on day five, I rounded, exhausted and refreshed, back through Wool Bay to find that the ice road had already closed for the season—ready to welcome the fresh spring melt waters. My Dad picked me up by Ski-Doo near T'è?ehdaà.

By the end of my journey, I had travelled almost a hundred kilometres, established a connection with my ancestors, and experienced the natural history of these shores on a level beyond words. I had received blessings from my family on my island, felt in spirit the suffering of our ancestors from past changes they could not control, and became more aware and concerned about the impact of mining exploration in this area. And with every solo stride I took, I received comfort and healing from the land itself. I pushed myself physically and mentally to the extreme. I learned that I could survive on my own—could survive the pain I was experiencing. I understood my own resilience.

I knew from that point onwards that no matter where I ended up in my life, I could always come home to these vast magical shores in my mind's eye and find my inner self there—singing as I skied or bundled up by the fire; listening to the night, reflecting on life, screaming across the ice shards or crying as a form of cleansing the past. I left so much out there with the ravens. In those thousands of steps, I let my ancestors know we are still here. I was back, we are back. We are awake and closing the cycle, acknowledging their pain and loss in our bodies. I prayed for safe passage for those buried in the shallow graves all along the Tu Nedhé shoreline and let them know their great grandchildren

https://www.cbc.ca/news/canada/north/board-gives-green-light-to-drybones-bay-exploration-1.634152; https://www.cbc.ca/news/canada/north/alex-debogorski-s-diamond-project-in-hands-of-federal-appeal-judge-1.3080125; https://indigenouslaw.usask.ca/blog/2015/yellowknives-dene-first-nation-v-canada.php.

are still pushing onwards and upwards through the frost heaves of shared grief, creating action on the ground and in academia. We are continuing and ready to advocate for the protection of the land itself, and the knowledge that lies upon and within it. And someday, we may even remember the language of the land itself, and all those beings seen and unseen who walk upon it.

> 'Land-based' is even one of those words. It's a beautiful, wonderful term. It is bringing people back to the Land and helping them become alive and remembering their humanity and their connection to all living things ... we are the Land. So, if we remember who we are, then the same miracle that we see all around us will be us.

To Wood Buffalo National Park, with love[16]

Chloe Dragon Smith & Robert Grandjambe

My partner Robert and I recently wrote an article about Wood Buffalo National Park published in *Briarpatch Magazine*. We wrote it as a first communiqué—set in the future and in the format of a story. You can find it below.

We wrote this story because we have been feeling the frustrations of our experiences in the park, where we have been based since the Covid-19 pandemic hit hard in March 2020. I have had the privilege of being involved in the Pathway to Canada Target 1 as a member of the National Advisory Panel, a federal initiative to support the creation of more protected areas in Canada. Although it wasn't a flawless experience, I contributed and left feeling hopeful about the future of the interrelationship between parks and the implementation of Indigenous Protected and Conserved Areas in Canada.

However, when I returned to my traditional territory, I was faced with the reality that although conversations are evolving nationally, there are still major obstacles and problems occurring locally. I have been shocked at the poor relationships between Parks Canada and Indigenous people on the Land. Now, through experiencing it firsthand, I can see some of the roots of the issues more clearly.

My Mother grew up in Fort Smith, on the northern border of the park. When I asked her recently if the proximity of the park to Fort Smith had affected her, she said that it had not. I then asked her if she

16   A previous version of this piece was published by *Briarpatch Magazine*, September 10, 2020, and is reprinted here with permission.

spent any time within the park boundaries in her youth, and she replied that she did not. We both let that admission hang there for a minute, the heaviness of the realization hitting us.

All that could have been rushed into my head and heart. Opportunities missed on my homeland, where tanning moose hide was taught to me over time by my Mother, and not a task I had to relearn at thirty years old. A life where I didn't step off the riverbank and sink deep into delta mud, because I was inexperienced. A life where I could speak my family's language and more clearly understand the worldview of my people. A life where I could have felt wholly confident with my birthright for a place-based identity.

The park DID affect my family. It affected us so much that our lives were altered, and within one generation we couldn't even remember what we had lost. Living and participating on the Lands of our ancestors had been taken away as an option. This is the injustice. It can be so tricky not to get bogged down in individual events, individual policies, and pieces of history. We can argue fault or cause, and we can dissect detail, but what it comes down to is that there are no longer Indigenous people on the Land in Wood Buffalo National Park. No one really lives here anymore and there are only a few who know the Land at all. The proof of injustice is in our absence.

Land needs people. We are part of the Land and that relationship is integral to sustaining a healthy environment, for people and Land.

Robert's experience—as someone who has managed to continue a relationship with the Land within the park—has also been telling. From my perspective, the fact that he is here today is nothing short of miraculous. Robert, at thirty-six years of age, has dealt with suppression from Parks Canada and lateral violence from our own Nations and Peoples. Both his Father and his Father's Father have had cabins denied within the park. His grandfather on his Mother's side had a cabin burned in the park, and that side of the family never returned, their relationship permanently severed. Robert, himself, had a cabin at Pine Lake dismantled and burned by Parks Canada in 2015. This was only five years ago.

It is confounding to me that when I share his story, the first thing I get back is often some form of suspicion or questioning of his approach. Did he build outside his delineated boundary? Did he follow the necessary steps? Did he abide by the rules?

This is where, tragically, the point has been lost. Here is a young, passionate Indigenous trapper on the Land in a park. He wants to live here with his family and share what he knows with others. He is taking care of the Land daily through the systems and worldview of his ancestors. He does all this without recognition, pay, or support. How is there anything he could possibly do "wrong" to deserve such dismissive treatment?

The answer is that an incident (like the burning of his cabin) was inevitable. The system was set up for him to fail from the beginning. The masterplan to remove Indigenous Peoples from the Land deemed a Canadian National Park has worked, and it has worked very, very well. As I see it, the details are unimportant once placed in the context of history. The governance and management of Lands and Peoples here have grown into an unhealthy spiral that is convoluted, divided, and seemingly impossible to untangle.

It is a discriminatory wrong that there are cabins at Pine Lake inhabited by folks who have no traditional familial ties here, who have raised their families on the shores of a "recreational" lake with secure leases, who are encouraged and sanctioned to make changes as they desire with the full support of the park staff—including fire abatement, regular meetings and communication, bear warnings, and control. They are even presented gravel for their personal driveways. In sharp contrast, the road we travel on (from where those coveted cabins turn off) is unmaintained, and the Indigenous people have few rights, sparse communication, and even fewer supports or services.

I accept the responsibility we have been given. With our passion and privilege, we feel compelled to give back and speak, while we spend time on this beautiful and abundant Land. We are committed to gaining full participation and asserting our opportunity to be here with all that comes with it: acknowledging the mess—the uncomfortable mess.

This is why we choose to speak out, why we want to open the conversation, and why we want to untangle what has gone wrong. Ultimately, our need is to be involved in positive change within this park, with cooperation, respect, and dignity. After all, this is the traditional Land and way of life of our Peoples. It simply cannot be lost.

Standing on the shores of Pine Lake, the wind ruffles my hair, rippling the surface of the water with the same gentle tendrils that envelop my body. We are one, the lake and I. We always have been, and we always will be. The contentment of being together again fills every cell in my body and manifests in a deep breath—of knowledge, time, and love. I look around and I see my home. I see the rocks and soils that carried my ancestors with grace. I see the trails of the bison that fed us and kept us warm. I see the temples where we prayed. Family who had long passed and were buried, they are here still.

Pine Lake is an oasis, a clear turquoise gem of an inland lake surrounded by thousands of kilometres of boreal forest. It's hard to imagine that violence occurred here, but it did. Some of it was obvious, but much of it was insidious, the kind that wears you down over time. My journey back home took generations and it took casualties ... however...

In Wood Buffalo National Park, we are now home.

After more than a century of outside control on the Lands of our ancestors, the colonial model of national parks was finally overturned in the largest park in Canada, Wood Buffalo. We did away with arbitrary borders and rigid regulations. People can breathe as part of the Land once again. Here's a cup of tea, dear seyaze—let me tell you how we did it.

First came the reckoning.

It can be difficult to reflect on our own wrongdoings and how they hurt others. This takes tremendous strength for anyone. You will learn this as you get older, sweet nipsi—it is a hard lesson that we all have to go through in order to grow. For taking this step, and admitting their wrongs, we are proud of the institution of Parks Canada. It was many years ago, in the year 2021—ninety-nine years after the establishment of Wood Buffalo National Park—when Parks Canada and the Government of Canada apologized.

As part of this apology, Parks Canada travelled to each of the eleven Indigenous Nations, councils, and locals who call this Land their traditional home. They shared their vulnerability as an institution, but also held themselves accountable for their actions as individuals with free will. They acknowledged the injustices that they carried out as an arm of the colonial system of governance. They called each injustice by name.

It is not out of bitterness or hatred that I share this history with you, seyaze; knowing what happened is part of the healing process.

Parks Canada began by apologizing for the trauma they inflicted when they created the park in 1922. The park was established with the mandate of "offer[ing] a variety of visitor experiences," but it was not in collaboration with the people on the Land. The entire concept of the park was imagined within a colonial mindset, which meant that our Indigenous systems never did fit the mould. Much like a museum exhibit, parks were meant to be preserved and admired, but not wholly participated in. That didn't leave much room for us, the people who lived here.

Indigenous Land-users spoke of a culture of fear instilled by park management practices—we learned to hide our guns and remove the feathers from our hats when the Parks Canada wardens came.

In fact, many of us were banished from the park, some even jailed for practising our ways of life, like hunting, trapping, and fishing. People on the Land were discouraged, shut out, and purposefully tangled in red tape up until 2021. These rules were written into Canadian law and Parks Canada regulations, so there was no disputing them. For ninety-nine years, it felt like death by a thousand cuts.

These are the reasons it took such an effort to get people back on the Land, like we see today. I know it's hard to imagine now, but up until 2025, there weren't many of us left at all. This wasn't by accident, seyaze. Our families lived through three generations of systemic obstacles to playing a role in the park's care. Our cabin applications were denied, and cabins were even dismantled by Parks Canada. There were strict rules around what animals we could harvest, and how, when, and where. Though there were trapping areas designated by the government, this wasn't our way and there were almost no active trappers remaining by 2020. When we were barred from accessing our traditional lands—for which we had a responsibility to care—we were forced to hunt and trap on others' traditional lands. This caused terrible division. Anyone who managed to live or harvest in the park had to be strong, for they had much to overcome.

Another piece of Parks Canada's apology had to do with the bison. One of the original inhabitants of the park were wood bison—they differ from plains bison on the Prairies. You can recognize a wood bison, nipsi, for wood bison are truly massive, with rugged humps on their backs. Because of their prominence in this area, the park was named Wood Buffalo National Park. (Although, as we know, "buffalo" is not the right term, since buffalo come from South Asia and Africa!) No matter what we call them today—"bison" in English, "ejëre" in Dënesųłiné, "mostos" in Cree—they have been important for our people since time immemorial. The way we protect ejëre is by maintaining a healthy relationship with them—understanding that our fate is tied to theirs and being part of one another's lives. This includes harvesting ejëre for food and all we do, including ceremony.

Fundamentally, protection means having people out on the Land.

I know you're aware, my nipsi, that the ejëre went through much turmoil under the governance of Parks Canada as well. Part of that was because the harvesting of ejëre was not permitted in the park until 2021, and, at times, Indigenous Peoples were prosecuted and expelled from the park for their harvests. Outside the park boundary though, anyone who wanted to shoot ejëre east of Highway 35 in Alberta, could. This is the utter madness of colonial borders.

Between 1925 and 1928, plains mostos were introduced in an effort to increase the number of animals in Wood Buffalo National Park. This brought disease—tuberculosis and brucellosis—which killed many of the native wood mostos. The herds of plains and wood mostos intermingled, producing a hybrid species. Parks Canada also sold mostos for meat until the early 1970s. They herded animals into pens, and many died in the process. Of the mostos that survived, an estimated 4,000 were slaughtered and sold down south. More were culled afterward, to try to eliminate the disease that was brought in. Because of the declining numbers of mostos, wolves were poisoned to try to lower the number of wolf kills. This did not help, as poison seeped into the ecosystem, affecting everyone and everything in the park—including mostos.

We know now that the treatment of Land, Peoples, and mostos was part of a larger governance approach aimed at control and commodification.

I know it hurts to hear these stories, my darling nipsi. It hurts me too to hear how ejëre have been treated here, and even more so when the injustices that were carried out against us were in the name of protecting ejëre.

It was never about the bison.

We know now that the treatment of Land, Peoples, and mostos was part of a larger governance approach aimed at control and commodification. Logging was carried out on traditional lands in the park and lumber was sold to support exploration and mining in Uranium City. Commercial fishing was permitted on Lake Claire within the park boundary. Profits did not go to the Indigenous communities in the park where they could have created circular reciprocity with the Land. Some will say this all happened a long time ago, but remember, these were not isolated events. Up until 2021, injustice changed shape, but it did not go away. Always look at the big picture, my sweet seyaze. It's not that commercial activity is a bad thing, but any activity without notions of balanced, local economies is bound to affect abundance over time.

The Land is rich, and it wasn't long before big resource extraction projects nudged up against the boundaries of the park. When the wind blew from the South, you could smell the foul odour of sulphur from the tarsands and see a haze in the distance. Even when we melted winter snow for drinking and other uses, we saw a sheen on the surface of the water. The threat of Teck Resources' Frontier mine—one of the largest open-pit tarsands mines ever proposed—loomed thirty kilometres south of the park, until it was (at least temporarily) defeated in 2020. The Site C dam, along with climate change and withdrawals of water from the Athabasca River, further dried up the waters of the Peace-Athabasca Delta. When the waters were low, it became difficult for us to travel along the rivers and lakes. Three dams along the river all released or retained water at will, making water levels and erosion patterns unpredictable.

Until the apology of 2021, the park was treated as a thing to be owned by Parks Canada—it was not self-determined, living, breathing Land the way we know it to be. With this mindset, it could be pieced away as different assets—for conservation, environment, commerce, or anything else. That's right, seyaze. Parks was trying to protect Land with the same mindset that caused the problem. That's why so many things went wrong under its care. For us, the Land never could be owned or categorized, nor could it be separated from people. The way Parks Canada understood "effective protection" of the Land was not the same way that we did.

So, along with Parks Canada's apologies came their recognition of the true guardians of this Land. Recognition that—before Canada stepped in—this area had been governed successfully for millennia by people on the Land, through holistic and cumulative worldviews and their own dynamic laws. They recognized that all our systems were built to work with the plants, animals, waters, rocks, and thick delta mud of this specific Land. They expressed deep sorrow for the loss of knowledge that had occurred over ninety-nine years. They promised to do whatever they could to support us in rebuilding our systems. Because of Parks Canada's authentic apologies and recognition, your ancestors decided to restart the conversation about solutions.

After agreeing to work together, the next step was to address the condition of the park. A century without proper care had left the Land in a dire state. In 2020, we saw declining numbers of mostos and wolves—the same species that the park was established to "protect" in the first place. Forest fires had been burning out of control, and invasive species were moving in. People had been almost completely removed. Without people on the Land, there was no way to stop, or even notice and understand, the deteriorations. The United Nations Educational, Scientific and Cultural Organization's (UNESCO) World Heritage Committee warned that if actions were not taken to improve the situation, the park was to be placed on their website's List of World Heritage in Danger. From every perspective, it was clear that we were at an all-time low.

How could we work together to build abundance once again?

Luckily, neither we nor our kin across the continent ever remained idle. In 2018, a passionate and dedicated committee developed recommendations for Indigenous Protected and Conserved Areas (IPCAs). IPCAs, by definition, are Lands that are governed by local Indigenous communities, according to their own laws and knowledge systems. Parks Canada supported this process from the beginning.

We decided there were steps we could take to listen to the Land and to each other once again. We could use IPCA models to rebuild Wood Buffalo from the inside out, with love.

As you know, my nipsi, we now call this governance system the Ejëre Mostos Relational Alliance in honour of our new-old governance approach. It wasn't hard to bring the people together—though for a time, it seemed as if it might be. Canada's politics of division tore us apart for many years, as they have all over Indian country. Once our leaders recognized what we had in common—namely, our struggles with Parks Canada and other Crown agencies—we were able to turn negative attention away from each other and move forward very quickly.

Instead of focusing on our individual rights, we were reminded of our collective responsibility to the Lands we share. We realized that we had no obligation to carry on as we had been doing, and with that we overcame the unhealthy jealousy, greed, and hierarchy that had poisoned our relationships for over one hundred years.

In the Alliance, each of the eleven Nations, councils, and locals who call this Land their home now govern together. We have developed a network of overlapping IPCAs within the park boundaries. Each one works not according to colonial borders, but with the contours of the Land. We each take primary responsibility for the areas closest to us. Guardians and Land users are the heartbeat of the system. They move as the bison do, informing the collective Alliance of what needs to be done to create and maintain abundance. In this way, while we govern the Land, we do not own it.

The Land tells us what needs to be done, and ultimately, our responsibilities are to listen and participate. We are all bound by the laws of the Land.

The laws protecting the park through Canada's National Parks Act remain; however, they are one layer of legislation that functions alongside—but cannot override—the Indigenous laws of the IPCAs. None of the Nations have veto power, either, and we must work through our disagreements by consensus. This can take a long time, but it is in everyone's best interest to find ways forward. We strive always for an ethical space of engagement, where our laws and our ways of knowing, doing, and thinking work respectfully alongside one another, never impeding or superseding each other. The Land tells us what needs to be done, and ultimately, our responsibilities are to listen and participate. We are all bound by the laws of the Land.

Today, instead of "bilateral" meetings with Parks Canada, all of the eleven Nations, councils, and locals meet with one another whenever needed. This is important, because to be accountable, we hear what is said firsthand. When we meet, we share food and hospitality. Everything that is said is made available to the public, and we upload videos of our meetings to a website. We use new technologies to achieve the long-standing cultural value of openness. Our governance structures are not permanent; rather, they are fluid and adaptable. We establish them when needed and remove them when no longer necessary. This means leadership is never absolute. Like the Peace River, it curves and winds.

As has always been our way, we welcome all people. Parks Canada is still here, too. They bring their strengths to the table, adding their voice and expertise, but they no longer make the rules. The Alliance hires them to do specific scientific studies. They also maintain and build roads to ensure people always have access to the park. They help to build cabins for guardians and community members. We believe they are doing their best to restore equity, and when asked they carry out duties in service of the Alliance so that Indigenous Peoples have time to be on the Land.

We remove red tape. We ask Land-users what they need, and we find creative ways to support everyone through our IPCAs, no matter which family or community they come from.

It is in the name of effective governance that the Alliance prioritizes Indians on the Land, above all else. The regulations and legislation of Parks Canada were once intended to ultimately eliminate us from the Land. But we long ago recognized that the systems of colonial control and division that were suppressing our Peoples had no power if we remained present. The Land has the answers we need. And so we do everything possible to support people getting out onto the Land.

Our goal is to create sustainable futures where our Peoples can live in two worlds—as part of the Land with all the integrity of our own systems, and part of the modern economy. Because the Land gives us the knowledge we need, it follows that people on the Land are the conduit between systems of governance, economics, health, education, and conservation. That is why guardians, trappers, hunters, gatherers, educators, and knowledge holders are essential to the success of the Alliance.

Together, seyaze, we have become the strongest "park" in Canada, because we have the advantage of diversity. We have so many different people who care. We all have our roles, our strengths, and also our weaknesses. We support each other in a messy and beautiful web of reciprocal relationships, just like the Land. And just like the Land, we cross colonial borders physically, mentally, emotionally, and spiritually.

We recognize that we don't fit within straight lines, and we must have the courage to continually cross borders to be true to our identities—being ourselves is the most basic tenet of our laws. Everything comes together on the Land, and so that is where we are now.

Glossary

We use both Cree and Dënesųłiné language to demonstrate the languages of our two families and the predominant languages of this Land.

Ejëre—"bison" in Dënesųłiné
Mostos—"bison" in Cree
Seyaze—"my child" in Dënesųłiné
Nipsi—"willow" in Cree (pet name for a child)

In this article, we chose to capitalize Land as a way to convey its encompassing importance. When we speak of (L)and, we acknowledge that it includes Peoples, cultures, languages, and knowledge.

Without the land, there is no understanding

Glen Coulthard in conversation with
Leanne Betasamosake Simpson

Glen: My name is Glen Coulthard and I'm a member of the Yellowknives Dene First Nation. I was born in Yellowknife to Christine Coulthard from Dettah, and my Dad is a white guy named Ric Coulthard. My Grandparents are Margaret and Napoleon Liske. We lived in Norman Wells where my Dad was a partner with a Métis man in a general store and motel. I spent my youth going back and forth to Dettah to visit my Mom's family. My Mom and her family were a big influence on me. She taught me Wıìlıìdeh when I was small and I apparently spoke quite well until I started school. I spent a lot of time on the land and on the water with my Grandfather and my aunties and uncles. I remember going for boat rides on the lake between Dettah and Yellowknife. I have lots of memories of my big extended Dene family at Dettah—playing into the evenings or out on the lake with Grandpa. In Norman Wells, we would spend time on the Dehcho or at Kelly Lake. I grew up around hunting and fishing in a big extended Dene family and being on the land was formative. It was more than formative actually, it was normal.

Leanne: That's a pretty beautiful beginning, spending that first decade largely in a Dene world through your Ama and her family.

Glen: Yeah, it was so nice, and it all changed when my family moved south to Kelowna, British Columbia. And while we kept in good contact with Dettah, I was displaced and thrown into this new city and culture that didn't embrace me. We lived on West Bank First Nation. The high school I went to had a lot of anti-Native racism, and I was a target. I remember being called "Eskimo" and punched in the face for wearing a parka. I was beat up regularly on the bus. It was a pretty brutal time for me, facing that daily racism that was often violent. I coped with it by distancing myself from my Dene identity. I internalized that colonial racism. In Fanon's words, I tried to escape or flee my identity as a Native person. I even avoided going north for about five years because I felt ashamed I was Dene. Of course, I realized later, that I couldn't escape it. I was a dark, Dene kid, and there was no getting around that.

Leanne: That's a pretty brutal set of experiences that a lot of Native youth face at a time in our lives that is already pretty challenging.

Glen: And because of these experiences, I didn't do well in high school. I didn't try. I skipped class a lot. I left high school hurt and angry and I didn't think about continuing my education. I spent some time living in Vancouver with my good friend John Munro. He read a lot of books and has an amazing mind. He is a professor of history at the University of Birmingham in England now, but at the time, we both worked in a bookstore—a book and map store on Granville Street. I was also partying really hard. We'd read books, drink beer, and talk about them. This is where I first read *Wretched of the Earth*—it didn't speak to me at the time. I remember thinking it was too hard. John gave me a copy of Howard Adams, which at the time, spoke to me more because it was more accessible and had similar themes to my own experience. John and I did a sort of book club together and we read all three volumes of Marx's *Capital*. There was lots of anti-gentrification organizing going on in Vancouver at the time and we'd attend some of those events as well, and that movement has always been big in Vancouver and has always had an uneasy relationship with Indigenous sovereignty and land struggles. I would have identified as some sort of anarchist at this time.

Needing a change, I ended up back in Norman Wells, working on a spec crew for an oil company. I was making good money. But there were problems. I had issues with how poorly the company treated people and the land. There was a lot of racism and sexism among the white workers. I would also have conversations with Dene people from Normal Wells and Tulita who knew my family and knew me when I was a kid. I grew up in an environment where Native politics was always a background structure with my parents. I knew a little bit about the Sahtu land claim, and because I had lots of free time on my hands after work, I started to read the land claim. I had an older Dene man from Tulita that was my roommate at the time, and we started to talk about the claim and Dene politics and the politics of working in the oil industry. I came to an understanding that what the company was doing was in violation of most environmental and working stipulations. This was the most money I'd ever made in a short period of time, but the payoff wasn't worth it. Seeing the racism and the sexism and knowing that they were operating in violation of Dene rights wasn't worth the paycheque. I was angry and I wanted out of the industry.

Leanne: This is such an interesting part of Indigenous politics to me. Having those early experiences on the land, being in conversation with other Dene folks, gives you the tools to form a critique of extraction, capitalism and even colonialism. You knew you had to get out. You knew you were part of a different embodied politic and ethic.

Glen: I did, and my way out of working in the oil industry was to go back to school to the University of Alberta as an adult Indigenous student. I got into a bridging program and took three university courses on a sort of probation. The idea was that if students did well in the courses, they could continue on and go to university full time. I took a history of science course, a philosophy of mind course and an Indigenous Studies course. I surprised myself and I did very well. I got A's. No teacher had ever told me that I was good at anything, yet here I was, doing well at university. It was the Indigenous Studies course that caught my attention because it was relevant to my life and to the North. I had a lot of experience with the things that we were learning in class. My Mom was a Residential School survivor. I had these early experiences on the land with her family in Dettah. I had this firsthand experience in the resource extraction industry and Indigenous Studies made a lot of sense to me. I ended up majoring in it and graduating with my degree. After finishing the degree, I knew I didn't want to head back into the oil industry, especially after I was beginning to understand the politics of land claims and the more radical liberatory political theory I had been reading. It was clear to me that without further education, this was something I was probably going to be forced into doing. One of my mentors at the time at the University of Alberta, suggested I consider graduate school. They suggested a program that was suited toward my theoretical interests but also my commitment to more radical Native politics. So I went to graduate school. I spent time thinking and writing on Dene struggles for land and sovereignty in the post war period and into the 1990s and Dene nationalism in the context of recognition. I got really interested in the Dene nation struggle for self-determination, and this extended into my Ph.D. work.

Things start to crystallize and click in my masters. I started to make sense of what had happened to me in high school. During this time, I did some archival work at the Dene nation and came across this file that had a memo from George Erasmus to the field workers talking about a library they had for the field workers in coming up with a development philosophy linking up international struggles with the wisdom of Dene Elders. There was a reading list that included *Wretched of the Earth* by Fanon, Paulo Friere, Howard Adams, Régis Debray and a bunch of writings from Nyerere in Tanzania. This was interesting to me because it showed me that at one point, these Dene folks were interested in how the Third World politics I was learning about in university in the South were useful and relevant to our circumstances in the North. I made a point as a project for myself to seek out and read this work.

Leanne: Is this where Fanon starts to really resonate with you?

Glen: Yeah, I made a purposeful intent to read Fanon after that. *Wretched of the Earth* starts to make sense to me now. I started to realize I only had half of the story—colonialism isn't just a structural restraint, it is the internalization of those asymmetrical structures that reproduce colonialism over time.

Leanne: Your Ph.D. dissertation then, gets turned into the very success-ful and influential book, *Red Skin, White Masks*. Tell me about that book.

Glen: It is a book that came out of my dissertation, but it is really a book that came out of my formative years—of going back home and spending time on my land with my family in Dettah. It started at the University of Alberta when I got interested in the Dene Declaration and Dene land struggles. I started looking into the history of the Indian Brotherhood of the Northwest Territories and the Dene Nation and the relationship between their struggle and the critical perspective that a defence of land provided activists at the time. The Berger Inquiry, all of that. There was all this engagement with Marxism and the Third World and it was all articulated through a Dene lens, through the land. I started to really understand how colonialism works and how it impacts individuals and collectivities. I came up with a program for myself to try my best to understand what that meant beyond a cognitive sense by re-immersing myself in that relationship, with my community and with my family in Dettah. This wasn't easy. It was a very painful experience as my past was catching up with me. I'd remember every time my Dad was racist, every time a friend said something racist to me, every time a girlfriend had made a racist comment and all of this came up and exposed itself. I had very raw nerves around it. It was very long and slow process then of building myself back up again. Slowly but surely rebuilding that relationship and embodying that critique that I found was so central to the Dene nation's proposals from 1975–1981.

Leanne: What was it like to reconnect with your family, community, and land?

Glen: It was like I had never left. I was still accepted. My Mom always opened our house to all of her family, so we always had a really strong connection to them even in Kelowna. But I had built it up in my mind and internalized this self-hatred and shame around being Dene and I assumed that was known by my family themselves. It wasn't. They were just lovely.

Leanne: At Dechinta, we've made a big shift over the last few years in the sense that we've really re-focused our work on community needs. In our work with Yellowknives Dene First Nation, your aunties and uncles are sort of the backbone of that program because they carry so much Dene Knowledge and are so good on the land. It seems like the work you are doing is much more than just returning home and reconnecting.

Your aunties, uncles, cousins, and community members are out on the land for extended periods of time with the purpose of providing others the opportunity to be immersed in Dene life and witness the embodiment of a Dene political economy and an embodied Dene set of ethics. Dene theory in motion.

Glen: I've always thought of my scholarship as sort of a private affair. I never intended to come back to my community in a professional sense to work, it just emerged that way. Because I had lost so much knowledge moving to the South, I had to rely heavily on the knowledge of others and it turns out my family is very proficient on the land and I drew them into the circle of Dechinta. The theoretical hook is grounded normativity—the perspectives that emerge from the practical ethics of relationality and so on inform our critique of capitalism and colonialism and the newer faces of colonial rule. It is theory. It is not abstracted. It is an embodied critique that comes from a practical ethics.

Leanne: What is it like to be on McKenzie Island with your family teaching Dene students?

Glen: It's really amazing to be out on the land with my aunties and uncles and cousins setting nets or hunting. It no longer feels forced. My shame isn't there. It's lovely.

Leanne: How does this Dene practice of being on the land influence you as a scholar?

Glen: It has made me comfortable in my own skin. It has grounded my work. It is not theory for the sake of abstraction. It is theory for the conditions for liberating our peoples, and this is grounded and rooted in the Dene practice of life. It has given me my approach to political theory. It has given me my approach to solidarity. This is all through a Dene perspective. It differs from the literature that dominated in the 1990s. It doesn't mean a disengagement with the perspective of others; it means that engagement is from a Dene perspective. That has given me a lot more freedom to explore other traditions and examine the interface between Dene and Marxism for example. It is a perspectival position that I'm taking. It isn't a little bit of Dene and a little bit of Maoism; it is a Dene interpretation of Marxism or Mao or Fanon.

I have a particular understanding of the interface between land-based practices and theories of decolonization. I think they mutually support each other. The normative frameworks that come from land-based ethics informs how we travel through the world, how we engage in structures of colonialism, how we engage in practices of emancipation, how we engage in political economy, and vice versa. Reading those traditions or reading certain texts from the Dene perspective sheds light on how we got here and the structures of oppression we face. That's probably the hardest thing about the Dechinta project is to hold up that Dene Knowledge as legitimate. Everything from accreditation at universities to the government sees Dene practice as "work," and what does work have to do with critical thinking or they see it as merely culture? As in, they believe it shouldn't inform how we make political decisions and how we make economic decisions. From a Dene perspective, our relationship with the land absolutely must dictate how we move in the world, how we engage, and how we make decisions. From our perspective, the land is absolutely foundational in terms of the politics of the North and the alternatives. Without the land, there is no understanding.

Notes on being in-between— A love letter to damaged Earth

Camille Georgeson-Usher

This is a love letter to the damaged earth of urban centres I have and continue to tread across, but also a process of understanding and embodying relations to lands that many have coded as beyond repair. Lands that have enveloped me and cared for me so deeply that it allowed me the space to forgive myself for everything that I don't yet know. The city to me reads in the form of suffocation and possibility. A space that we trace, draw, mark, and colour upon through the very presence of our bodies. For those of us from elsewhere, it presents an invitation for us to melt into anonymity yet propels us from getting too comfortable. I consider this particular space one of unknowing, urgency, mystery, and eagerness to learn from the often-faint watermarks of matriarchs, as *spaces in between*. To be in between, to be folded in and out of what is known and unknown, to exist in ongoing moments of abstraction, and in spaces as the uninvited but also the reparator.

The urban is often marked as land that is "too far gone" and within a general set of values that prioritize what occurs on top of the land versus for the land itself, with the goal of a population to be able to consume more. The urban prioritizes the mass versus the individual, making it feel impossible for one person to be able to make any kind of significant change. As I move through these spaces, I have enjoyed the anonymity at times, but am constantly reminded that my body and my skin does not allow for me to move easily nor to ignore a history that I don't know. I had originally hoped that living in urban spaces would afford me the time to figure it out, but it has made it unbearably visible that I am far from where I come from. It has made it more clear that my body is a result of dispossession and of colonialism's desperate attempts to erase histories of those it tried hardest to eliminate, but simply going back to live on "my" territory often seems impossible.

It is a complex universe of being, living, moving, growing in territories in between. I continue to come back to theories around these in-between or unknown spaces of possibility or impossibility. Ashon Crawley's concept of the "otherwise" sticks to me as a possible futurity. Otherwise presents an opportunity to imagine moments or spaces outside of dominance, outside of pre-established structures or systems, and outside of the displacement and dispossession many of us have endured. Crawley writes: "The otherwise is the disbelief in what is current and a movement toward, and an affirmation of, imagining other modes of social organization, other ways for us to be with each other. Otherwise as plenitude. Otherwise is the enunciation and concept of irreducible possibility, irreducible capacity, to create change, to be something else, to explore, to imagine, to live fully, freely, vibrantly."[17] I imagine how we might read a city if it were written by Black people, Indigenous people, and People of Colour. What shapes would inhabit it? How would the structures anticipate and care more deeply for our bodies?

There is something within me that is connected to another dimension outside of these cities I have lived in for the past fifteen years, but I care deeply for these lands that are not my own. This care has manifested as a practice of building ecosystems that reinvigorate these "irreparable" lands. Through this I have imagined and attempted to enact otherwise possibilities where small pockets of distinct ecosystems might offer reparations. I often question the place for protocols (in their many forms) in urban spaces as a mark maker and a community gatherer. I have also questioned the role of land acknowledgement within these protocols; how the foundational incentive for doing land acknowledgements is exactly what the path to reconciliation has done wrong, but that the

---

17   Ashon Crawley, "Otherwise, Ferguson" *Interfictions Online* (blog), no. 7, accessed July 2, 2020, http://interfictions.com/otherwise-fergusonashon-crawley/.

practice of doing a land acknowledgement has become so co-opted that it has forgotten those foundational values. Being from another territory entrenches us into living the land acknowledgement in so many ways, but there is little space to discuss how this comes to play. I often wonder where the space is for those of us not raised in specific protocols? What is the protocol for those of us who are deeply hurt or unable to begin the process of engaging with these protocols because colonization has cut us and our ancestors so deeply that it has become nearly impossible?

There is so much of my family's history that is unknown and perhaps will never be known. As urgent as this knowing feels, the process has been lethargic; filled with more abstractions than fillable voids. There is a lot that was "erased" from history for my family. Some of what we do know is that my grandfather, George, was a mix of multiple Coast Salish nations primarily in relation to the territory now known as Vancouver. But our families have mostly moved among the Gulf Islands which is where I was raised. My aunt Rosemary Jr. has done a significant amount of research on the history of our family. I cite my aunt's work, but my personal understandings have come through relation with her.[18] I remember a conversation with her in my living room in Toronto where she explained the process of uncovering information about the matriarchs in our family, or, more appropriate, of feeling deep frustration over the lack of information about our generations of grandmothers and great grandmothers. So what do we do with generations of information that ceases to exist? How do we be accountable to protocol in these circumstances?

My grandmother is beautiful. I have images of her when she was my age and in between points in her life—similar to how I feel right now—I feel her energy in those photos within me and perhaps I always have but I'm not spiritual enough to say anything significant about that. I have one photo that was taken of her as she was being removed to go to Residential School. The photo was taken in Aklavik, Northwest Territories, most likely in 1931 when she was two. That's all I know. When she was diagnosed with dementia almost ten years ago now, I remember exactly where I was when I found out: I was standing in the depanneur at the corner of Saint-Marc and Sainte-Catherine Ouest staring blankly at a pack of sour keys; someone had just spoken to me in Portuguese and were shocked to find out that I wasn't from Brazil *even though* it was during the 2014 FIFA world series final game. I looked at my messages and forgot where I was for a second. I realized my opportunity to really know my grandmother vanished in that second.

I had been living in Montreal for nearly four years when I began sifting through texts on urban Indigeneity. What I found was statistical information for thousands of peoples who may or may not have connections to their own communities who were/are moving to urban centres in waves. I read texts about the importance of nation-specificity and its place in research; I read accounts of Indigeneity from non-Indigenous scholars; I read us as numbers, but I found little space where I saw myself in these texts. So I entered academia with the intent of providing one small place of self-recognition or knowing in an ocean of unknowabilities for people who might have travelled a similar path to mine. I have done this work through research and I have done this work as an artist. As a street artist I wanted to see a part of myself and those in my carefully crafted community represented in the city. I wanted us to be able to *read* ourselves on the facade of buildings, to bring that deep love we have to bubble to the surface of a city. But what is it to mark a city if it is not the territory of our ancestors? Is it enough to do it for that specific earth that has been pillaged and suffocated? Or are we trespassing on protocols that there have been few opportunities to discuss? I began creating stickers of little brownish me riding bikes and put them along de Maisonneuve so that at least I knew that a part of my story was making a mark in the world with the possibility of perhaps one other person seeing it. Maybe this person would recognize themselves in this moment and feel as though there would be someone there for them if they were ever in a dangerous situation.

These small moments for the potential of recognition come in many ways. It was in the late winter in Vancouver that I was being led through a small piece of green space wedged in between buildings in Chinatown. Skwxwú7mesh, Stó:lō, Hawaiian and Swiss media artist and ethnobotanist T'uy't'tanat-Cease Wyss created a garden installation, "x̱aw̓s shew̓áy̓ New Growth 《新生林,》" that was built up through deep and caring work with the land, youth, and many communities. The garden offers a brief moment for quiet in a city overwhelmed by commercial dominance and modernization. Wyss told us stories about how the youth showed up each day during the construction to carefully put each plant into place. She told us of some of the responses she has received from people who came to this newly transformed space: some came there intentionally to spend time with the carefully selected plants from that territory while some were surprised to see it and did not know that something like it could exist in such a small part of a concrete city.[19]

As I walked through Wyss's garden, I was reminded of what it means to care for earth that has been left without care for too long, but it also gave me an opportunity to imagine how a city's energy and vibratory sensations might shift if it were built with the value systems of this garden, for example. What if space was built with the intention of togetherness and care for the bodies that have been pushed to the margins? In many urban centres we don't have the luxury of being in expanses of green, so we have to make do and build the moments that we feel might uphold and provide space for communities that don't often have that space to *be*. Spaces for and by Indigenous people, Black people, and People of Colour need to be built by ourselves otherwise they cease to exist. In New York City, Yup'ik dancer and choreographer Emily Johnson has worked with Cree scholar Karyn Recollet to create events that hold space for community to come together and share stories, poetry, and music, as well as create, dance, read, listen, or sit in silence. These gatherings are called *Kinstillatory Mappings in Light and Dark Matter*; before the global pandemic people would come together around a fire and sit on quilts as part of these gatherings. There would often be food and people could create in ways that were untethered by expectations.

Through all of this, I imagine the city as space ready for intervention; ready for *otherwise possibilities*. But more specifically or pointedly, I would like to think through how the city might begin to provide moments for Black people, Indigenous people, and People of Colour to feel protected, invited to contribute, invited to participate, and expected to succeed, and that those moments transform into permanence. The urban is a space for a lot of us who come from elsewhere, who may or

---

19   Oscar Domingo Rajme, "T'uy't'tanat-Cease Wyss," *Canadian Art*, accessed July 2, 2020, https://canadianart.ca/reviews/tuyttanat-cease-wyss/; Wyss, T'uy't'tanat-Cease, "T'uy't'tanat-Cease Wyss," *221A*, https://221a.ca/fellows/tuytanat-cease-wyss.

may not know the histories of our ancestors, who are trying to create small pockets where we feel okay. These small gestures to build kindness on lands "beyond repair" have to be seeping through in small ways. While there are many discussions that we still need to have about how we engage with land politics in urban spaces, especially as those who are *in between,* we are seeing incredible acts of resurgence through radical community building where we are enacting new protocols as we imagine futures outside of dominance and shame.

This is your home

Ski-Doos, caribou, and mosquitoes

Jeneen Frei Njootli in conversation with
Leanne Betasamosake Simpson

Jeneen: My name is Jeneen Frei Njootli. I'm from the Vuntut Gwitchin Peoples and our home is in Northern Yukon in Old Crow. I wasn't raised there but I'm really grateful to have a strong relationship with my family and community there now. I was able to spend time there as a kid and a young adult. Those things really shaped me—growing up with my aunties telling me, "This is your home. This is your home." I grew up moving around a lot, and it's always so grounding to just be told and be held in that.

My family on all three sides of it are really creative and are makers. I grew up being stitched into clothing by my family. I'm working on a show in the Yukon right now. I'm hoping to borrow my late auntie Alice Ross's baby belt. She made the belt in the '70s or '80s and it is part of the Metropolitan Museum of Art's collection in New York City. How cool is that?

I just got back from visiting Old Crow for five weeks. I was struck by and so appreciative of just being able to reflect on how many of my family are makers. Everyone is sewing something or learning new songs. Growing up, this was just part of the world around me, or worlds around me or communities around me. My moms owned and operated the Lesbian Women's Publishing Company in Prince Edward Island, called Ragweed Publishing Books. My moms are Sibyl Frei and Louise Rebelle Frei now, but I've had many moms all throughout—people giving that kind of care and nurturing, and I'm really grateful for that. My Dad is Stanley Njootli and my grandmothers from his side are Joanne

Njootli, Jenny Lord, and then my great-grandma is Rachel Cadzow who was married to Dan Cadzow who ran the trading post outside of Old Crow, called Rampart House, which was there before Old Crow was there—and Old Crow is only 110 years old. My great-great-grandma is Margaret Black Fox—just to situate this kind of thing. My Dad helped settle our land-claims and also helped form the Porcupine Caribou Herd Management Committee in the Yukon, and then my Mom ran for NDP in Yukon when she lived there in '88 or '89. Then my moms got involved in organizing community support stuff in PEI, and so my moms moved there.

Leanne: I'm grateful for your sharing of that personal history and context because it situates your body of work in a body of politics and a body of meaning.

Jeneen: Sometimes artistic practice is just sitting at home and water colouring, but it's often a political engagement, or being engaged with sets of politics. Yeah, I think the question of how did you become an artist, or maybe when did you know you were an artist, and then in like what world, too? In the community world or in the, like, white cube art world? There are different modes of trying, and I feel way more impostor syndrome in the institutional art world. It kind of scares me how easily I can code switch sometimes. The fluency in that institutional art world I find alienating to myself sometimes, but it also feels good and empowering to be able to hold those tools in my hand and be able to manoeuvre through and use all those eight-syllable words and what not.

Leanne: The white cube art world is not necessarily a welcoming space for Indigenous Peoples, or a space that we're invited into very much. There's a lot of rules and surveillance, and there are security guards—you're not supposed to touch, and I'm always made to feel like I'm not supposed to be there. When I went into Art Space to see your show in Peterborough, ON, I felt like I was supposed to be there, and that was such a gift because I saw a code that told me that I was supposed to be there and I feel a sense of belonging in your work—oh, there's snowmobile parts or a Ski-Doo part, that's not something I normally see in galleries, but it's something I see in my life all the time, and I have a lot of affection for—and the caribou antlers, or caribou antler vest. All of these things—the hide tanning, all those mitts, all of those elements made me feel like I belonged. There was also a sense of refusal because here you were in this gallery, in this institutional setting in the South—in Nishnaabeg Territory—with all the big words and the institution of art, and you were telling me that I wasn't a fraud and you weren't a fraud. We are supposed to be there, and we are supposed to be everywhere. Our work is generative, it's smart, and it's intelligent, and it's full of meaning. I could feel all of your family connections and your homespace in the gallery—that was really visible to me.

Jeneen: I'm grateful to hear you say that because you just don't know how it's going to land with people. One time this non-Indigenous curator told me that my work is obtuse, and thought, "That's so good. I'm glad it feels like that for you."

I spent six years at Emily Carr University of Art and Design in Vancouver in my undergrad and then did another year for my masters. So, for folx out there that are—there are so many journeys and paths within education to take, and it takes time.

I remember feeling so far away from what I was learning about. It felt un-enterable; it didn't feel like it was made for me, but I felt so driven to understand it or to be able to use that language even though it felt like it was pushing me away. Sometimes I get grumpy and I want my work to do that. And I also wanted to be there to engage with that language and practice. Tania Willard invited me to participate in a project she was curating called *LandMarks*. Tania came to Old Crow and my Dad was like, "What's your last name?" And she said, "Willard." And he said, "Willard ... Willard ... Mike Willard is your Dad?" And she was like, "Yeah, why?" It turns out our dads went fishing together when they were in their late twenties/early thirties in Secwepemc Territory. And here Tania and I were decades later, on our way out to caribou hunt with my brother. This is part of storytelling and making community relations around work and that way it's not the same as coldness of the studio visit, or a show produced in a white cube gallery space. There's reciprocity and deeper connections.

In *LandMarks* we made these Ski-Doo blankets. I had been look-ing at our traditional dog blankets and was interested in pushing the boundaries of museum culture. Peter Morin introduced me to the word belongings, instead of artifacts or objects, because belongings bring those things into presence and into our families and our communities. When non-Indigenous people see our belongings in museums, they don't necessarily know that some of those things are still being made in community, or that that knowledge exists in community still, or that sometimes it doesn't exist anymore because of pure colonial violence, or it just exists in different ways. With the dog blanket project, or the Ski-Doo blanket project, we looked at dog blankets in museums like at the Museum of Natural History in New York City and the Museum of Civilization (now History) in Ottawa. I got to visit with these ancestor artists' dog blankets. My people made regalia for our dogs to honour our transportation. I know it was pretty big in the Gwitchin community and Northwest Territories, too. So, getting to visit those, and then looking at the Gwitchin word for Ski-Doo, which is a metal dog team, I started thinking about what are the ways we still honour our transportation? People are still travelling with dog teams, but not in the same way. It's in a different way now. How can that knowledge still be alive in our community or practised actively? And so, we made seven of these Ski-Doo blankets with the community in Old Crow to honour our transportation. What does it mean to make regalia for the machine? The Ski-Doo blankets stayed in Old Crow. Galleries have asked for them, and I agree they are beautiful, but I didn't want to give into consumer culture in that way. If you want to see them, come to Old Crow or there's a brief moment in the film, *Being Skidoo* (2017), where you see them. Other than that, I wanted them to be these intimate close-up shots of the land, of like, I don't know, my Dad's hands, my hands, and it's not. You don't get to consume our land you know, what do they call it, our material culture in the same way.

Leanne: So that's something that I also really respect about your work is how you have those boundaries between what you share with wider audiences and what's shared with the gallery setting, and then projects like this that are for the community, or projects that are for the land. I saw a clip of you speaking about or asking the question, what does it mean to make something where the audience isn't human? And that's something that I always think a lot about because I think in our making cultures, that was something that our ancestor artists would have thought of and would have considered in this idea that we make stuff that gets consumed by whiteness; it's something that our generation and probably the generation before us had to deal with. So why are those boundaries important in your work?

Jeneen: I think I've learned from a young age that refusal is a survival tool, and it sometimes feels impossible, and then when it feels possible, I just want to hold onto that as much as I can. Seeing how my body or our bodies are consumed or treated, and then also seeing how our material culture is being devalued by whiteness. Like with beadwork, when you're wearing it, people want to touch it. It's an extension of your body. If it's another maker, or if it's another community member, or a close friend, I'm like, "Yes, yes, yes, touch all this beadwork." But when it's a stranger, when it's a non-Indigenous person, which it almost always is, who reach out and touch your earrings, or your hair, or your neck, or your wrist—it feels like a small violence. It's this entitlement to our work and bodies that feels pretty awful. Or like people being upset at how much some of my family charges for moccasins. I mean, maybe not upset, but it gets met with a frown, and they want it to be cheaper or something, and I just find it so upsetting.

In 2013 or 2014, when decolonial aesthetics really popped off, and then on the heels of that there was quite a few texts that came out around this idea of refusal. With decolonial aesthetics, the term itself is a problem because even decolonial doesn't feel accessible to people, and then that word comes from a specific set of geopolitics, and then even in Latin America their relationship to it is what Walter Mignolo calls the colonial matrix of power. Their relationship to that is so different than in what is now known as Canada versus in the North, like the homelands of Dene and Gwitchin and our northern relatives. In talking with community members, I remember going back to university and I was visiting with my friend Angela Code and her Mother Mary, and she's like, "What are you studying? What are you working on?" And I was like, "decolonial aesthetics." And she was like, "What?" She's a hide tanner and a bad ass filmmaker and owns her own productions. The danger of academia co-opting or theorizing and then profiting off certain ideas is that the language isn't accessible to the people who are doing it, and not wanting to reproduce that, and that's why I so deeply love Tania Willard's work and the Bush Gallery Collective. In their manifesto they talk about streaming films through the trees, and that was something that really got me thinking like, what does it mean to have this non-human audience? When I was applying for school, my nation always asked me, how does what I'm doing benefit Old Crow?

Leanne: What does it mean for you to work with the sound of Gwitchin life?

Jeneen: How do we pull knowledge through our bodies? Honestly, I just get elated hearing the sound of driving a Ski-Doo over the land. And then even when you put in those earplugs, you hear it in your body. Having those embodied sonic experiences are so powerful and informative. I equate those drone sounds with time on the land, so it makes sense for me to create those drone sounds or sonic environments outside of that space to summon it. The sounds of our land are diverse.

The sounds in all of our communities are changing, and it's because of colonization, and climate change caused by colonization, and our land use patterns are different, and our trees are growing taller—which means it's damping the sound—the weather is warmer, so sound doesn't travel as far in the winter, and then it doubly doesn't travel in the winter because the trees are getting taller and thicker.

And so, in thinking about the dog blankets, my Dad and I are now working on a project of dog whips. They're a sound tool. They're kind of like a polarizing belonging—people might look at it and immediately think about animal cruelty and animal rights, but it's a sound tool and it gets the dogs excited to get going. The crack of the whip sounds different now in our communities. Does the land miss hearing dog bells? Does the land miss hearing that dog whip? Or barking in the morning? Or the sound of those bells echoing in the canyon coming home? So, with this project with my Dad, we're thinking about, I mean the grant terminology is like, "We're rematriating sounds to the northern landscape." We are remaking some of those belongings, getting to visit with ancestor artists, dog whips and blankets, and hopefully being able to bring some of them home just so we can visit, but then being able to remake some of them.

Northern Indigenous Voices on Land, Life, and Art   69

Sound work is thinking about how we pull knowledge through our bodies, through another's body, so maybe like a belonging's body, and giving voice to something that is maybe small or could be unheard, like an antler or beadwork—like having the sound of beadwork fill an entire room and spill out and disrupt and hold that space; making beadwork is so loud that some people have to leave the room. I call them sound tools, so I make my own contact microphones and put them on, and make different sound tools using contact microphones, and then run that through distortion and effects pedals, and then run that through a guitar amp and subwoofer. It's amazing to have those lower frequencies because you really feel them in your body, and sometimes your shift will even vibrate. You know I've had some people tell me that they can hear the land in the work. Like one piece on my microphone, or sound tool that I made, was a beaded hair barrette that my godmother made for me, which has a moose toe bone through it. I'm using that to sound.

Leanne: Tell me about you and caribou.

Jeneen: Movement is such a big part of their lives. I like being able to use those moments to talk about the porcupine caribou herd and the importance of protecting their calving grounds as a sacred place where life begins.

There was sad news released on August 17, 2020, that Trump's moving forward with resource extraction in their calving grounds. We're going to fight like hell against it as we have been for decades. When I include caribou in my work, I get to talk about caribou—that caribou is, it's a caribou that my brother harvested and tanned and gave it to me and said, "Make something with this." And then I said, "I'm going to make contemporary art."

In 2018, the show for the Sobey Art Award was interested in that work, and then I was like, well it's a collaboration with my brother, and we need to acknowledge all the labour and knowledge around harvesting. The title of the exhibition was *I Can't Make You Those Mitts Because There Is a Hole in My Heart and My Hands Hurt,* and it was so true for me at that moment, and I did want to make him something out of it. Instead, I asked him if he wanted to be listed as a collaborator on the work itself. We went to Ottawa together and showed the work at the

National Art Gallery. His name was on the wall with me, and it was just this huge moment for us. Stanley Grafton Njootli.

We first met when I was nine. He had these sketchbooks that were just full of some of the weirdest stuff I'd ever seen, and it really inspired me in my work and motivated me. He was living in Old Crow; there's a documentary about him and my Dad called *Artic Son* (2007), about him coming home from the streets of Portland. It was just a really significant moment from when I was nine and meeting him—seeing his art and then being able to be at the National Art Gallery together with the caribou that he harvested.

Leanne: How would you characterize your aesethetics in your creative practice?

Jeneen: Recently I've been thinking about the body and bush aesthetics, or just like Indigenous aesthetics, and spending time thinking about mosquito bites—picking berries and picking tea, and, like, paying for them with your blood. I've been spending time at my late uncle Grafton's cabin, and my great-grandma Rachel, who I talked about earlier, used to spend quite a bit of time there, too. I was being chewed up by mosquitoes there and I started wondering, do mosquitoes have blood memory? And I'm wondering if mosquitoes are a way of paying the land? Those mosquitoes' ancestors had a relationship with my ancestors, literally through blood. I was so grateful to be bitten by mosquitoes and think about the history of my grandmothers in that place, and our history and relationship to the mosquitoes there. Seeing the welts form and watching them dissipate and turn into smaller bumps, and then fade back into my skin. I thought about those bites as an image, as a temporary or fugitive image on the land. Our bodies hold these fugitive images, and hold memory in that way, and that that memory can be a shorter time moment, and these can shift over time like the caribou antler desk images or even the grease print of beadwork on metal smear and shift, rust and change over time. Tattoos on bodies and these skin stitches as lines that have been displaced from our bodies, just like how our people have been displaced from lands. This got me thinking about what symmetry is, and unlearning what a perfect tattoo line is, and what a clean line is and how messy it actually is. It's always shifting and always moving, and I think that's why I'm really drawn to sound and performance art because they are also able to bend and grow and shift, and then dissipate, and then we have to hold that memory—or maybe there's an accountability that happens because you have to hold that memory, and that memory lives in our bodies in different ways when we encounter a mosquito or a sound, or when we are tattooed very literally.

Leanne: I love your bush theories or bush aesthetics. So brilliant. You have me thinking about mosquitoes and their sound when they're stuck in your tent—that vibration—how they're always moving, the reciprocity you pay with as they're taking your blood, and this idea that we've had a relationship with them for tens of thousands of years. In my language, bug is manidoonsag, or little spirits. It can be challenging to think of them that way! It seems like the land is a very generative spot for you artistically.

Jeneen: Yeah, we have stories of mosquito ancestors as pterodactyls. I have a show opening in Winnipeg at Platform Gallery called *Small Mounds of Flesh Form*, and I'm making these twelve-foot mosquito legs. I was going to have a video of my back being chewed up, to think about reciprocity and the land. They really unite... sometimes we can feel really separate from our non-human relations, but we're the same to mosquitoes. You know they keep the caribou moving. Like one time I was just really cursing them, and my Dad was like, "Well they keep the caribou moving." And then, the caribou are our relatives, and we've had an interdependent relationship with them, forever, and we're part of each other. I'm just really enjoying thinking about mosquitoes right now.

Code shifting, listening, and trusting ourselves

Inuksuk Mackay and Tiffany Ayalik of PIQSIQ in
Conversation with Leanne Betasamosake Simpson

Tiffany: My name is Tiffany Ayalik. I am born and raised in Yellowknife, Northwest Territories, but my family comes from Kugluktuk, Nunavut, up on the Arctic Ocean in the Kitikmeot Region. I grew up in Yellowknife way back when there was only the one territory—Northwest Territories— before Nunavut split and had their own territory. So, that's where I was born and raised, along with Inuksuk.

Inuksuk: I'm Inuksuk Mackay. I also grew up predominantly in Yellowknife. Tiffany and I are sisters, so we have the same Mother but different fathers. Our fathers come from different regions. So, I did grow up visiting Kitikmeot Region—Kugluktuk predominantly. As a kid, we spent a lot of time there, so I have an interesting split of Inuinnaqtun and then Inuktitut because my Father is from the Kivalliq Region, so they're from the Rankin Inlet/Arviat area. They speak central Arctic Inuktitut there. We grew up travelling between the communities, but our home base was always Yellowknife.

Tiffany: We did our whole school and education in Yellowknife up to grade twelve, and then, as everyone had to do back then, we went south for any postsecondary education—especially if it was related to arts or writing or any kind of performance or anything like that. So, we both had to, at different times, go south and get educated. Inuksuk went for writing, and I went for acting.

Inuksuk: At that time for me, it didn't really click for me that you could be an Inuk in a postsecondary environment. It was almost like, "Oh okay, this is what the white side does and it's necessary," but I didn't really consider myself an Inuk in a postsecondary setting. There was a weird separation that I don't think I was super conscious of, and it wasn't until I had been working with a lot of other artists in the North that I realized, well, you're just Inuk all the time and you can just be Inuk and do what you're doing. We'd always been into music and we'd always been into throat singing. That was just a normal part of growing up for us. Putting things together and allowing myself to not split off between white zone and Inuk zone was so important.

Tiffany: White zone!

Inuksuk: This is Inuk zone now!

Tiffany: Here, let me put on my code-shifting accent!

Inuksuk: Yeah, she does code shifting.

Tiffany: Let me put on my Caucasian voice for this phone interview.

[everyone laughs]

Tiffany: We always joke that we are different sides of the same coin. We're always saying, "Oh, same different," because the two of us experience issues in vastly different ways with different experiences, and then somehow end up at a similar conclusion. When I was at acting school, my otherness was always brought up, like, "Oh, you're a generic ethnic, you're ethnically ambiguous, oh you're racially ambiguous, this is perfect, we need one of you." This kind of thinking was in my face every day. It wasn't healthy. It was super extractive. I was never allowed to just be an artist or an Inuk. I was also 'in service to' something else because of the way I look and because of, you know, "you could be Chinese, you could be Hawaiian" ... or, "Oh perfect, we're doing some weird Saigon play and you're the only one who doesn't have to be in yellow face or whatever." I wasn't allowed to be who I am but was kind of forced to be someone else every day, because it served some other purpose. And to clarify, I was one of three Indigenous students on campus at that time.

Inuksuk: I went to school in the South for writing. In a similar way, my heritage would come up. I said I'm from the North; I'm Inuk. My professors would respond by saying, "Oh, you know what you should write about" ... I had a lot of really obscure instruction from my professors on what they figured I should be interested in writing about based on their limited knowledge and assumptions of who I was as an Inuk. I didn't want to write about how there are sixty different words for snow because I'm not sure that's true and I don't care about that. [laughs]

Tiffany: In the South, there are a lot of mental gymnastics that go into just existing. Now, we approach our art as whole people. We've always known who we are. We've always known we're Inuk. There's never ever been a question about that. We have always been surrounded by community in that sense, by family and by extended community of Inuit, so our identity has never been a question. We know who we are and we know our roles.

Inuksuk: It's more like, how you compartmentalize your experiences in the educational system that come from a predominantly white settler lens. And so you're like, what space am I in right now? Is it one where those are the rules, or is this a community setting where I can just be?

Tiffany: We grew up on the land, a lot of the time. We've spent months, and collectively years of our life in the bush. We've always had really meaningful land connection. Throat singing, culturally, is born out of a deep listening to land. It is hard to do authentic throat singing if you don't have land connection, because the sounds in throat signing are literally the sounds of the land. The songs are called creek or river or mosquito, or there are geese—things that are literally informed by land practice. If you're not engaged in land-based practices, then you're missing out on this whole iceberg of the meaning of the music.

This relates to how we're doing our work as Inuit in 2020 in Vancouver. In our online performances, we've taken to doing sonic land acknowledgements. We acknowledge through song the land we're currently on with the Musqueam, Squamish, and Tsleil-Waututh. This is more meaningful to us as Inuit.

Inuksuk: We listen!

Tiffany: We listen and think about how we can meaningfully reflect back on what we're hearing from this land, and from the people who have always lived here.

Inuksuk: We ask what does the land sound like here and then reflect that back.

Tiffany: This is how I hear your land, let us make it into a song for you! There is almost a cute element. Little kids like to mimic and repeat. There is a back and forth. It's joyful and playful. You know when kids are little and they mimic.

Inuksuk: The land makes sounds, and you listen, and then you say it back how you hear it.

Tiffany: What you are hearing in our music is us remembering a huge part of our life where we were out on the land for three or four weeks—or we're remembering on a deep level our feelings of being in the Arctic, being in any of our communities. We love to blend things like throat singing with our own aesthetic because we also love choral music, and we love the emotional power of many voices singing something in a complicated harmony with soaring, heart-throbbing vocals.

Inuksuk: It is lyric-less, and I think folks engage in a different way because they're not being told what to think about it. There's a lot more room for interpretation in terms of feel by the listener.

Tiffany: I sometimes feel—I was thinking and feeling sometimes that lyrics would kind of get in my way in terms of how big the feeling was. And that if I have this big feeling, I'm like, "English is not doing it justice. Inuktitut or Inuinnaqtun is not doing it justice," so I'm going to sing in this other non-lyrical language because that's when I can be authentically expressing something. There's something that grounds it in the here and now. It feels more authentic to express it through a wordless sound than reading it in something as pedestrian as English.

Leanne: What work do you hope that your performances and your recordings are doing in the world?

Inuksuk: Our work is an opening of portals. There is a teaching in Inuit Qaujimajatuqangit about where thoughts originate, and so a group of Elders were asked, "In Western thinking, thoughts originate in your brain, so where do Inuit think thoughts originate?" The Elders had a conversation about it and the paper that came out of this conversation explains that in Inuit belief, thought originates in the middle of you. And your brain is just following suit, being prompted by something in the middle of you. When we experience traumas, unresolved traumas, it is described to be 'gumming up' the pathway between your heart and your brain, and the communication isn't great anymore. So, in our work, that's one of the strong images that guides us, is that we want to be opening up that portal in the middle between where your thoughts originate and your brain. It is sort of like a healing thing for us too, to open up, so there's also the question of time. What's time, and can it be opened up? Is it really linear? So, it's a portal between the past and the future. We are a connection between the past and the future; it's just true. A lot of the time we feel like we serve as a portal that connects people to something that is sort of hard to put into words and experience that's hard to put into words.

Tiffany: We are performing as Inuit in a mainstream, surprising, cool, dynamic, and modern way. I hope this paves the way for other Inuit imagining what is possible. I hope we are collectively moving us forward and that we are advocating for Inuit because even in Indigenous circles, Inuit are marginalized.

Inuksuk: We are so isolated.

Tiffany: We are so quiet, we're so isolated. How we express anger is so different. People don't know anything about us.

Inuksuk: People don't know how different we are.

Tiffany: People know nothing about Inuit. So, I feel like even within Indigenous circles it's important for us to be gently and firmly holding those boundaries to let Inuit also occupy space because we're so easy going. And culturally, how we deal with conflict and the harsh conditions that we grew up with and live in is to 'just make it work,' and that is beautiful, but it can also let people take advantage of us. Yeah, I hope that the work we can be doing is taking up space and allowing Inuit to also claim a bit of space as well.

Leanne: Before the pandemic, you were touring a lot and you were all over in Europe. You're connecting with audiences, non-Indigenous audiences, non-Inuit audiences, and there's an intimacy to what you're doing. I notice from my own experience with performance, often times when I walk on stage I can tell by the look on people's faces that I am not what they had in their mind when they thought they were going to see an Indigenous musician. What is the work that you're doing in terms of Inuit internationalism? You are connecting with groups of people that, if you weren't doing this work with the band and with touring and with performing, probably wouldn't be in contact with Indigenous people. And certainly, wouldn't be in contact with Inuit people. So, what is that part of it like?

Tiffany: It is good to get out of Canada. As Canadians, we absolutely love our own propaganda and our own buy-in to the idea that we are blazing trails, reconciliatory trails, and like "Look at us, we don't have a tinder date without a land acknowledgement." I feel like we just love to buy-in to like, "Yes, I know there are ninety-four things out there somewhere that say how bad we are as Canadians and I love that I know about that document."

Sometimes it is harder to be sharing this radical practice about Indigenous people to audiences that think they know so much already, and their cup is so full already. They've already made up their mind that they know everything, and when we are in the lobby after a show in Canada the questions we get are not questions but statements to show us how much they already know about us. Earlier this year when we were in Germany and Switzerland, people have a blank slate. They might have a few racist ideas in terms of Eskimos and igloos but other than that they are open and easy to correct.

Tiffany: So, it's funny, like I actually ... even though some people might get more flustered by the ignorance I'm like ... it's sweet. It's a sweet ignorance as opposed to Canadian which is like a...

Inuksuk: Staunch.

Tiffany: A weird knowing, informed ignorance. Which is harder to fight in a way. It's subtle. It's a subtler enemy. It's easier to combat something that's out in the open and more blunt, which I feel like a lot more Europeans are. So, you can meet something like that. But when it's a deep-seated thing, it's harder to call people on.

Tiffany: As tiresome as colonization 101 chats can be, in any context whether that's Canadian or international, it is kind of refreshing to be in conversation with people who are horrified to learn about Residential Schools for example.

Inuksuk: And in Canada it's like, "Yeah, but that was a long time ago." Europeans aren't as desensitized.

Leanne: Where are your favourite places to perform? Do you get to go home and perform in the North?

Tiffany: We've never performed in either of our communities. We've preformed in Iqaluit, Yellowknife, and in the Yukon. We've never been able to perform in our Inuit communities. Who knows when we'll be able to do that but that's something that I really want to do as soon as we can, to go and reground and be at home and do this. As touring musicians, up until basically this year, the idea of work has always been you have to leave home to do the work, and you have to travel and tour, and you have to suffer for three months on the road and not see your loved ones or your kids or eat good food or have a decent cup of coffee.

That's the work and it is hard work and you have to love the suffering of that in a weird way. So, the pandemic has turned that totally on its head to really show how we can innovate our practice and...

Inuksuk: Be home.

Tiffany: Be home and do a show in the garage, film something, and then come in and have dinner with the kids.

Inuksuk: Honestly, for me this is the best-case scenario. Being home is life-changing and we've been at home for probably the longest stretch in our adult lives during the pandemic and its magical. Being with my kids every single day, not missing them, it's so good, it's so good. Weird, I mean I am not saying what's happening is good, but that one spin-off has been very, very good.

Inuksuk: The burnout and the exhaustion of touring isn't there.

Tiffany: We've been producing so many of our own shows because of COVID. Now we're not only the artists, we're the sound techs, we're the lighting techs, we're our own camera crew, we are editing our own stuff, we're marketing ourselves as filmmaker-artists, which I think people have to do now, and we're producing these shows. We just did an album a few weeks ago, a new album, so we are still creating, just not from a place of exhaustion.

Inuksuk: I notice our sound has changed and is evolving.

Leanne: How has it changed?

Inuksuk: It's more dynamic.

Tiffany: We also are always communicating, all the time. Especially when we're performing, and because we're preforming more it almost feels like we're in a bit more constant communication and we're homing in on what our little nonverbal performance language is.

Inuksuk: That's what it is. Communication—there's a thread you can follow through.

Tiffany: We're getting to know our tech better; we're having more time to just play and experiment, and it's like, "Oh, I didn't know my pedal could do that. Shit, let's bust that out."

Inuksuk: Time and energy.

Tiffany: We have the time to experiment and not feel like festival stage mode where you've got three minutes to set up, line check thing, it's Sunday morning, hope you got people who are not too hungover, and then you're off to the next thing.

Tiffany: That's artist as product in those instances and so now we're like artists as artists and having the time to play and experiment a lot more. It's really making it more sparkly and dynamic and unknown and kind of weird—it's awesome.

Inuksuk: Being a small-town kid, especially a woman—especially a brown woman—it is really easy to underestimate how valid and important your processes are. It is easy to defer to the way quick-moving city folks do things and to assume that their way is right and yours is not quite right. If we've learned anything from the pandemic, which I really hope we have, it's that the way that things are being done in general doesn't work. So, they're not the standard for perfection in how processes should take place. And our small-town, small-kid Indigenous northern views are very, very relevant and useful. Not just to us, but to anybody that we're collaborating with. It is hard to feel confident in that. Especially if the sort of general message that you've had repeated growing up is that those are small, weird, back-country ideas [laughs]. So, it can be hard to develop but from this place looking back, I would say trust that what you might think is a 'limited' perspective, is not actually that limited. You have a lot to share.

Aural cycles

A conversation between Niillas Holmberg and Tiffany Ayalik on Inuit throat singing and Sámi yoiking[20]

Niillas: When I was a child I got connected, so to speak, to the traditional way of Sámi singing that we call yoiking. It's often said that you cannot really learn it if you didn't hear it as a child. It's always very evident. You can hear if someone didn't start as a child, or if someone learned it as an adult. I heard it enough to learn when I was young. When I was a schoolchild, I was lucky enough to have Sámi cultural activists around me, who were doing their best to preserve our traditional ways. Yoik was taught a little bit in our school—we had workshops and I was hearing it here and there—but then I turned eleven, twelve, and I started listening to rap music and rock music and so on, and I wasn't really thinking about traditional yoiking. I guess I didn't really want to do it or I didn't even consider it an option for years. It came back when I started making music on my own, playing guitar and singing. That was a road that took me back to yoiking. Now, during the last two or three years, I have come across an archive of traditional yoiks from my home region.

Just a short description of yoiks: we have personal yoiks for people, for animals, for places. When we yoik those yoiks, we're not yoiking *about* that person. We are *yoiking* that person. So, it's also said, and I think this is very essential, that the yoiker does not create a yoik, but merely channels it from their surroundings. That's something that says a lot about our Indigenous worldview.

In recent years, I've come across those traditional person-yoiks from my region, and many are the yoiks of my ancestors—my family members who lived in the nineteenth century, for example. Very often yoiks have lyrics in them, but they're not very wordy. They're very poetic. Often they tell a lot about the person being yoiked. Learning these yoiks in the past three years, I've felt myself become much more rooted. One way to explain it is that some of those people lived such a long time ago that there are no more people who knew them personally. They were not famous people; there are no literary descriptions of them. These yoiks are the only way for me to know what my great-great-great-grandmother was like as a person. To know what she did and how she lived. It can be heard through the lyrics but also very much through the melody and the whole expression. And, by yoiking them, it's very evident to me that I can feel the people I'm yoiking around me when I'm doing it.

Tiffany: Like you're conjuring them a bit?

Niillas: Yeah, something like that. One of the most famous yoikers, Wimme, actually told me last summer that he never yoiks human ancestors when he's doing a concert abroad because he doesn't want them to come there and stay there. He feels that it's somehow risky. So he sticks with animal yoiks and stuff like that. So that's a way of...

Tiffany: Reading time?

Niillas: Yeah.

Tiffany: Was yoiking ever banned by the different governments?

Niillas: Yes, they were very much not allowed. In the 1600s, you were condemned to death if you yoiked in some areas. It was considered a sin by the church. For example, my grandmother, who died last winter, never accepted yoiking. A lot of people from her generation were very affected by the church. I remember when I was growing up, there were yoiking concerts. When a person started yoiking, a lot of older people would stand up and walk away, because they were completely brainwashed by Christianity. The church was used as a political tool to get rid of all the elements that were seen as strange, and thus hard to control. So yoiking was banned. Different elements of our clothing were banned. Yoiking is very much connected to the mythical—well, I guess you could say, the religious background of our people.

Tiffany: It's so similar with Inuit throat singing. All across Canada any sort of cultural practice was at one point punishable by fines or imprisonment, not just for Inuit but for anyone Indigenous.

Inuit throat singing is usually done by two people as a partner song. When we're carrying our babies on our backs, it's a way to soothe our babies to sleep. There's also a game element to it—it's really fun and since there are two singing, they can compete with each other. So there is this playful element. How [the songs] come about is just through being inspired by the natural world around us, by the sonic world. We're listening to those things.

Throat singing, when the missionaries were around us, was very severely tabooed and shunned. I think this is a really common theme with missionaries: they see something they don't understand and immediately it's evil, satanic, or sinful. Especially in terms of how the church suppresses women. Misogyny was also an element in the demonization of throat singing, because you have two women who are supporting each other and learning and bonding and spending time together, and standing very close. It's a very intimate thing between two women. A beautiful bond like that is seen as sinful. We're also making noises that, if you have no reference for them, can sound scary; it's this sort of guttural, animalistic, deep, powerful thing. It's no wonder the church was terrified.

There was a time, in the mid-1900s, when throat singing almost went extinct it was so taboo. Many people were afraid of practising and many Elders who held traditional songs died and took that knowledge with them. That's pretty devastating. But in some areas it did stay active, and there were still women who practised it and eventually it started to come back. There are some very old wax-cylinder recordings of those songs and, thankfully, they survived and [throat singing] didn't become another one of those practices that went away because of colonization. There's been a real resurgence of throat singing and huge wins in that sense, where people are reclaiming the practice, taking it, and making it their own. And doing really cool, fun, innovative things with it: mixing it with electronic music, country music, hip hop or beatboxing and just really owning it, so that we can also make it adaptable. Inuit are making it accessible in ways that we feel are exciting and relevant. I feel like that's a sign of a strong culture, that it can remain grounded in tradition and things of the past but also allows for enough flexibility to adapt to changing times. And that new generations still find it relevant, and important, to keep incorporating traditional elements into their everyday lives. So, it's a really cool place, where throat singing is right now. There are really brave, awesome people who do this, despite what others may say from their couch at home, saying: "This isn't traditional. This isn't the Inuit way," and finger-wagging, you know.

Niillas: The throat-singing police.

Tiffany: Yeah, throat singing policed by people who probably don't throat sing anyway. There is a lot of that and I think that happens with anything as time goes on. It is probably the same with yoiking or other things about Sámi culture—there are the purists.

Niillas: Yeah. As the for the resurgence of traditional music in Sápmi, it really started flourishing again around fifteen years ago and has really played such an important role in making our youth feel proud of their background again, to help them see that there is a future for their cultural heritage. It's a very important thing when it comes to being healthy. Something that is important with yoiking is the cycle of it—I wonder if you share this? It's very evident that the yoik goes around and around and around. That's why it's said that it doesn't really start anywhere as a musical piece. It doesn't end anywhere. It just exists and you can jump in wherever. I'll give you an example. [yoiking] You can go on forever, forever, forever, and that is something that symbolizes the cyclical conception of time relevant to Sámi people, and I think to most Indigenous people in the world. We live by seasons. I think we understand that nature works in cycles. Everything is about cycles.

Tiffany: I feel that, especially for storytelling in the Western tradition, we're obsessed with the set-up, the rising action, conflict, climax, and then the resolve at the end. Everything follows a very Aristotelian way of looking at the arc of a story. This is sharply opposed to an Indigenous way of telling stories, where we don't think of time as straight and linear—like past, present, future. Many things are happening simultaneously, and I think that's so cool, on a sort of quantum physics level. I always make this joke that when people say, "Well there's no time like the present," I always say, "There is, it's just the past and the future—it's exactly the same!"

Niillas: That's also about basing one's life on process instead of on goals. One could say that process is the only goal.

Tiffany: The sensibility of time is very cyclical. It happens in cycles and seasons. Even things like life and death; it's not really that you live and then you die. I think this idea that Spirit can still be very present in our lives really changes how we think about death or the finality of something. Instead of being the end, it's just a continuation.

Niillas: It's about them being timeless. It's about the cycle of history repeating itself. I don't think it necessarily repeats itself in a way of identical things happening again and again. They take new forms and this is what we are seeing.

Tiffany: Are there people who are taking yoiking and being very contemporary about it and mixing it with all different kinds of musical styles?

Niillas: Very much so! It's exactly as you said. Fifteen years ago it was rock and now it's basically whatever musical genre is popular. That is what the Sámi youth are doing; they are making a fusion of yoik with the genres of music they hear all the time.

Tiffany: And are there also purists who are wagging their fingers and scolding them about it?

Niillas: There are yoik police around. Fifty years ago, music pioneer Nils-Aslak Valkeapää (or Áillohaš as we call him) was the first one to bring yoik to the stage and to mix it with other music—Western music. He was very much condemned to hell and whatnot, but he kept on doing it and then other people started following. Little by little it started growing and now it's played on national radio in Norway, Sweden, and Finland.

Tiffany: With this rise in popularity and the taboo falling away, are there non-Sámi trying to adopt yoiking?

Niillas: Yeah, there's always going to be something like that. There's always something, no matter how positive things are. I don't think there is a phenomenon which doesn't have a single negative side effect to it. There's always a counter phenomenon. And this has happened. There are television shows with celebrities trying to yoik, like top-notch Norwegian musicians and vocalists trying to yoik, and learning them.

Tiffany: Same here too, especially when we travel to different cities or countries where people might not be as familiar with throat singing. People will come up to us after and say, "How do you do that? It's so amazing. Can you teach me?" Did you not just hear the history? This is something that we just got back. We just got this back. In the history of things, in the scheme of time, we just got the baby back, so let us hold it for a minute. This is something that non-Indigenous people shamed and shunned us for. All of a sudden now you love it. And now you want to use it for your own.

Niillas: We are expected to teach everyone...

Tiffany: And share. When you go to a museum or an art gallery and you look at the beautiful things on the wall, you look at these beautiful pieces. You can see a piece of art, look at it, and appreciate it. You can support the artist. You can look at the craft and the skill, but in order to fully appreciate it you don't have to go and cut a little piece of the painting off and bring it home, as though that's the only way you can appreciate it. We do it all the time. We let things be, we let things be on the wall and we appreciate them. To think that we have to then own a little part of it in order to fully appreciate it—it isn't true. We recognize that with visual art and with a lot of cultural things, it's the same: just appreciate the skill. Appreciate the history. Marvel at the artistry. Support the people who do it. You don't have to be inside of it to fully appreciate it.

Niillas: You don't have to own everything. You don't.

Songs of gratitude and hope

Beatrice Deer in conversation with Leanne Betasamosake Simpson

Beatrice: My name is Beatrice Deer. I am from Quaqtaq, Nunavik, on the Hudson Straight, Ungava Bay of about 400 people. I am Inuk and my Father is Mohawk. My Mother is Inuk. I grew up in my Inuit village and that's why I mostly identify myself as Inuk. I work full time and I am also a singer-songwriter. We've been a band for over ten years. I've been doing music much longer than that. I started singing in festivals when I was eighteen. My first song when I was fifteen with my cousin, so I've been making music ever since. I'm thirty-eight now. I also sew a lot. I make outdoor clothing—traditional and contemporary outfits. I've lived in Montreal now for almost fourteen years. I have two grown children and I am now pregnant so that's a big part of my life too now.

Both my parents are musicians. My Dad plays guitar and bass. He had a lot of guitars around. My Mom plays accordion and organ. They were also pastors at the church, so I grew up going to church and playing and singing at church. My older cousins in Quaqtaq are great singers too. There was always music around.

It took many, many years for me to muster up my courage and finally move south. I thought about moving for a long time and I made excuses to stay for a long time because I was scared. I had a very troubled marriage that ultimately gave me the push to leave. Key people in my life told me that I could be much more than a school secretary. That I had more potential. That I should go to school. So that's what I finally did. I always struggled to find musicians to play with, so I left so I could be a musician. I had a lot of personal problems that I couldn't find help with in my town, so I left to get help—to get therapy. There were no therapists in Quaqtaq. I wanted my kids to have a better education. I had to make the sacrifice of having my children miss out on their culture, language, and identity, but it was what we needed to do as a family.

Leanne: Yesterday I watched your music video for "Immutaa." It is such a beautiful piece of work. There is so much Inuit joy in this video—kids, smiling, dancing, high fiving, thumbs up, Inuit kids learning from your band mates—and I could feel the Inuit pride and joy watching. Tell me about that song and that video.

Beatrice: That's the song that we all learn as children. It is a traditional song—it has no date; we don't know who wrote it. It is ancient. The words are gibberish—they don't make sense. We started spontaneously playing it during a rehearsal. I just started singing "Immutaa." The first time we played it, people loved it and we kept playing it. Because it was so loved by people we put it on the album. It is such a happy song. So during the launch of *My All To You*, we made the video at the official launch of the album in Quaqtaq. I wanted to launch my album in Quaqtaq, so I got a grant and we flew the whole band there with a videographer. I just wanted to show everyone where I come from, and I wanted to have kids in the song because it's a children's song, and I wanted to show that even though we are from a very small town we can accomplish fun things by working hard. I wanted to show the warmth of my hometown. The kids are so enthusiastic and welcoming when I come home. We had an afternoon of music workshops at the church and you can see the kids learning from my band. It is very cute.

Leanne: It is always so hard for Indigenous musicians, but particularly northern Indigenous musicians to play in our hometowns. I'm so happy you made that happen. There are so many Inuit women making rad music videos right now—PIQSIQ, Elisapie, Asinnajaq and of course Leela Gilday, who is Dene. Collectively you're making a very different sort of visual experience than mainstream music videos. You're centring joy, community, land, and children. Is this deliberate—because it breaks so many stereotypes people have of the North, but I think it's also doing other work.

Beatrice: I wanted to show the happy side of the North. We are more than what the media portrays us to be. We work with good people. The video for "Quajimagit" features Deseray Cumberbatch as an Inuk athlete in the one-foot high kick. It is about making a choice to change if you're in a place in your life where you don't like your circumstances, you're bound, you're not happy, or your past is controlling you. The song tells you if you don't want to be there, get up on your own and walk. I want the message of my songs to come through for me and for other people. In spite of all the struggles, it is ultimately our choice to change and evolve in life.

Leanne: "1997," from *My All To You* is a very moving song for me. I listened to it for several months without googling what the Inuktitut lyrics meant. There is a sadness to it, but also a calm in the music. When I finally found out what the song meant, I learned that the music without the lyrics were communicating with me and talking to me about my own trauma. It is such a gorgeous piece so full of courage and humility. Could you talk about that song?

Beatrice: In 1997, my family had a house fire and we tragically lost four of my siblings and my cousin in that fire. We lost everything. I wrote the song as a song of gratitude to my friend who stuck by me for almost three months after that. I was only fourteen years old, going through so much loss. My family was completely shattered. My friend Charlotte, just stuck by me. Slept with me. She was with me all day and all night. We didn't know how to talk or to express our grief at fourteen. Many years later, she had a huge role in supporting me and that song is a song of gratitude although it comes from a very, very, painful life-changing gratitude. After many years of working on myself and healing and understanding that death is the most painful thing you can experience as a human being, but if you can see beyond that, and know that life is more than just a series of tragic events, then you can come to a place of gratitude. In that song, I wish her the best life that she can have, and I want her to know that I love her.

Leanne: You write songs in French, English, and Inuktitut. How do you decide what language?

Beatrice: Most of my songs are in Inuktitut because that's the language I'm most comfortable expressing myself. I come up with the melody first. The more I'm working on it as the lyrics come to me, they sort of determine the language. Whatever makes sense in the songwriting process.

Leanne: The racism and patriarchy of the music industry can be pretty difficult for Indigenous women, particularly for the emerging Indigenous musicians from the North. How have you navigated that?

Beatrice: I don't focus on who is going to accept my music. I'm a full-time musician and I have a day job. I'm not solely relying on music for my income. I love performing. I love being on stage with my band making music. I don't focus on the industry. I'm not a touring musician either because I've chosen to work and have a steady income for my family because I've been a single Mom forever. I didn't want to go on tours and leave my kids behind. That felt selfish to me. I worked full time instead. As a band, we go to one off shows and festivals instead of two-, three- or four-week-long tours. I chose not to do that. I don't really rely on the music industry. I don't pay attention to if the music industry pays attention to me or not.

I hope my music is helping someone realize that life is not always easy, but it is ultimately our decision to determine how happy we are. We all have a history. We have all gone through different forms of trauma at different times. Some have gone through hell and some have not, but we all go through hurt. We all have issues. I hope that my music breaks down the stigma that we have to hide our past. We shouldn't have to be ashamed with who we are because shame really kills people. I hope my music brings hope.

Leanne: I think that's the perfect ending to this conversation. Miigwech.

I am a woman, I am Indigenous, I am Inuk

ᐃᓕᓴᐱ Elisapie Issac in conversation with
Leanne Betasamosake Simpson

ᐃᓕᓴᐱ **Elisapie:** I am Elisapie Isaac. I'm an Indigenous woman, I am a woman, I am Indigenous, I am Inuk. I was raised in Salluit, Nunavik—one of the most northern villages in Nunavik. I grew up there until I moved to Montreal when I was in my early twenties. It has been twenty years now of exile life in the South, as we call it in Montreal. I started really getting serious about singing when I was twenty-three, after having met some guy in a café who knew a musician friend (instrumentalist Alain Auger) and we connected. A lot of my dreams that I kind of held onto for myself, because I was very shy about it, became true very quickly when we made an album as a duo called *Taima* (Inuktitut for "that's all" or "it's done"). I led the life of a musician, and it's never really stopped. I've done four albums so far and did a documentary film with the National Film Board when I had just arrived to Montreal. It's called *If the Weather Permits* (2003). It's been a very busy life and I've been very fortunate to get to do what I do and tour. I love being on stage and performing and communicating to different people. Right now, I'm working on new songs and thinking a lot about filmmaking.

Leanne: Did you grow up with music and singing? Is that something that was part of your life in Salluit?

ᐃᓕᓴᐱ **Elisapie:** Oh yeah, for sure. There was an Elder in Salluit, she was very old and she called me grandmother because I was named after her grandmother. I would go see her once in a while. She was a relative, and I think she had some connection with the shaman world. These are things we didn't talk about then, but there was always *something* about her. I did some research in the archives at the Avataq Cultural Institute in Nunavik, and I got to hear her Ayaya (personal songs put into story). Ayaya is this chanting describing things, incidents. You see a lot of Ayaya with the drum. People chant these very meditative songs; you could almost fall asleep listening to them because it's so soothing. Sometimes these are stories about events or tragic things that happened between two people and sometimes they're definitely not love songs [laughs] ... like far from love songs. Listening to this Elder at Avataq was so magical and I realized my goodness, I grew up listening to her. Sometimes she would chant with her very old voice. So, I guess a lot of those magical moments existed with the generation before me, but they were somehow not practised anymore because of Christianity.

I was with these Elders who had adopted me—maybe not Elders, they were older people. I called her Anaana (Mom) and I called him Ataata (Dad). I'd say they were one of the last people who were from that old world. Life was very simple. I grew up in the early 1980s with a lot of church songs, because my uncle was a born-again Christian, but my parents weren't so I wasn't exposed to this heavy religious way of life. My uncle would sometimes practise in one of the rooms of his house; that was my Mother's sister's husband, though I called him Father because they kind of adopted me also. You know how Inuit are very loving and we like to just take in a bigger family. Every time he practised—he was a violin fiddle player—he would practise with the bass player who was also in a band with my other uncle, Sugluk, a rock and roll band in Salluit. He would join Mark on the bass and he would practise for an event that would be happening in a month in the community. He would also call me "little grandmother" because I'm named after another lady that is his grandmother. They would always bring me along, and so here I was as a kid among these old guys. In my head, they were really old but really they were in their early forties. My uncle would play the fiddle, like really Scottish background kind of music, and I guess they just wanted to expose that world to me. A musician's life. He knew I loved singing. I loved the hymns they would play at church. I used to go to an Anglican Church when I was young and that's where I got to hear music and learn to sing. There were no music programs or a music teacher at school. Every year for Christmas I would be the only one who was like "Yeah I want to be part of the Christmas show!" [laughs]

I took what I could. My other uncle, my biological uncle is George Kakayuk. In the 1970s he formed a band during his Residential School days in Churchill, Manitoba, among many amazing people like Willie Thrasher, William Tagoona, Charlie Adams. These young Inuit boys formed a rock and roll band! My uncle was very, very, very talented. He's a great singer-songwriter. He has a group called Salluit Band. Back in the day they were called Sugluk. My uncle called me "Little Mother" because I'm named after his Mother who died the year before I was born in the same hospital in Moose Factory, Ontario. I have this strong connection to him.

I mean I took what I could. Knowing that I'm related to George Kakayuk ... music has always been kind of a secret love of mine, I guess. Of course, as a teenager I learned to love a lot of pop songs and a lot of folk songs. I would watch the Grammys like any kid and I would say, "One day I want to go there." Then I heard Susan Aglukark for the first time and that's when it hit me and I'm like, "What!? You can actually make a CD as an Inuk girl?!" I held onto her words, in her first album. She was a huge, huge, huge influence for many of us, for young girls. I don't really remember when I wanted to make music or if I wanted to make music. When I came south, I realized the feeling of wanting to leave the North is very related to wanting to express myself and feel free. When you are from a small northern town and you are surrounded by biological and adopted family there can be a lot of choice in family life. My parents passed away, my siblings. There were a lot of feelings of guilt and music became like a therapy for me.

Leanne: That's perfect, that's amazing. It is amazing to hear of the influence of your community and your family, especially your uncle. I love that you hung onto the words of Susan Aglukark and that her work made you realize a musician's life was an option for an Inuk girl like you.

Your album, *The Ballad of the Runaway Girl*, it's one of my most precious records for many, many reasons. It is so honouring of those Indigenous musicians that have come before us. And so I'm really glad you talked about Sugluk because I think that dedication in the albums to Willie Thrasher, Willy Mitchell, it's so beautiful. It's so moving for me because I think that generation of musicians, it was so difficult for them, such a struggle, but they had that love of music and they did it anyway and it's such an amazing inheritance for us. So, can you talk a little bit about why "Call of the Moose" and then "Wolves Don't Live by the Rules" made it onto the album? Why was that important to you?

ᐃᓴᐱ **Elisapie:** After I gave birth, it was my spirit that needed a lifting. I needed to shift my way of seeing myself and I needed to grow up. When I had my second child, I had a weird situation where I had just bought a little house, everything was great, I felt safe, I felt connected to the Mother I am. And then all of a sudden I just crashed, and I had no idea why this was happening, and it was so powerful to the point where my ear would ring and I would get unbalanced.

And it's funny because my biological Mother went through a depression. She was a very strong, bubbly woman that went through this and as it was happening to her she would lose her balance also, something to do with her ear. This is my biological Mom; I didn't grow up with her but I knew her. I know her, she's like a friend in a way. It was so weird; it was so strong.

My life was calling to me, trying to wake me up. I connected to that call and the fear it brought to everything. It was powerful. I felt I owed it to myself to go deep, deep, deep into it instead of being afraid. And that Willie Thrasher's album *Spirit Child* really became the soundtrack for that year in my life. I listened to it every day for so long, to a point where my kids and my boyfriend were like, "Oh ... old '70s folk music is cool but there's a limit."

I became attached to it. I needed it, or else I was going to collapse. That's how it felt anyway. It allowed me to cry, without feeling like I was going to collapse. You know when we go through something like this, we feel very bad. We feel like, "Oh, I'm crying again. I'm depressed again," and when you have a child and children at home you can't collapse.

This time also opened an old wound that I had been carrying and that I tried to minimize—my adoption, my biological Mother, the connection with her that all of a sudden became weird. And I was like,

"Why am I feeling like this? This is a very natural thing to do. Inuit would adopt a child. Inuit would give up their child. You know, it's a form of friendship and it's an Inuit way of life. Why should I doubt that?" I wondered if I was just being a white person, if I wasn't Inuk enough to accept my adoption and understand it. It's hard, right.

I just couldn't do it anymore and that's when I realized I never really asked for guidance ever. I always, always thought I have to be strong and on my own because I sacrificed moving to the big city and left my family and my community.

Working through this became really important. Thrasher became like a foundation of *The Ballad of the Runaway Girl*, of course with my uncle's songs. They were all related—it was Residential School survivors. They had to face so much, probably more guilt than I've felt, because they were told, "One day you're going to be an amazing person because you're going to get a job. That's why you have go to school." And my uncle, George for instance, speaks English ... he knows how to communicate in such an amazing way because that's what he held onto.

So, yeah, I'm really drawn to Willy Mitchell's songs. I really felt the spiritual connection of these songs in "Call of the Moose." These guys didn't have the opportunities I've had. We have the tools now and the confidence. These old guys were just like, "I know how to write songs," and it ends there. I need to pay tribute to them and also say, "These songs are also my songs. They're everybody's songs." It was really fun covering their songs. That's the story of *The Ballad of the Runaway Girl*, which is my uncle's song title.

Leanne: That's so amazing. That's so amazing to see that trajectory and that energy flowing through that generation. I really identify with that. I feel like when I had my children I lost myself, and I lost my own voice, and actually that's why I started performing as well. I think as a way of finding my own self again, so I've never heard anyone else talk about it like that but that's so much more meaningful to me than depression. These videos that you made, are so beautiful and so centring of women, community, and Inuit joy. It's such a celebration of the North and Inuit culture and such a different intervention in the world. Can you talk a little bit about the image of the young Inuk girl on the ATV doing donuts in the video for "Arnaq"?

ᐃᒃᓯᓕ **Elisapie:** I know she's badass. It's so blunt. It's so raw. There was no planning. She came up to me and asked me if I was Qupanuaq (my name among many like Elisapie, Lissie, Akumalik) and we started talking. And I figured out she was one of my relative's kids. She said we're related (connected) by name (namesake) and she started calling me "Saunik," which means bone in our language—in our tradition names come from somewhere and we try to make that ancestor live through our names; we become the spirit of that person. I asked her if we could film her on her Honda four-wheeler because she was doing all these spins. She agreed. So, there was no planning or preparation. If you plan, you're just going to create a headache. You have to recognize it is another rhythm. In the North, if you don't show up, it's not the end of the world. If you show up, that's cool. This video is based on spontaneous moments. That's what I wanted to show. The rhythm of the North, our own rhythm.

It was so much fun. I think what I'm also trying to show is the pride we have, because we need to see ourselves on TV and in videos. We need to see more of ourselves. I think images are so much fun since forever, for Inuit anyway, when we see videos or old pictures we're really captured.

And also, for southerners, they have these images of the North; it breaks their stereotypes of us in the snow, never changing. I'm like, no—don't forget Inuit were always inventing, we were always moving, we were amazing inventors. We adapted to anything that would arrive. Any modern stuff that arrives in the North, Inuit take in and we're like, "How can we adapt this to our environment?" We're excited about it! The South has to stop thinking that Inuit are in this very 'pure' world. No, we also want to invent stuff, so just bring them whatever and they'll figure something out that's going to be exciting and useful for us. It's fun for me to show that. Every time I'm going to go film—and the next shoot I want to do is *When the Darkness Brings the Light*—I make sure the images of us are not like *National Geographic*. Forget that view. We are going inside. That's what I want people to see. To feel like you're inside Inuit culture because then you can start to understand that we're human beings, you know. We're not your historical figures; we are human beings.

Leanne: You tour a lot, and you've toured internationally. What do you hope your artistic practice is doing in the world? What is the work that it's doing?

ᐃᓕᓴᐱ Elisapie: I think in order for people to really connect and want to be with us and want to contribute to change they have to start seeing us as humans. As individuals with feelings, emotions, dreams—like anybody. I want to continue to do this because it is an amazing tool to connect with people. When I started to go to France two and a half years ago with my boyfriend who is from France, I wondered how I was going to relate and connect to French people and get through to them because they are so different. I thought they would be whispering, "Oh my God, an Inuk." At the end of my shows, they were the most gentle people. They didn't overtalk. They just spoke to me as a human, a person, a woman, and it was nothing more. They were very emotional because they were still trying to take it all in. That part is more important to me than say going to a university and speaking to Anthropology students. I gravitate toward simple human connection. I think that is a good base for understanding. People will be more open-minded or they're going to be more open-minded.

Leanne: You are a Mother, and from the way that you've talked, that's been a source of inspiration and it's been a generative spot for you. It also, I know for myself, it's difficult to balance those responsibilities with the responsibilities of an artist and an artist life. How do you navigate it? Parenting, and touring, and creating art...

ᐃᓕᓴᐱ Elisapie: I think *The Ballad of the Runaway Girl* has been one of the most exciting things that's happened in my life because it also allowed me to grow and embrace my strength as a woman, to flirt with my vulnerability and my strength, because that's what these songs demanded. I tried to deliver them in the most genuine way and they've actually been very helpful in my life so I can face many things in a much clearer way, because these songs, this music, and this journey with this album gave me that. I owe it to the Willies for their songs that became much bigger than just a song. I have a feeling by doing that my kids, they see a much ... less doubting Mother. I easily doubt and I easily feel guilty and then I get to be all over the place. I can't do that anymore. It's cute to be vulnerable, to show your vulnerable side, to show that you can change. You fall and you get up and all that. It's great, but I think at one point I have to say, "Kids, I'm your Mom. I'm doing the best I can so, you know, I'll show you that I assume every action I make." Touring was very hectic because I had a newborn baby. I left him for the first time for a two-week tour when he was only six months old, but I was very well surrounded and I think the whole time that I would leave that year before he was two, not once did I feel like, "Oh my god I feel so bad." I mean, maybe once, but because it's a choice that I made I was like, "You know what, if you're going to do this Eli, go for it, or you don't." So, I was like, I'm going for it, and actually they're okay. I don't feel like they missed out because this was almost like a family project. They knew that this was a big deal, to go tour Europe and to have a team out in Europe. So, it was a big deal. There was a lot of excitement also. I mean the little ones didn't really realize it, but my daughter certainly knew that it was exciting to be doing this and to get good reviews. It didn't become this "Oh my, I'm so great," it was more like. "This is a sacrifice, so I might as well be celebrating it right."

Leanne: On Christmas day 2020, everybody is under stay-at-home orders because of the pandemic, streaming the Disney+ premier of *Soul*, and Inuit, Nishnaabeg, Mohawk, and Indigenous families all over North America get a few minutes into it and we hear Inuktitut; the first time in a Disney movie! Seeing your name in the credits, it was such a celebration. I was so proud of you. Hearing you in that movie was one of the high points of the pandemic for me.

ᐃᓕᓴᐱ **Elisapie:** Aw, it was very special, especially because we're in a pandemic. We did the same; we went into the basement and we're chilling watching the movie. For me it was just like one little line that I went to go do almost a year ago and I kind of had forgotten about it, but it is a big deal for people, you know? For my little cousins, they hear their language, but also for my people, "It's someone we know. She's from our town. It's so precious."

I've learned to accept, to praise myself once in a while because if I don't do that I'm very stupid because my people are so proud. People want that, they are proud of you, and I wonder how can I get all that praise and not be able to say it to myself? That's like not really living it. I've done that so much in the past just because I feel guilty of having success. I'm like okay, people are suffering, but actually people who are suffering love seeing things like that.

Leanne: It's just this tremendous practice of humility that comes through in your records and even in this interview that I just cherish. It's just so beautiful, so thank you so much for engaging and doing this with me. Miigwech.

Many voices walking together

ᐊᓯᓐᓇᐃᔭᖅ Asinnajaq in Conversation with
Leanne Betasamosake Simpson

Asinnajaq: My name is Asinnajaq and I'm from Inukjuak, Nunavik. My parents are Jobie Weetaluktuk and Carol Rowan and I grew up in the suburbs of Montreal, so that's where I come from.

Leanne: I know you as a visual artist and an editor, curator, writer, filmmaker. How did you find that path? How did you find your voice?

Asinnajaq: When I finished high school, my parents decided to move to Victoria so my Mom could finish her masters, which she put on hold until her children were able to be on their own. Me and my Dad decided to go out with her. My Dad and I would go for drives and walk on the beach, like beachcombing, and taking our cameras and really look at the world with our instruments—our cameras. I remember one time the salmon were spawning so we went—especially to go and see them and I really practised looking. I was doing online school for grade twelve because I had been living in Quebec and we just went to grade eleven. In grade twelve, they gave me, like, all A's on every single class which I thought was unacceptable, because you can't grow if you just have A's everywhere. Especially I would say because I didn't feel I was trying.

I decided to move schools back to Montreal to do CEGEP. I was having a really good time and I was in a really good flow, feeling challenged and doing sociology. Then one of my best friends from my summer job on a cruise ship killed herself, and I was broken. I felt so bad because I was in such a good place and someone I loved so much was having the very opposite experience and I had no idea. I developed great anxiety and I was unable to go to my classes. I would try to go, see the door, and be unable to go in. Or, I would enter and have to leave. The only class I could continue doing was printmaking. So, I was spending all my time there doing hands-on art. I always loved art and connected with it, but I didn't want to go to school for art. After that experience I decided it was important for me to do crafts and to do very hands-on work. So, I moved to New Brunswick; there they had a college for art and design—of craft and design. There I was learning everything that was very tactile and I very fearfully scaredly told my teachers that I had anxiety and I might leave class. I only had anxiety once and the teacher sat with me outside until I was calm. It was the most amazing place for me to have a transformation. It was very loving and I was able to learn things that I was very interested in. They encouraged me once they saw me in my video class. They encouraged me to go to NSCAD (Nova Scotia College of Art and Design) and told me that I should go to the film school. I went to NSCAD and looked at it and it was exactly what I wanted. So, that's how I ended up being pushed into the arts.

Leanne: It sounds like that practice of hands-on work and making things was very grounding and therapeutic for you. How was it when you got to NSCAD?

Asinnajaq: When I got to NSCAD, at first it was kind of confusing because I had just done a foundation year at a craft school, and basically when you start at NSCAD you also do a foundation year, but I hadn't properly been explained that. So, I did a repeat of a lot of classes, but the amazing part was once I entered into film. The other students were very interested in film and we would make recommendations to each other, and I really got to be a super-nerd on film history, which I loved. I think that there was a tension that I felt in certain classes, where I knew there was an answer if we did a test that was expected of me, but I knew that it's not how I saw the truth. I had to have some very difficult moments during school where I had to decide whether I was going to be honest about what the truth was in my eyes, or if I was going to get a good grade, and I almost failed because of those hard decisions.

Leanne: I'm sorry you were in that position. A lot of Indigenous students still face that. So, you leave NSCAD and you live the life of an Indigenous artist, as an Inuk artist. What does that look like for you? What does that mean?

Asinnajaq: I think that I work hard but I'm also lucky at the same time, because I know it's not just luck or hard work that gets you somewhere, but you have to be lucky for your hard work to pay off, I think. I was lucky enough to have started making a film before I graduated, whereas I think a lot of artists from any background might not ever get a shot in the field that they're looking to be in. I was able to start on that path before I graduated and so I remember some friends in the final year of school wondering, "What am I gonna do?' and having to figure out taking a coffee job or things like that. I definitely felt lucky at that time to have an arts job lined up and to be able to go right into my filmmaking. It's definitely not easy to be doing contract work and I think the hardest thing is not having jobs to do because I think Indigenous and Inuit artists and curators are very needed and important. It is sometimes difficult to figure out what to put your time into—your own projects, other people's projects, and sometimes you have to just try things. Like, I'll say I tried TV; it's not for me. It is also hard because security is important and of course helping out family financially is important, but you also have to set limits of what you can do in a day and take care of yourself. I'm always trying to find that balance.

Leanne: It seems like it's been really important to, in addition to your own practice, to be creating space, and holding space for Inuit artists—I'm thinking of "Tillitarniit," a three-day festival in Montreal that celebrates Inuit culture that you are a co-creator of, and of course the issue of *Canadian Art* in the Spring of 2019, which you co-edited. Why is this work important to you?

Asinnajaq: I think it's important to me to have an artistic practice because I love making art, and it's equally important to me that my voice isn't the only one. One of the things that I appreciate a lot about being Inuk is that my people demand to have their own voice and they recognize that everyone can have their own perspective and their own opinion on things. I think it's important to me to remember that and make space for many voices and also to, like, be together and get to walk together.

Leanne: I love that because I think, I know in my culture, making creative practice and arts and crafts and music used to be something that everybody did but also very communal. Leela Gilday talks about that too. And now, under colonialism and capitalism it's such an individual pursuit. I really have a lot of respect for you and your practice, about that collective ethic and bringing up those other voices. I really, really love your film *Three Thousand* (2017). It's so gorgeous the way that you've woven together animation and archival footage of Inuit and there's so much joy and happiness and hope, I think. I watched it again today during the pandemic, and sometimes hope is sort of lucid. That film is just so breathtaking and beautiful and thank you for that work. Can you talk a little bit about why you made that film and where that film comes from?

Asinnajaq: Definitely. I used to go on the website Tumblr a lot to share photos with people and kind of be a part of that community. But, like, the danger with anything online basically is that there's always people who are volatile and have no idea about where you come from in an aggressive way. So, I remember my first idea for why I made this film isn't very positive, but during the process it definitely changed what the purpose behind it was. First, the notion was that I could see people posting on this website and they had no idea how I could be behind the computer at all as an Inuk. Some people could not understand that idea. They only think of snow and igloos when they think of Inuit. So, that was the initial motivation for the idea. One of the reasons I really like filmmaking and also anything that kind of takes time and effort and thought, is that you get the chance to grow while you do it. As I was making the film, the intention for it changed. As I went through the process, rather than being for people who I don't know on the Internet, it really became for my immediate family. For an understanding of ourselves and also to be able to see strength in ourselves. So, yeah, it shifted a lot and I'm really happy it did because then I got to make it from a very loving place, rather than a sarcastic place. [laughs]

Leanne: I felt the love watching that piece.

Asinnajaq: It's a lot of love because I think that once I started looking at the archives and talking to my family, it's the feeling that was there.

Leanne: It seems in some ways it was like a visual conversation across time and space with your ancestors, and you all recognizing each other—at least that's one of the beautiful things that I noticed in it. As someone who is working and living in the South, how do you carry your homeland and your people with you?

Asinnajaq: I think our Inuit philosophy and way of being is all formed by the relationship with the land. What I know about how to be human is informed by where I grew up personally and then also where my ancestors grew up, and that's Nunavik. Over thousands of years, people learned how to be in relation to that landscape and relation to the animals and the elements and everything. All of that kind of knowledge of how to be, that's what makes me Inuk, and there's so many incredible lessons in the way that people learn to be in the world and sometimes it isn't so obvious how they apply in this world, but they definitely do. So, I really try and always remember that even sometimes when the answer of how to behave or how to interact with something or someone isn't clear, that there is a good way to do it.

Leanne: A lot of the Indigenous women artists that I've talked to in this book have talked about how they, I guess had different understandings of success. They've talked about how the process of making and creating, and the fact that they get to do that and keep getting to do that is the important part, and that's why they feel successful, rather than that other kind of Western "I made it to Hollywood" and "I'm a billionaire" sort of idea. I'm wondering if you could talk a little bit about your hope for your work in the world. What is the work that it's doing?

Asinnajaq: I see my work as a loving environment for growth and learning for people, and especially I think about youth. I try to make work that can be long lasting and that can still help people grow many, many years into the future. But I also hope that it's not the best artwork ever made because the people after me are going to be even smarter and better than me, so I hope it can help them and then they can be even cooler.

Leanne: What are your hopes for the future?

Asinnajaq: Same as always. I hope that I can pretty much learn how to be true to myself and how to be kind to others and to help other people do that. That's pretty much all I want to do; I want to be nice and I want to help other people be nice.

Leanne: Miigwech, Asinnajaq.

The Harvest Sturdies [21]

Tanya Lukin Linklater

21   This is an excerpt from *Slow Scrape* (Montreal, Quebec: The Centre for Expanded Poetics and Anteism, 2020) and is reprinted here with permission.

cheap memory foam cushions a cheaper mattress, under goose down comforter and flannel I'm wrapped composing before I open my eyes, there's a woman whose name means to harvest, to provide.

a crimson ribbon skirt to ground, a down coat, tanned moose hide mitts braided with yarn rest at her sides held at her neck. moose hide, smoked and tanned, collide with red and white beads. those hands pluck geese chop wood snare rabbits stoke fires lay spruce boughs for warmth, the harvest sturdies.

here, I bleach black mold lines on window frames, scrub the septic tank toilet, wash re-wash bathroom counter tops, he pine sols the floors, stacks rugs on deck snow. together we dust scrub bleach to prepare our home for visitors.

from a hand me down couch through the window, an ice-fishing hut appears driven by a truck I can't see, it hovers on a dirt road to launch onto the frozen lake. this view from our 900 square-foot home on someone else's first nation.

surrounded by blankets hanging inside raw canvas and scraped trees, spruce boughs on ground to insulate, she rests. a woodstove pipe creaks toward december sun. the girls crouch on unthawed land near a fire, she sits mantled in blankets against wintry damp. she listens as they speak about a day when every child in Canada feels they are worth something. I watch as she brings her lips to each cheek and brow and I plot a line for her as these james bay mitts rest at her neck. to harvest provide dispense, she enters her twenty-first day.

the eve of a new year on the unmelted river.

mitts : astisak

women : iskwewak

James Bay astisak worked by women's hands astisak. And from the life of an animal, you say it's a year to fix a moose hide or longer, your hands

clip

scrape

smoke

wring

tan

stretch

wash

Your hands work hides beads fur linings. Stitches thread cloth. Both your hands work these objects that aren't *objects:* astisak warm the hands of   awasisak   napewak   iskwewak on this land, astisak. Women who work in this way, mothers grandmothers aunties, I'm telling you. I don't know this work. Nimbly, James Bay iskwewak craft astisak. Swiftly, they sew astisak. Astisak, in repetition they stitch, swift repetition, they clothe their families.

Nohkom I call you. Ask about sewing mitts, instead you tell me you grew up in a tipi, on the land. In the bush near Hudson Bay 95, 200 miles from Peawanuck. Your Dad hunted caribou, trapped beaver otter mink and nowadays the young men trap martens.

Years ago in my Mother-in-law's kitchen you fried caribou with onions, ruddy on a spring afternoon in Timmins. After tea and visits in your daughter's house I told you my grandmother passed away, I was only seven. *I can be your grandmother* you said.

Now as we talk on the phone, you in Peawanuck me on Lake Nipissing, I wonder why I never asked you more. I waited so long. Nearly 80 this May and you can't cook in the tipi nor teach the kids how to snare or to speak Cree. But you sew fierce and scrub the floors from your wheelchair.

I never saw my own Mother sew stitch cook.
Ghoulash canned corn dropped in macaroni
second-day. Grandmother, it was a wooden red-
handled rolling pin tiny bread tins the feel of dough
flattened on my palms. Girl fingers, just play. Who,
among women, showed me. How to [   ] *small*
objects *in seventh-grade Home Ec. How to* [   ] *a*
blue frock for performance [   ] *beads on a silver*
skirt [   ] *a patch. Among women, I tape the hem*
on slacks for an interview, sewing machine
untouched.

"

They need

to   understand   the

whole

concept

of   our

craftsmen.

"

Auntie

So it's done like this, Tanya:

seam thread needle hem seam thread needle hem seam thread needle hem seam thread
oo:::|| astisak ||:::oooo:::|| maskasina ||:::oo
seam thread needle hem seam thread needle hem seam thread needle hem seam thread

oo:::|| petal leaf stem ||:::oooo:::|| yellow purple green ||:::oo
oo:::|| daughter & son & daughter ||:::oo
oo:::|| petal leaf stem ||:::oooo:::|| yellow purple green ||:::oo

seam thread needle hem seam thread needle hem seam thread needle hem seam thread
oo:::|| astisak ||:::oooo:::|| maskasina ||:::oo
seam thread needle hem seam thread needle hem seam thread needle hem seam thread

Instead, with accent hues of moss and
lavender shades of rose, I follow a map of
syllabics

I write on ‖ a t i k o w a y a n ‖

and build my lines like this

nohkominanak
‖:::oooo:::‖ ‖:::oooo:::‖
iskwewak iskwewak iskwewak
‖:::oooo:::‖ ‖:::oooo:::‖ ‖:::oooo:::‖ ‖:::ooo:::‖
askiy askiy askiy askiy askiy askiy askiy askiy askiy askiy
‖:::oooo:::‖ ‖:::oooo:::‖ ‖:::oooo:::‖ ‖:::oooo:::‖ ‖:::oooo:::‖ ‖:::oooo:::‖

"

When it's

my   own   time

my   own   sewing

my   own   ways

it's like I go into a little

place   of   my   own.

"

Auntie

practice practice practice practice practice practice practice practice practice practice

....

a stitch a bead another stitch repeat a stitch a bead another stitch repeat a stitch a bead ano

ther stitch repeat a bead a stitch another stitch repeat a stitch a bead another stitch repeat

o-o-o-o-o-o-o-o-o-o-o-o-o-o-o-o-o-o-o-o-o-o-o-o-o-o-o-o-o-o-o-o-o-o-o-o-o-o-o-o-o-o-o-o-o

hands deft every stitch straight each bead nimble repeat hands deft every stitch straight e

ach bead nimble repeat hands deft every stitch straight each bead nimble repeat hands def

....

gentle   gentle   very gentle   repeat gentle gentle very gentle repeat gentle gentle very

"

You connect with your loved ones. For me I connect with my Mom it's my Mom
and grandma mostly my mom though and my aunties. I have their patterns
their mitts their slippers. I pull them out I look at them. I see her writing I can
see the style of my aunts I can see the style of my mom and these papers
are little whittled now they're just thinning out. You start thinking
about them it's healing it brings real comfort in your soul
when you're sewing I get a lot of comfort. That's why
when things go on *ah I'm goin' to do some*
sewing I go in another world it's hard
to explain just with you and God
you're thinking you're praying
your mind goes you're
in another
atmosphere

"

"

I don't let it   go.   I won't let it

go.

"

smoke of the canvas skirt you bind on

a t i k o w a y a n in the cook tipi eddies

we spark the spongy wood

for this last part you show me

over the phone, Nohkom

raising one delica bead

from the cache, I fire the caribou broom

turn it over in my mind

as I cannot see its texture

weight color, the light

You say, only three or four left

in Peawanuck and perhaps two in Fort Severn know

how to *fix* the   hide   of   a t i k

Nohkom, I am not with you

Notes

"The Harvest Sturdies" was written in the winter of 2012–2013 in response to Chief Theresa Spence's hunger strike, a 44-day action that began December 11, 2012. She fasted for treaty in a tipi on Victoria Island in the Ottawa River not far from Parliament Hill, Ottawa, Canada. The mitts Chief Spence wore in many of her press engagements may be understood as a symbol for the people of James Bay. Agnes Hunter, Marlene Kapashesit, and Lillian Mishi Trapper agreed to be interviewed about their experiences and knowledge of sewing, beading, and hide tanning during January and February 2013. Their discussions of making traditional James Bay mitts supported the development of this poem and are cited through direct quotations. "The Harvest Sturdies" was written during a mentorship in poetry with Layli Long Soldier. Excerpts have been published elsewhere, including in Tanya Lukin Linklater's first collection of poetry, *Slow Scrape*, published by The Centre for Expanded Poetics and Anteism in 2020, and performed and installed in galleries and museums in Canada, the United States, and Europe.

Agnes Hunter and Duane Linklater provided spelling and translation of Cree words in "The Harvest Sturdies."

askiy: earth
astisak: mitts or mittens
atik: caribou
atikowayan: caribou hide
awasisak: children
iskwewak: women
napewak: men
nohkom: grandmother
nohkominanak: grandmothers
maskasina: moccasins

Encountering Cree language privileges Indigenous language as a way to enter, or to be refused access to, Indigenous thinking. Indigenous Peoples continue to work to recover Indigenous languages as a result of colonial projects such as Indian Residential Schools, a system that actively worked to dismantle Indigenous languages, families, and our relationships to the land. Indigenous Peoples have historically experienced a range of emotions in relation to English language. At the very least, we can describe this experience as discomfort and not knowing. I cite Cree speakers whom I describe as intergenerational language learners and teachers that I am in relation to.

The song we should all be listening to

Why a Dene worldview, embedded in Dene music, is more important now than ever[22]

Leela Gilday

Snapshot 1975: The community hall was packed. The drummers had been drumming for hours now, swapping out to mop their brows, have a drink of water, have a smoke, or share a laugh and a chat. They then move back toward the front of the hall to join the twenty or so Dene men passionately singing and playing songs passed down through generations. Songs to dance to, songs to move a community and unite a nation. Songs as prayers to the ancestors, songs about the love of the land, songs that tell the people who they are and where they came from, where they are going. The people danced endlessly, moccasins hitting the floor, snaking in a circle almost as one entity. Young people, children, Elders, adults, babies, everyone dancing together, weaving our stories into the air, into our DNA, and out into the universe.

Dene music came into a more international focus during the time of the Berger Inquiry. Community gatherings were the backdrop for intense hearings on the proposed Mackenzie Valley gas pipeline. The people raised their voices against the pipeline like the sound of rolling thunder and became the first Indigenous nation to stop a multi-national resource development project on our land. And in every community

---

22   A previous version of this piece appeared in *Up Here Magazine* and is reprinted with permission.

where the people gathered there was a feast and a drum dance to finish things. In a way, the music was the companion to the speeches where people talked about Dene way of life, centralizing the land and water. The people spoke and the music brought it all together.

The Dene Nation as we know it stretches across the northern part of this continent, with relatives all the way into Alaska, and as far south as United States with the Apache, Ute and the Dine (Navajo). As Dene from Denendeh (Northwest Territories) we have four distinct styles of music that have existed from time immemorial: Ets'ula (Dene love songs), Iliwa (Tea Dance songs), Handgame songs and Drum Dance songs.

Ets'ula (also known as Dene love songs) are sometimes the source of teasing and fun at talent shows, performances and community gatherings today, but they are more deep-rooted than they might first appear. The songs, often sung by women but sometimes by men convey a love or longing for another person—be it a family member or a romantic interest, alive or dead. But they can also tell the story of an event, give thanks to the Creator, or express a deep love for the land, water, animals, environment, seasons, spirit world, ancestors—things all central to a Dene existence.

Tea Dance songs (Iliwa) are sung without the drum but danced in an inward-facing circle. These are among the most ancient songs and are a beautiful expression of unity as everyone in the circle sings and dances together.

Handgame songs are the songs that accompany the stick-gambling games that teams play against one another. Originally for fun but also to gain wealth and supplies to make it through the hard winter, handgames have gained unprecedented popularity in recent times because of the considerable cash prizes—and opportunity to gather and celebrate a facet of Dene culture. The songs for these games have now become just a few amorphous songs as the focus is on the players.

Drum Dance songs are by far the most popular style of Dene music, known across the north, and are the focus of drum dances and gatherings, the crux of which is community connection. They are filled with strength and resilience, fun and laughter—attending a drum dance generates a powerful energy and brings people together in a unique way.

Throughout the history of Dene music there have been some standout singers and drummers, people whose rich and powerful voices lead the rest of the singers—like Joe Tambour, Randy Baillargeon and Lawrence Manuel—but "stars" in traditional Dene music don't carry the same weight as in Western popular music because **the emphasis is on the community, not the individual**. This is also central to a Dene worldview. And the reason why even well-known contemporary Dene musicians like Johnny Landry or David Gon write anthemic songs that people can't help singing along to. "Hina Na Ho Hine" (Landry,1980)—or as it is better known, "Hina-Na-Ho-Ho" the de facto Dene anthem, is based on a traditional Tea Dance song. When Susan Aglukark covered/adapted it in 1995 it became an international hit that people all over the world sang along to. The music and the message resonated across cultural divides. Digawolf's Juno-nominated record *Yellowstone* is celebrated across this country and I have personally witnessed how his Tli Cho lyrics and songs based on Drum Dance songs make people move, dance, and cry.

The common thread in Dene music is that the stories woven into the songs, sung in the language or else in vocables (musical syllables that don't necessarily have a referential meaning such as Hine- Ho- Heya- Eh-Eh and so on) are the distilled knowledge of place, people, events, geography, skills, and spiritual values. Dene history is embedded in the songs. Dene ways of life and Dene laws are encoded in the songs; Dene worldview is subtly pervasive throughout the whole repertoire of Dene music.

I read an interesting theory that the sound waves of "traditional" music reflect the shape of the environment in which they are created. It makes sense. As does the connection with the drum—the first heartbeat of the people—what we hear in our Mother's womb, the first sound, being the most important one in almost any Indigenous society.

The time is now to embrace that Dene worldview, to be reminded of our sacred connection to this land and to this water. We are not separate from our land, and we are not separate from each other. Thinking otherwise is what has got us as a human race into hot water with climate change, pandemic-level disease, race wars, and the ever-widening wealth gap between the rich and poor.

As northerners we have an important role in this new world—to use our traditional knowledge to lead the world into a sustainable future where every human is treated with dignity, equality, and justice. I learned this from my Elders: when settlers first came to Denendeh, my ancestors welcomed them, shared knowledge with them, taught them how to survive. Elders have always said to be kind and treat one another with love and respect. To work hard and to respect the land. These lessons are in the Dene laws. Dene music is rooted in these values and beliefs, and this is the song that resonates throughout Denendeh: the song that we should all be listening to.

Resources:

Listen to Dene Tea Dance songs:
   https://www.nwtexhibits.ca/teadance/

Info on the Berger Inquiry:
   https://www.pwnhc.ca/exhibitions/berger/

Susan Aglukark adaptation of Johnny Landry's song:
   https://www.youtube.com/watch?v=NrLL8n4fIe8

A fun Tli Cho drum dance, shuffle-style:
   https://www.youtube.com/watch?v=ExU22gcYQw4&t=42s

Awesome Contemporary Dene musicians:
   Johnny Landry
   Digawolf
   David Gon
   Stephen Kakfwi
   Paul Andrew
   The Bushman NT
   Kenny Shae
   Lawrence Nayally
   Leanne Goose
   Katłı̨à (Catherine) Lafferty

I was given a gift

Randy Baillargeon with Leela Gilday

This is an excerpt from a conversation that took place inside a tent frame on McKenzie Island during the Dechinta Centre for Research and Learning's fall semester 2020, in the homelands of the Yellowknives Dene, between Leela Gilday and Randy Baillargeon. Both Leela and Randy were instructors in the program. They were co-teaching a class on Dene music for our Indigenous arts course.

Leela: So I've already told the students how amazing you are Randy. They already know that because they have seen you around camp and heard you singing, but I don't think they realized how you are a cultural song carrier and how you are probably the best signer of Dene music, well maybe Joe Tambour is better. [lots of laughing] It is a real honour to have you here to teach us. I've known Randy since 2014. Jackson 2bears came up here and we did a collaboration between myself, Randy, Gordie Liske, Leory Betsina, Paul Andrew and Lawrence Nayally. We wrote some songs and did a performance. This is where I first learned of Randy's voice. In this class we are talking about the value of Dene music and how the Dene worldview is encoded in the music.

Randy: I started singing with my grandfather Alfred Baillargeon when I was a little boy, around five or six years old. Aflred was one of the old Dene drummers. He is from around Jennejohn Lake—up ahead of here; two portages. My grandma, Mary Louise Baillargeon (nee Crapeau) is from Enodah. When I was little, I would sit in the corner near the drummers and hit my hand. My grandfather would crawl me into the circle. He gave me a gift, to be a signer.

The drum I use today was given to me by my grandfather. It was made by Paul McKenzie's Dad, Alexis. Alexis gave it to my grandpa. Alexis had a vision in his dream that I was going to be a singer, that I would sing for the people and be a lead singer. He told my grandfather about his dream and gave him the drum for me. My grandpa saved it, and that is the drum I use today.

When I was a kid, I sang in the corner, in the low section. For some reason slowly, I moved up into the middle and then into the centre. Ever since I was small, my grandpa told me that once I turned eighteen he was not going to lead anymore, that I would become the leader.

I guess I got his voice.

The New Year's Drum Dance at T'è?ehdaà (Dettah) is big. Everyone comes—Tłı̨chǫ, Délı̨ne, Tulit'a, and **Łutselk'e**. Almost 200 people come. The year I was eighteen, I was looking around for Alfred because it was time for him to lead the Prayer Song. Chief Eddie Sangris asked me where my grandpa was. I didn't know. I was looking around for him. I finally found him in the audience, dead centre looking into my eyes. I asked, "Are you coming?" He gestured no. I said, "Come on." He gestured for me to lead the song.

WHAT?!

I had never led a Prayer Song in my life.

All the drummers were looking around asking who is going to lead the song.

I said, "I am."

Leela: Wow.

Randy: They were worried it might be embarrassing, but I said, "I'm leading." When I started to sing, my grandfather's voice came out.

Leela: Wow.

Randy: It was high pitch, good tone. By the end of the song my grandpa gestured that he approved.

Ever since then, I've been leading. There are lots of drummers older than me, but for some reason, they always wait for me to lead.

My grandfather gave me an awesome gift.

ᐅ⁻ᒍ / ūdzi: The art of Dene Handgames/ Stick Gambling

Angela Code

The Dene are a group of Indigenous People who are part of the Na-Dene language family. The Dene are also commonly referred to as Athabaskans or Athapaskans. We are one of the largest Indigenous groups in North America. Our land covers over four million square kilometres, spanning from across northern North America to the American Southwest. There are three distinct Dene groups: Northern, Pacific Coast and Southern/ Apachean. There are approximately fifty distinct languages within the Na-Dene language family, and various dialects.

There is a game that the Northern Dene have been playing for many years called Dene Handgame, also called Stick Gambling, or simply referred to as handgames. Dënesųłiné yatiyé, also known as Chipewyan Dene, is one of the more widely spoken languages from within the Na-Dene language family. In the Sayisi Dënesųłiné dialect, Dene Handgame is called ᐅ⁻ᒍ (oodzi).

There are different rules and various hand signals of the game across the North; however, the object of the game and how it is played are essentially the same. Basically, Dene Handgame is an elaborate guessing game. It is a fun pastime that requires a good sense of "reading people" and concealment. The players who compete with high energy, humour, good sportsmanship, and performative gestures are often the most fun to play with and to observe.

Gwichya Gwich'in men and boys playing Dene Handgame while a man drums, Tsiigehtchic (Tsiigehtshik, formerly Arctic Red River), Northwest Territories (a102486), photo reprinted with permission from Library and Archives Canada.

How to play Dene Handgame

There must be an even number of players on each team. Tournaments will specify how many people per team will play—the number varies from region to region, and it often ranges from four, six, eight, ten, or twelve per team. Two teams play against each other at a time. Each player must have a personal token—a small object that can be easily hidden in one hand (for example, a stone, a coin, a button, a .22 shell).

When players are not personally competing in the game, they, as well as some onlookers, will hit individual caribou-skin hand drums with handmade wooden drumsticks in a fast-paced, rhythmic beat. The music of the drums, whoops, cheers, chants, and songs fuel the high energy of the game. Drummers who are not personally playing in the game will often drum behind the team that they support. They drum when their "side" is hiding their tokens, to encourage them and protect them from being guessed out.

Each team has a captain. To begin the game, the two opposing team captains will play against each other. They will each hide their token in one of their hands, and then they will simultaneously indicate which hand they think their opponent's token is in.

Once one of the captains correctly guesses where the opponent's token

Men playing Dene Handgame, photographs from the Royal Commission on Aboriginal Peoples visit to Tadoule Lake, Manitoba, the community of the Sayisi Dene (Denesuline), 1992–1993. Back (left to right): Brandon Cheekie, Peter Cheekie, Jimmy Clipping, Fred Duck, Ernie Bussidor, Tony Duck. Front (left to right): Unknown, Evan Yassie, Thomas Cutlip, Ray Ellis. (e011300424), photo reprinted with permission from Library and Archives Canada.

is, then their respective teammates will join the game. The winning captain's team becomes the first team to have the opportunity to win points.

Each member of a team will line up side by side, kneeling on the floor or on the ground, facing the opposing team. Because handgames can often go on for long periods of time, players will kneel on something soft like a mat or a bed of spruce bough.

It is not necessary, but often one or two designated, unbiased score-keepers/referees will keep a keen eye on every player to ensure that scores are tallied correctly, no one cheats, and any disputes are settled fairly. They sit close by on the sidelines between the two opposing teams so that they have the best vantage points to view the players and have access to move the winning handgame sticks.

The sticks are placed between the two teams and are used to keep score of the game. The number of sticks correlate with the number of players. For example, when four people are playing per team then twelve sticks are used; when six are playing per team then fourteen sticks are

An Elder (Charlie Learjaw) observes a Dene Handgame match, Tadoule Lake, Manitoba, 1992–1993 (e011300421), photo reprinted with permission from Library and Archives Canada.

used; when eight are playing per team then twenty-one sticks are used; when ten are playing per team then twenty-four or twenty-five sticks are used; and when twelve are playing per team then twenty-eight or twenty-nine sticks are used.

The team whose turn it is to hide their tokens will place their hands under a cloth covering (like a blanket or spare coats). They will move their token from hand to hand until they decide which hand to hide it in. Then, when they have chosen their hiding hand, they will take their fists out from under the cloth covering and face their opponents. Commonly, players keep their arms straight in front of them or they cross them over their chests; however, players also develop their own elaborate and unique positioning of their hands. Players will use facial gestures, body movements, and sounds to try and confuse or "psyche out" the opposing captain, who is the one who will guess and signal to where they think each token is hidden.

Before the captain makes the hand signal indicating where they think the tokens are hidden, they make a loud sound—a big clap, or they hit the floor with their hand—to let everyone know that they are ready to call.

Men drumming and playing Dene Handgame, Tadoule Lake, Manitoba, 1992–1993. Left to right: Brandon Cheekie, Peter Cheekie, Fred Duck, Jimmy Clipping, Ernie Bussidor, Tony Duck and Ray Ellis. (e011300426), photo reprinted with permission from Library and Archives Canada.

There are many different signals that can be used; however, there are four main ones that the Arctic Winter Games follow, which can be learned here: http://www.denegames.ca/dene-games/hand-games-rules.html.

Once the captain reveals their hand signal, all the opposing players must then open the hand that the captain has indicated so everyone can see if the token is there. If the token is not there, meaning that the captain was wrong in their guess, the opposition player(s) must then show the other hand containing the object. Each time the captain is wrong in their guess, a stick is awarded to the opposing team. For example, if the captain guesses and makes one correct guess and three wrong guesses, the opposition will receive three sticks. The player who was guessed correctly is eliminated from the round, and now there are only three players remaining. This will continue until the captain has correctly guessed all of the players remaining, or until the opposing team wins all of the sticks. If the captain guesses all of the opposition players correctly, it is their team's turn to hide their tokens and for the other team captain to try and guess which hands the tokens are in. The team to win all of the sticks wins the game.

Gwichya Gwich'in men and boys playing Dene Handgame, Tsiigehtchic (Tsiigehtshik, formerly Arctic Red River), Northwest Territories, ca. 1930 (a102488), photo reprinted with permission from Library and Archives Canada.

Handgame tournaments

There are many small Dene Handgame tournaments happening all across the North all the time. My home community of Tadoule Lake, Manitoba, aims to play every Friday evening. There are also some very big Dene Handgame tournaments that happen a few times a year in various regions. Some of the prizes for winning teams are in the thousands of dollars!

Historically, there have been stories told about when people would play handgame—they would gamble goods such as firearms, bullets, axes, and so on. I have even heard about men losing their wives to a game and having to win her back at another game!

Gender controversy in Handgames

Children, both boys and girls, are taught how to play Dene Handgame at home and at handgame tournaments. In some regions, they are taught how to play at school as a part of physical education.

However, for adults, the sport is predominantly played by men. This is because some regions, particularly in the Northwest Territories, do not allow adult women to play. However, in the Yukon and in some northern Prairie provinces, women are not only allowed to play, they are encouraged and widely supported. This inclusion of women makes

A man (Peter Cheekie) hits a caribou-skin hand drum with a wooden drumstick while a teenage boy (Christopher Yassie) and a small child (Brandon Cheekie) watch a Dene Handgame match, Tadoule Lake, Manitoba, 1992–1993 (e011300426), photo reprinted with permission from Library and Archives Canada.

the games much larger and more fun to participate in and to observe. Tournaments will state whether they allow men's teams only or mixed teams. There has only been one women's handgame tournament (that I know of), which was held in Whitehorse, Yukon, in 2016. The inclusion of women to play handgames is a hot topic in the North. Some say that it is not "traditional" to allow women to play and that women "have too much power—so they would just win all the time." Some communities do not even allow women to drum.

Others say that women played a long time ago, but that this changed with the imposition of Christianity. Some Christian missionaries actually banned the drum and playing Dene Handgames altogether. The drum in Dene culture is very important. It is spiritual and some Christian missionaries saw it as heathen and therefore unacceptable. They actually burned drums in some communities. Some people continued to play handgames in secret, but in other communities it only came back into practice in recent years. In one community in particular, I heard that handgames were not played for a long time, and it was the women who brought it back, encouraging the men and others to play again.

Author photo, playing handgames in Ross River.

I think that in this day and age, it is not fair to exclude women from playing Dene Handgames, or to prevent them from drumming, for that matter. Gender dynamics change and shift within all cultures. I believe that more gender inclusion to compete in this fun pastime is a good, positive change for everyone.

I personally love to watch people play, but I much prefer to compete in the game myself, and I would love to see more women participate and have fun playing handgames as well.

Ringing drums, talking land

Antione Mountain

"These places, the landmarks, they talk with each other, every morning."

So said my brother-in-law Michel, married to my sister, Judy Lafferty, for many years before her passing in May of 2020. They spent their half century of marriage together, inseparable, mainly on the land. I now have quite a number of nephews and nieces from their union. Through thick and thin they were proud to be of the land, carrying on our Dene culture, the old way.

Most of my questions for Michel had to do with his experiences as a drummer. He is the DrumKeeper for our local Radelie Koe Dene Drummers and is always ready at a moment's notice to join the rest for a practice or an event. The Fort Good Drummers have long made a name for themselves, having even represented the North at the Winter Olympics in Vancouver.

Knowing that I love the details in our Dene stories, Michel brought me all the way back to when he was just a boy. Our town didn't have much more than a couple hundred people then. Everything was done by hand, including the wood he sawed up and split every day. He said that even though he was brought up Métis, at the time there was no difference among the Dene and Métis Peoples. Everyone had the same kind of hunting, trapping, and fishing way of life and everyone shared.

Michel said that every morning while he cut up the family's wood for the day, he could hear the sound of drumming, and faintly, that of a human voice, in the cold wintry air.

Michel Lafferty of Radelie Koe, Drum Keeper.
Photo credit: Antione Mountain.

It came from the Chief's home, several hundred yards away.

Even being so curious, it was also beyond Dene etiquette for a young boy to just go and enter another home. The usual way was to offer to do something useful for the family, to cut some wood, or bring ice from the river for their tea. Once invited in, he could only stand by the door until actually allowed in. If he was lucky enough, he would catch the man, Gabriel Cotchilly, just finishing up a song and hanging his hand drum back to the wall.

Now almost eighty years later, my brother-in-law came to be commonly acknowledged as a Dene drummer! He said that the last of the drums made by one of the best, Michel Grandjambe, are the ones only he uses. There are no nails holding the wooden hope together, taking it all the way back to the ancestors. He told me that one of them not only sounds the beat, but actually rings—rings like a bell. It's the only one he's ever had or heard of that does that!

Then he started talking about how the drum is an extension of the person who made it and on to the drummer. He made me understand that the drum is no less than the voice of the land, and our language the same. A man of the land such as Michel Lafferty loves to hear stories coming out of Denendeh, our country itself. We come from a very traditional family and have learned to share and learn from one another.

Michel told me of our late uncle, J.B.—Jean-Baptiste Gully—who talked of the four major landmarks of our K'asho Got'ine, Big Willow People. The four, the nearby Yamoga Fieh and Rigosho, join with the other two, Kahbami Tue's Eyoniki and Beziayu, and talk—just talk among themselves every morning. The four must have a lot to say, for legends of them go all the way back to our cultural hero, Yamoria. This, from a time, according to storyteller and statesman George Blondin, who spoke of When the World was New. These landmarks were there when dinosaurs roamed our lands! Yamoria, He Who Walks Across the Universe, the peacemaker, had a warrior brother named Yamoga.

This giant had a major battle with a rival named Ko Hedi, Without Fire—a man so tough he walked even the coldest winter without shoes on! When the smoke cleared Ko Hedi was left frozen into the rock at Yamoga Fieh.

Another of the four landmarks who talk, Eyoniki, involves two brothers who shot at an owl. The bird fell dead and the two claimed to have brought it down. The argument carried on into their family, the tribe and to all of the peoples there. All separated to every corner of the world, to eventually become the Gwich'in, Inuit, and other Dene far away. Much of Dene culture is exactly like this—an embodiment of our human relationship to the land. Our language, too, is so complicated that only a very few outsiders can even learn it. It is no surprise then, that the Diné of our southern relatives, the Navajo, would be used as a military code which saved democracy in the Second World War!

As an extension of the human soul, our language has an organic elasticity to it, like Shakespeare. You can manipulate it at will, even to make artistic, personal expressions. As you can well imagine, this creative use of language marks Radelie Koe as a major source of storytellers.

Upon arriving back home for the Summer of 2020, I began some research into traditional Dene burial practices. This involves much more than just putting a relative's body into the ground. The practice, Ehst'ehch'i, literally "starving oneself" or doing without, was not only about the death and grieving, but was something that an individual would take upon themselves to basically become an outstanding community member.

This person would set out to live an entire year on the land, alone, with strict physical and moral rules, concentrating on their dreams.

They wanted to come back a better person.

These steps, small though they may appear, will leave their mark. When I mentioned to our Radelie Koe Elders Council that we should have our own Dene be the principal and teachers in our school, not only janitors, they sat up and paid attention. We should include our Dene Knowledge in the curriculum. One of the Elders, Thomas Manuel, told me that now, finally, we're beginning to fulfill the prophesies of Ehtseo Ayha of Délı̨nę—to carry on our Dene traditions! And so it should be with the youth of today.

My generation of Dene were born right on the land and we made an effort to relearn our Dene languages. This gave us an advantage; we were familiar with the land and no stranger to Mother Nature's feel. We have a strong relationship to the land. Speaking the language, we think in Dene.

A few years ago, I was invited by one of our youth at home, Cara Manuel, to help with an event they were organizing. I thought my part would have to do with putting the conference together. When I got there, though, all they wanted from me was a mural to highlight what they had already planned, fundraised, and organized, complete with a detailed agenda! When I asked them where they had learned such expertise, they quoted Leanne Betasamosake Simpson and, to their credit, were conversant with Taiaike Alfred and Jeff Corntassel.

From my recent work with the youth I've found them to not only be artistically gifted but curious enough to pick up and verbally appreciate the nuances of their Dene language.

Our younger generation is able to organize for hide-tanning camps and are even able to make the thinnest, yet tasty, smoked dry meat!

There have been a lot of major changes in the last twelve years I've worked with the youth. Back then they were acting out and getting into trouble. In our community, every willing and capable adult began volunteering to help with our Dene language, drumming, and other cultural activities. My part was painting the large number of murals now in the Sahtú, Great Bear Lake Region. We wanted to help our youth. Now young people return with trophies and other cultural accomplishments!

For the ancient now,
ringing drums,
our talking lands
aspire
to Dene tradition.

Mahsì.

Land stories

Josh Barichello

yíbā guja. k'ón disk'ān. ts'ū yigē tsisestīh, gohgahi zāgé edésts'ék yéh.
espāne shenetīn. ekūdē dih chō kā ejedzedū'āź ī. dedi dena kēyeh
lēt'ā. sōganessén, jānī sésda yéh.

it has become dawn. fire burns. i kick back under a white spruce and
listen to voices of tundra swans. my friend sleeps. soon we will hunt
blue grouse. this is dena country. i feel grateful to sit here.

They call this Canada's north. Yukon. Land of gold; the last frontier.
Home of big moose and big mountains. Big wilderness. Dizzying.
They say this belongs to Yukoners, to be governed for the public
good. They make large statements. *Larger than Life.*

łą́ tso'ālla tū gād́ zenetą̄ñ . īd́ ā, miyēdzedīh. dídū łagah mekā
gidzukeh. shobāt'āne kégeneshān gūdedīł. ekūjé' tenebeh.
seni k'ī lā, łą́ īś dā.

slowly and with care we watch water. (s)he is alive, we remember.
this evening we travel on top. poplar leaves will soon come out. a
young beaver goes under. me too, you know, i'm really alive.

Pelly was an officer of the Hudson Bay Company. They name this
river after him. The river supports four of the ten proposed hydro
dams in Yukon. The dams will mean massive flooding, but

Photo by Josh Barichello.

this is considered a necessary cost. They say these projects are
critical to the territory's economy. They tell me this economy
supports me; they say I depend on this economy.

---

kādzenet'éde nādzu'āh́ i. dena tégedéglū. got'lis łah ezés négejin.
gudzįhzés. jānī˜

gudzįh yedādzedī. dena tsį' négedi.

all together, we play hand games. people are laughing. skins sing
among dust. caribou skins. here we respect caribou. they help people.

Photo by Josh Barichello.

Caribou are tranquilized with darts shot from planes. Their necks
are cuffed with radio collars so professionals can track their
movements from desks in Whitehorse. Caribou are not
asked. Dena are not heard. This looks like farming.
But *renewable resources need to be managed*, after all.

łūge nḗgegān. gēs tené gagah nédeł. ts'édāne kégenet'ąh,
getsųe gegāǵ enetąñ yéh. mesgą dena łą́ gutiē keīh lā.
echō sek'āde miyḗgedīh.

they dry fish. they camp beside salmon trails. kids play
while their grandmothers watch them. raven person did really
good work. elders still remember.

They advertise "world-class fishing." Catch-and-release in the
"pristine wilderness of the Yukon." Fish are taken from here to be
displayed on southern walls, or thrown back to the water—
after a photo, of course. They call this country unspoiled.
They call fish trophies.

---

geden'íā. gúle łets'íh elīh dōk'āde sā ní'ān yéh. kedātséné' nédzet'āś .
hés tah tédzedeglū.

they stand up tall. willow smoke dances and the sun hasn't set yet.
we cut moose meat. we laugh among mountains.

Faro Mine produced so much money. But the water will need to
be treated for hundreds of years. We are surrounded by mines—
Wolverine, Ketza, Sa Dena Hes. They tell us mining benefits us; that
it is *part of Yukon's history*. The road to Ross River isn't paved. In
the village the school is unsafe and houses are condemned. There is
no cultural centre—not even a café. They say we need more mines.

---

det'ele guja. nededhay. dena dzídze negebeh. etsíe gugáń etąń .
nédetē. kuhsāze tah gédzedah īyéh dena k'éh gūs'ān gha dedeszets.
dūłą́ mezí yedessīn.

it has become red. fall time. people pick berries. the grandfather
watches us. the dreamer. we walk among buck brush and i am
mindful of dena ethics. i don't say his name.

Photo by Josh Barichello.

Photo by Josh Barichello.

They sell hunts of him. Foreigners charge foreigners for the
thrill of killing him. His life is converted to dollars. *He is demonized
by an industry that profits from hunting him.* His skin is
displayed to feed macho pride. We are told he is too numerous
and that this is predator control.

---

men ejin, shenéten yéh. sā dena dedi tahmā gégedah. gekāǵ e sek'āde
negúlīn. gedah sek'āde selā. gedīǵ e sek'āde gúlīn.

lake sings as (s)he freezes over. long-time-ago dena walked on this
shore too. their tracks are still here. their things are still around.
their positive thoughts remain.

They call this shore Crown Land. They claim ownership of historic
artifacts found here. Indigenous nations only own artifacts found
on the 8 percent of their territory that agreements of paper and
ink name "Settlement Lands." Here there are no
Settlement Lands. So they say it all belongs to Her Majesty—
a Queen from a far away island.

---

ts'ussę̄ ele estōn. echō ts'édāne gedugedech. dena k'éh gudedéh. gutiē gedīǵ e dege. negedehtih gha gudech. mā guyānde getlą̄ yḗgedūt'ī.

i hold balsam boughs. an elder tells kids a story. (s)he speaks in dena. it's good for their minds. (s)he tells story of mammoths. whoever is thinking will carry this on to their descendants.

Yukon Government does a strength of claim analysis. Without Land Claims they need another way of demonstrating that this is not Dena land. A legal way. They look to written records of anthropologists. Objective observations, they call them. They will prove what they seek. *In English, in writing.* They will sound convincing. Inside the walls of Western thought; within the standards of Europe.

---

tahtené' guja. dechintah łą̄ kāǵ e néstlōn negū́līn. gudzįh kā gidzukeh. seni kuskāni eslīn. ahlāde esdena łą̄ kuts'ī́t negudedéh yḗgedīh. kēt'ēghólī́ dedi dūłą̄ kuskāni kēyeh lēt'ā lā. dedi dūłą̄ canada lēt'ā. miyēsdīh.

crust time. the bush is full of tracks. we travel around for caribou. me i'm a white person. some of my people really know how to tell lies. even so, this is not white people's land. this is not canada. i remember.

Photo by Josh Barichello.

Some Notes on Language

Dena language is the language of the land where I live. It is the language of the land and people that have inspired this piece. I believe that spaces that centre this language are important both for language resurgence and in the political statement that comes with centring Dena language: this is Dena land. But building this piece around Dena language didn't come without challenges. It is not my language. I have been gifted some knowledge of the language through many Dena Elders. As a non-Dena speaker of the language, I believe we must walk here with deep accountability and reciprocity; teachings that are embedded in the Dena ethics of this place. I choose to centre Dena language in this piece because it should be centred here, but I am also mindful that as a non-Dena speaker of the language, my use of it must be tied to ongoing accountability and reciprocity to Kaska Dena land and people to whom the language belongs.

Also, in the community of Tū Łīd lini (Ross River), there are multiple dialects spoken, and there is not a universally agreed upon writing system among speakers. Some Elder speakers feel that we should use the writing system developed by linguists (what I have chosen to use here), while other Elder speakers believe we should write it without the introduction of characters that we do not use in English. In light of this, even the choice to put the language in writing has its challenges.

Finally, translation is complicated when moving between languages as structurally and ideologically different from one another as Kaska Dena and English. I believe that much expression inside Kaska Dena language doesn't lend itself to English. And in colonial relations, translation has been used as a political practice to hide deep meaning and force equivalence despite profound ideological incompatibilities. In this piece I have done my best to translate meaning as close as I can, while still writing something that makes sense in English, but I acknowledge the sometimes incompatible differences between the two languages.

Language needs land needs language

Chloe Dragon Smith

On the Land
we feel
the roots beneath our languages—
twisting and turning, gnarly, knowing.
On the Land
we learn
with bodymindheartandsoul,
the truths that shaped our words
long before they were spoken.
Language is more than words and
words hold more than any language
could ever explain.
Simple rhythmic sound waves from
throat vibrations transferred to consciousness;
words are the brief physical manifestation
of something
that is only a tiny bit physical.

Words are portals.
My love,
that's why it feels so good to learn them . . .

Our languages come from deep
within the souls and unconditional loving of our ancestors—
human and otherwise.
To do soul learning
you must meet on soul terms.

So, you say you want fluency?
PLEASE,
Let us meet our languages.
Let us feel our languages.
Let us love our languages.
Give us a fighting chance to get to know one another,
before you send someone to instruct them to us.

The gate

Dian Million

We pray the sacred land
allowing
time without end/
the mountain sends
a storm which mounts a wind
rides down

we sit among the rock people
watching light retreat
I feel the first gentle touch of rain
and you are crying without sound
tears warm rivulets mix on the cool wet of your cheek
I cannot breathe
The wind has caught it up in my throat

We carry our children
to the mountain
to pray for courage to live
we know it will not be our decision
only our children's
they must want to live
to know the motion
to know to live with the motion

we defend the possibility
of love,
the northern stars to travel by
and our sacred knowledge to pick our way
among each place;

to acknowledge our seasons
the certainty of our change
and the spirits we evoke,
released into the world.

to learn old stillness
i walk toward you
through the mouth of the gate
a half moon arbor where we find the bones
of a young deer
and wonder at the faces of the rock people
knowing they lead out.

Dedicated to Tyghe and Simnasho artist, scholar,
and visionary Susana Santos

The Housing Poem [23]

Dian Million

Minnie had a house
which had trees in the yard
and lots of flowers

she especially liked the kitchen

because it had a large old cast iron stove
and that
the landlord said was the reason
the house was so cheap

Pretty soon Minnie's brother Rupert came along
and his wife Onna
and they set up housekeeping in the living room
on the fold-out couch,
so the house warmed and rocked
and sang because Minnie and Rupert laughed a lot.

Pretty soon their mom Elsie came to live with them too
Because she liked being with the laughing young people
And she knew how the stove worked the best.
Minnie gave up her bed and slept on a cot.

23   This piece is from Gloria Bird and Joy Harjo, *Reinventing the Enemy's Language: Contemporary Women's Writings Of North America* (New York: W. W. Norton & Company, 1998).

Well pretty soon
Dar and Shar their cousins came to town looking for work.
They were twins
the pride of Elsie's sister Jo
and boy could those girls sing. They pitched a tent under
the cedar patch in the yard
and could be heard singing around the house
mixtures of old Indian tunes and country western.

When it was winter
Elsie worried
about her mother Sarah
who was still living by herself in Moose Glen back home.
Elsie went in the car with Dar and Shar and Minnie and
Rupert and got her.
They all missed her anyway and her funny stories.
She didn't have any teeth
So she dipped all chewable items in grease
Which is how they're tasty she said.
She sat in a chair in front of the stove usually
or would cook up a big pot of something for the others.

By and by Rupert and Onna had a baby who they named Lester,
or nicknamed Bumper, and they were glad that Elsie and Sarah
were there to help.

One night the landlord came by
to fix the leak in the bathroom pipe
and was surprised to find Minnie, Rupert and Onna, Sarah and
Elsie, Shar and Dar all singing around the drum next
to the big stove in the kitchen
and even a baby named Lester who smiled waving a big greasy
piece of dried fish.

He was disturbed
he went to court to evict them
he said the house was designed for single-family occupancy
which surprised the family
because that's what they thought they were.

Golǫdhé

Kristen Tanche

I have a moose hide. Gifted by family, the moose is from the Dehcho. It sits in my shed as it thaws. This is my hide story. My story.

In the fall of 2019, I was gifted a hide by my brother-in-law. I didn't have time to deal with it then so thankfully I was able to freeze it and store it in my Mother-in-law's freezer, with the promise I would take it out by the spring. Even the act of putting it into freezer made me anxious. I texted people, asked around. How do I even store a hide? Can I? For how long?

I am Dehcho Dene of mixed ancestry. My Father is Icelandic and a mixture of everything, Settler Canadian. My Mother is Dehcho Dene and part of the Liidlii Kue First Nation. I am a capable 35-year-old woman in today's society, yet I don't know much about hide tanning and I am a baby language learner.

Sixty years ago, this would be unheard of.

Throughout time, my Dene ancestors were told that their way of life was no good. Our cultural practices were not ok. Sent to schools. Sent to towns. To learn the molah way.

Put the drum down!
Outlaw gatherings.
Not allowed to vote.
Not allowed to drink.
Sign your land away!
Peace and Friendship, we promise!
As children were taken from their homes.

New materials started coming to the Dene People, like different types of fabric and new forms of shoes. Hide was once an essential part of life. I have heard that people would go through numerous pairs of moccasins in one year. So moose hide tanning was a necessity for the survival of people. Moose hide tanning was not practised as much as the times changed.... Not because of want ... but ... maybe out of necessity ... in order to survive in a changing landscape.

When I say changing landscape, I mean that in multiple ways. Society was different from what the Dene knew. Colonialism brought new people and a new way of life. The economy was changing. The land was changing. Everything was changing.

To survive in a changing landscape, there was not a whole lot of choice but to adapt. Dene people are good at that. We adapt to everything around us. We are used to it. You didn't change the weather as you were travelling. You changed your route. Or you waited. You adapted.

So here I am. A 35-year-old Dehcho Dene learning something that sixty years ago every 35-year-old Dene woman would need to know. Here I am adapting. Putting my hide in a freezer, texting moose hide questions to people, paying attention to social media posts about hides. About to start fleshing a hide in my back yard in the middle of a municipality.

What does this hide mean to me? Why am I so anxious about it? Why is it important?

I'm anxious because I'm scared. I'm a grown woman, yet I know nothing. I need help. Admitting that is hard.

> It's scary.
> I want to do well.
> I want to learn.
> I need to learn so I can pass the teachings on.

It's urgent to me.

We are losing more and more knowledge as we lose our Elders. If I don't step up to do my part, learn the teachings, what is going to happen to all that knowledge?

It's important to me because my Mother is still here. My grandfather was the survivor of a pandemic that swept the Northwest Territories. He, two other children, and their Father survived. Many passed.

I'm still here.
And I'm tanning my hide for them.

I want to proudly show my parents my hide. I want to gift it. I want to provide some to my Mother. I want to share it with my teachers and my helpers. I want to leave a piece of it for family. It is my way of saying.

See.
We survived.
We thrive.
Our people will continue our practices.
We will tan hides.

Not out of necessity for materials anymore. But out of necessity to practise our culture, traditions, and language.

It's more than the act of tanning. It connects me to my past. Connects me to my family. Beginning my first moose hide is one of my many ways of connecting to my people, the land, culture, and language.

My first connection came when I was walking on the land during a Dechinta program. When I came to the realization that my shame, my hatred of self was not because I was a bad person. It was because over time and throughout my experiences, I was taught through society that being Dene wasn't really a good thing. Where were my Dene princesses in Disney movies? Where were any Indigenous heroes really? Why did our people have to go to schools to have the "Indian taken out of them"? Why wasn't wearing moccasins cool when I was a kid? On top of those feelings, I also come from a mixed background. So, I didn't feel as a child I fully fit in either, with my non-Indigenous Father, in a largely Indigenous community. I think of that realization as a turning point in my life—when I truly started to love the skin I was born into.

When you think of a moose hide, it is not one colour. One hide can be multiple shades of colour. It's still beautiful.

It requires hard work to get to that final step of a completed hide. Weeks for one. But when put it into perspective, the time is longer. Because you are not just tanning a hide with your own knowledge. You learn from teachings that were passed on from generation to generation to generation. Hundreds of years of knowledge.

My moose hide is one step of mine. I used to think to decolonize you needed to do really Indigenous things. Learn to live on the land, hunt, speak your language. But I have come to realize that is not it. Maybe it's a part of it. But it's an individual journey where you need to find your own path. Whether it is changing your thinking, relearning a language, or learning how to cook a traditional dish from your family. It's about finding your path.

My moose hide is part of my journey that has been encompassing many from my community—and hundreds of years of knowledge.

The knowledge we carry from the land is medicine

Justina Black in Conversation with Leanne Betasamosake Simpson

Justina: Our Dene Laws remind us to *Share What We Have*, and while working in my home community I was able to spend time with community members who were generous enough to share their knowledge of how our ancestors lived on the land. Growing up I often heard the saying, "It takes a community to raise a child." This saying applied to my life immensely because if it weren't for my community, my school, and all of the people who were there for me growing up, I would not be where I am today.

My roots to the lands in Denendeh come from my late grandmother Bella (Eyakfwǫ) and my late grandfather Johnny Base on my late Mother Lucie's side of the family. My Father is Mark Johnson who moved to the North from Halifax, Nova Scotia, in the early '70s.

I was born in Yellowknife, Northwest Territories. It is commonly referred to as Sǫǫ̀mbak'è, which translates to "the place where the money is" in many dialects spoken by Dene people in this territory. In the early 1920s gold was discovered by a Yellowknives Dene Elder Liza Crookedhand while she was picking berries. This later brought many jobs to what is now known as the Giant Mine site. Elders have also referred to Franklin Avenue as ekwǫ̀ tı̨lı̀ı̀, which translates to "caribou trails," that scattered across the shores of the Great Slave Lake long before gold was discovered.

I grew up in the community of Ndilǫ where I attended K'alemi Dene School. The school was built to ensure that the children in the community would have access to an education that represented themselves, by integrating the language, culture, and Dene way of life taught by the people from our community. I grew up surrounded by Indigenous education and Dene values, learning from Elders, community members, and the land. Throughout the school year we learned the traditional way of life and the knowledge that my ancestors carried with them as they lived on the lands. We would pick berries and medicine, set nets, set rabbit snares, learn about hunting and trapping, and had an annual duck plucking day with a community feast at the end of the school year. It was a great privilege to be raised in a community that embraced our culture, and it made me appreciate it even more when I relocated during high school.

Leanne: Take me back to when you first decided to come to Dechinta as a student. What attracted you to the program? What was your experience like? How did this change your life?

Justina: In the Summer of 2014, I was an international participant in Northern Youth Abroad and was travelling to Guatemala to work with Habitat for Humanity. My friend Jasmine Sangris who I grew up with in the community of Ndilǫ, where we went to K'alemi Dene School, was also a participant. She had mentioned that she had applied to a Dechinta semester in the fall and told me that she was going to be spending two months on the land while doing post-secondary studies, and I was sold. I immediately started printing off forms and sent them out. I was so excited to return back to Canada and begin my post-secondary journey in my home territory.

Over time I have witnessed how the lands and the community in my home territory have changed with more and more people arriving and settling here. It is unfortunate to see how many people have become so disconnected from the lands we have inherited as Dene people and have become consumed by drugs or alcohol to cope with this loss. Growing up I was fortunate to attend culture camps while in school that gave youth the opportunity to learn from community members and reconnect with land. At a very young age I knew that I wanted a career that would influence the futures of youth in the utmost positive way. I was unsure of which route would be best to help guide the youth into having a brighter future, while educating themselves, but also keeping a strong sense of pride in their culture. Many of my own family members have become consumed by substance abuse and the traditional Dene lifestyle is no longer being practised, so I've had to take it upon myself to learn about the Dene way of life and what it means to be a person of Denendeh.

During my semester at Dechinta we spent four weeks in a community we created out of blue rope, canvas tents, tarps, spruce poles, and spruce bows for flooring. Our kitchen was set up on fold out tables under a blue tarp and a frame made from spruce poles we chopped and peeled. Our classroom was a wall tent and the berry patches behind our camp that were full of Labrador tea and other medicines. It was also the lake where we set and pulled nets to make dry fish and hauled our drinking water from. It was hard work, but it was all rewarding work.

Until I had attended Dechinta Centre for Research and Education, I was truly unaware of how much colonialism and the impacts of intergenerational trauma was affecting my life as an Indigenous woman of the North. This was the first sort of unveiling of the world that surrounded me and why I was being raised in an oppressive environment that has impacted the lives of many First People in the Northwest Territories.

Following our four weeks on the land, we spent an additional four weeks at a lodge where we focused on academic reading and writing while working on caribou and moose hides. In this time on the land, we began to study the history of the lands and the political struggles our people have faced to protect our lands in Denendeh and we learned from leading Indigenous academics and community leaders. It was the first time I heard and understood what decolonization, self-determination, community governance, and sustainability meant.

Leanne: After you completed the program, how did you continue to deepen your land-based skills?

Justina: During my eight weeks on the land, I gained the knowledge and tools that allowed me to transfer to the University of Alberta in the fall of 2015, where I studied in the Bachelor of Native Studies program for a year. Attending a school with a student population that is in very close proximity to the entire population of the Northwest Territories was a huge culture shock for me. I felt a lack of community support and guidance that I was so used to growing up in a small community—support that allows for our Indigenous students to succeed. I quickly became influenced by the rush of the city and lost interest in my studies. In the springtime I returned back to the community of Ndilǫ where I felt grounded, and began to work with the youth in the school as a student support worker.

In the fall of 2016, I moved to Fort Smith to continue my educational journey in the Bachelor of Education program. In my second semester at the college, my auntie who raised me fell ill and passed away, which took a toll on my mental health. I began closet drinking in my apartment where I lived alone. When I returned in the fall, I continued on with my drinking habits, put in the bare minimum when handing in my assignments, and would rarely make it to my classes because I was too hungover to get out of bed. I was put on academic probation and returned to Yellowknife where I was still surrounded by drinking in my family life, which was not healthy for me or the work I so desperately wanted to do with youth on the land.

In the spring of 2018, I was asked to assist with childcare at the Dechinta Centre where we would spend two months out on the land creating a community similar to the one in my semester. Only this time I was facilitating a space to engage youth in the process of inquiry-based learning to encourage self-determining youth who were in charge of their own learning on the land. The land has so much to teach us in each season it goes through. We had morning check-ins to see how we each felt physically and emotionally; we checked the weather forecast and would check in with what the rest of the community would be doing that day. I worked with the Elders and the youth to make sure they were learning the knowledge that was useful in the season we were in while we were out on the land. We spent our days walking in the bush discovering tracks on the snow and plant medicine that laid beneath it. We tapped birch trees and would deliver sap to the Elders. We learned the language by being immersed in a community of fluent speakers.

During the Dechinta programming, drugs and alcohol are not allowed to ensure the community is safe. Once our two months were up on the land, I returned back to Yellowknife and I tried to continue on with my regular drinking habits but my body could not keep up. I would be sick for days, and by the time the weekend would come I would go out drinking again and put my body through the same cycle. I never considered myself an addict or someone who struggled with substance abuse, but as I look back on the times I would drink a bottle of vodka with a group of friends, or a bottle of wine alone to fall asleep in my apartment, I know that I was not in a good place. Instead of drinking on the weekends, I started staying with my sister and nephews on the weekend. My Mother would come over and we would sew together. It has now been over three years that I have not consumed or allowed alcohol to control my life. I'm not saying that sobriety is for everyone, but healing definitely is. Healing is not easy, and it is not something that we can or should do alone. There was no one in my immediate family that could take me out on the land, but I was blessed to work with and learn from the community the Dechinta Centre has created for me.

Leanne: What barriers exist for Dene women and Two-Spirit and Queer youth in terms of land-based learning and getting out on the land? What can organizations do to break down these barriers?

Justina: As a young Dene woman, learning from people who hold onto the traditional knowledge of how our ancestors lived has helped me on my healing journey. Hearing how the land has cared for and healed our people since time immemorial made me want to continue to immerse myself in those settings. I've been so fortunate to have a community of people who have held space for me to heal, to learn, and to pass on those teachings. There are so many barriers we face when accessing education in the North, but we have so many community members who hold archives of knowledge from the land. However, the impacts of colonialism, Residential School, and intergenerational trauma have affected the way in which knowledge is being transferred in our communities. We have slowly become isolated in our individual homes and are no longer acting as a community. It can be challenging to find people in the communities to facilitate spaces for everyone to learn this knowledge without having the Western knowledge systems dominate these spaces.

The ways of the settler society have changed how our communities engage, and the patriarchal behaviour seeped into our Dene beliefs changing the way that women would engage in the community. Traditionally, the women in our communities would have many roles to maintain livelihood on the land. Women would have to hunt and fish to feed their children while the men would travel long distances to hunt caribou and check their traplines. They would have to protect their camps from predators. They would have to haul water and tan their hides to clothe their families. The bush life was a hard life, but the land always provided.

In the work we do at Dechinta, our programs are always reflecting what the needs of the community are. We recognize that Indigenous people have every right to create programs and services that are going to support the unique cultural teachings and the socioeconomic status of each community. Providing trust, flexibility, and the autonomy for community members to bring people onto the land will allow for safer environments for community members to share traditional knowledge, ensuring it stays within the community.

Leanne: I know language and language learning is very important to you. Can you talk about why language is close to your heart?

Justina: Language is and has been so vital to the livelihood of Indigenous Peoples, as it creates a relationship and deeper understanding to the land, the place, and the people. Our words have such a deep meaning to the root of each word. In the Dene languages of the North, it was a way of communication for each distinct group that travelled on the lands, and many times Dene people would speak more than one dialect which allowed for people to make trades. I have heard stories of my grandfather being able to speak in Tłicho, Dëne Sųłıne, Dehcho Dene Zhatiè, Nêhiyawêwin, and English. He would often be asked to translate for Elders and Chiefs when visitors would come. In 1959, when Prince Phillip arrived in Yellowknife for the official opening of Sir John Franklin High School, he was an interpreter for Chief Jimmy Bruno of Behchokǫ̀, and Chief J. Lamalice of Kátł'odeeche.

In the summer of 2019, I was a land-based coordinator during a Dechinta semester in the *Nío Nę P'énę*, which loosely translates to "the backbone that holds our lands together." The lands we were immersed in for a month is in the shared territory of Shutáot'ine and Kaska Dena on the Yukon and Northwest Territories border, where the Canol Road was built to bring oil from Normal Wells to Whitehorse during WWII. An Elder I worked with in the heart of the mountains that summer, Frank

Andrew from Délı̨nę, would always say before he would speak that he would be speaking in his language because it connected his head and his heart. He would always speak with so much love and passion when he would share his stories of his time on the land.

Speaking from my perspective as a young Dene woman who has tried to balance the traditional and modern worlds our people have been brought into, I have stumbled many times when trying to speak and understand the language that my ancestors have spoken on my homelands since time immemorial. Indigenous Peoples in the North and across Canada have faced colonization and resisted the attempted assimilation into a settler society where we were forced to learn the English language, customs, and beliefs. Our languages and way of life on the land were taken from us, but I feel that in the North we are at an advantage to learn our languages because we still have access to our lands. The work to stabilize and revitalize our Indigenous languages is already being done on the land, in our communities, in our homes, and in our schools across the North. Indigenous people must continue to work together to hold our territorial, provincial, and federal government bodies accountable to assist in the preservation and promotion of our Indigenous languages. It must be acknowledged that in order for this shift to be successful, each language group will have a different approach to ensure they are rooted in the Indigenous knowledge and customs from their respective communities. It is time that our communities take back what is rightfully ours and strengthen our people as a whole.

Leanne: I know you've been working with an Elder to learn more about medicines and healing.

Justina: During my semester at Dechinta in 2014, our Bush Professor Paul Mackenzie shared his knowledge of plant medicine with our cohort. We would spend our days going on bush walks to find dechı̨dzèh (spruce gum) deep in the bush. We picked gots'agoò lidì (Labrador tea) to keep us healthy while we were working on the land. In the work that I have done with Dechinta in the past few years, I have had several opportunities to immerse myself in settings on the land that allowed for Elders to share their knowledge of how plants would traditionally care for people on the land.

When learning about these plants, I always make an effort to learn the name of the plants in the language of the lands that we are harvesting them on. This allows for me to have a relationship and pay my respects to the spirit of the plant, the land, and the ancestors who traditionally harvested the medicines. I thank the plant for the medicine and healing properties that they provide and lay down tobacco or return the energy by simply giving thanks to the land.

As a youth programmer with Dechinta, I have been working to create spaces for youth to learn this knowledge. In addition to the traditional knowledge we learn from our Elders, we study the medicinal properties of each plant and when is the best time to harvest plants using textbooks. I share with them the importance of having consent and the relationships we must have when we are taking anything from the land by studying them, and to remember the importance of having good intentions when harvesting on the land. As Indigenous people, our spirit and our intentions will attach themselves to our surroundings and we must remember to follow the Dene Laws and *Be Happy At All Times*. Especially when working with medicine that may be shared with others.

Leanne: During the fall semester of 2020, you and I were moose hunting with a group of staff and students. I heard you call a moose. This was the first time I've heard a woman call a moose and it was so powerful to see you reclaiming the practice of hunting. How can we encourage more youth to follow in your footsteps?

Justina: In the modern world we are being pushed into, it can be so easy to lose sight of the values that allowed our people to thrive on the lands together for generations. As Dene People we have the ability to create so much change with the voices we carry from our ancestors. We understand the interconnected relations between all beings, the people, the animals, the water, and the land. The lands we have inherited as Indigenous people have a way of healing us and bringing our people together, but we must go through the process of learning and unlearning to take care of ourselves before we can take care of others, the animals, the water and the land. Youth must be guided gently and safely in the process of learning the importance of land-based skills and how they can be transferred into life skills. Through self-discovery, I have seen firsthand how youth can work together to develop a sense of resiliency, self-governance, spiritual awareness, and take on leadership roles to confidently engage within the community roles that are created in our Dechinta semesters.

Leanne: Your work at KidsU has been supper important to my kids and is a critical part of our Dechinta programming. Why is Dene land-based learning important for kids and families?

Justina: The land has and always will be there for us as Dene People. We learn from the land because we are the land. We are able to connect and understand ourselves at a deeper level when we are connected to the land. We take better care of ourselves and our surroundings when we are living in a community setting with infants, children, youth, adults, and Elders. The setting teaches individuals to work together and care for one another. Each person in the community is a key component to the learning process that takes place when we are on the land. As Dene People we must decolonize our ways of learning and connect to the land, because we are the land. I truly believe that the land has a way of holding us and caring for us as Indigenous Peoples, and learning from our Elders is the medicine we need to heal from our traumas.

It is important to remember that the knowledge we carry from the land is medicine, and that we are strong because our ancestors were praying for us to have that knowledge.

Consent: Learning with the land

Kyla LeSage

Pick, Pack, Weave

What's the key
to warmth and protection
sleeping bag? blankets? pillow beneath your head?
no, he says
Mother Earth is
our warmth, she is
our protector, our healer, our blanket.
pick these, pack these, weave these
is a single branch
protection?
No, he says
a single branch is
a gift
roots, trees,
b r a n c h e s
are gifts waiting
to be given
they whisper take me
with you
so I pick, I pack, I weave
and I leave tobacco,
Mahsì Cho

I walk to you next
You are
hesitant and stiff
Your branches firm and
attached
No you cannot
pick me, don't
pick me
you say no and you hold
on to
a gift not ready to be given
they say
Mahsì Cho but
no.

I smile and
move on.

This is what consent from the land, consent from a spruce tree, looks
like to me. I was taught by the Dene Elders that consent is not confined
to verbal cues but rooted in experience and teachings that can only be
understood if we take the time to listen. My poem tells the story of
my experience where I was introduced to a Dene approach to land and
consent that was embedded within a sacred practice where we used the
branches from a tree for warmth and protection as flooring in our wall
tents. By practising this tradition, the Elder, Paul Mackenzie, explained
how when we are picking spruce boughs, we must receive consent
from the tree in order to use their branches. Paul taught us that while
picking spruce boughs we must be conscious of what we are doing;
if you pull on a branch and it does not come apart from the tree, you
leave the branch and continue to a different tree. This resistance from
the tree is the tree's way of saying it isn't ready to give that branch to
you. By acknowledging this, we also acknowledge the agency of the
tree and its right to say no. If the branch does however break when you
pull down on it, this is the tree's way of consenting to you taking that
part of them. I then lay tobacco and say Mahsi Cho. This practice of

consent extends to all living beings while harvesting, whether that be berries, medicine, plants, water, or animals.

I have continued to pass on this teaching while I'm out on the land or teaching others on the land. In my role as a youth educator with an on-the-land program, one of the youth was creating a fort in the snow for herself to live in. She was digging, piling snow, and creating a home when she realized that she was getting cold sitting on the cold, snowy ground. I asked her, "What can we use from the land to provide warmth and protection for the cold, snowy ground?" She looked around to find something that wasn't already covered in snow. "The trees," she said with excitement. "Yes, let's go pick some spruce bough branches to use as your floor," I said. This was when I shared with her the teaching of consent that I had learned from Elder Paul. I explained to her how to know whether or not the tree is consenting to us taking its branches for our warmth. She then went off on her own and I heard her say, "This one says no," as she pulled on a branch. She then continued to a tree that had orange-coloured pines and pulled on it. Snap! "This one said yes. Look, look!" she came running toward me. I asked her how she knew to pick the orange-coloured branch and she explained that the green pine needles are young trees that aren't done growing yet so they need time for the branches to grow stronger for us to use. She went on to explain that the older trees have grown long enough for us to use their branch so that they can regrow stronger again. I was in awe of the teachings she was telling me without knowing it. The land is our teacher.

Land leads the learning

We not only learn on the land, but we learn *from* the land. Land is central to Indigenous thought where traditional practices are grounded within the roots of creation. The land, or deh is responsible for all the life on earth—the bodies of water, plants, animals, and humans. We were all created to grow together, to nurture each other and to live in kin together. We are all connected, even though our roots have been pulled apart time and time again from greed that stems from colonialism and capitalist extractions. We take and take from the earth without ever taking the moment to ask or understand the sacredness that comes with what we are removing from the earth. We continue to take and extract from the land for our own needs and desires without receiving or asking for consent. This is because Western notions of land have degraded the value and meaning of the land and its beings. We are only taught that consent must be between two humans, yet when we are on the land and learning from the land, we are taught the meaning of consent and what it looks like. The meaning that is grounded within Dene practice is what I experienced in my first interaction of consent with the land when I studied as a student on the land with the Dechinta Centre for Research and Learning.

Returning to the land

Growing up I was far removed from my traditional roots, my traditional territories and my cultural practices. I was not raised knowing how my Gwitchin aunties would spend weeks in the spring and summer tanning hides or when my uncles would go hunting for caribou in the wintertime. I was not raised with my Anishinaabe aunties from Garden River, harvesting manoomin (wild rice) or picking sweet grass. Although I was never introduced to my own traditions as a child, I have been grateful to learn the Dene way of life from Elders and community members in Treaty 8 Territory. It was by returning to the land and learning from Dene Elders that I realized how much of myself I was missing and my passion to learn the Dene way of life in hopes that when I return to my traditional territories, I will have similar teachings and skills to bring.

In addition to the spruce bough experience, the Elders taught us the ways to receive consent from the land in order to be gifted with a moose for harvesting to feed our community. The Elder took us to ask the Old Man spirit of the island to gift our community with a moose. This moose would not only provide food for subsistence, bones for tools, and hides for tanning and sewing, but also a learning experience on Dene harvesting practices. We greeted the spirit of the island by leaving an offering, giving a prayer, and also asking for a moose. A few hours later, we received the message from one of our bush professors that they had shot a moose. This news came as a shock to us considering the practice the Elder taught us on asking the spirit of the land for not only consent to harvest a moose but to be gifted with one. Being gifted with this moose was embedded within the Elders' traditional teaching which Dene have practised since the beginning of time, and shows the intimate spiritual and physical relationship these Elders had with moose. This was a crucial practice to ensure that Indigenous Peoples had the resources needed in order to survive. But instead of simply appropriating the land without consent, the knowledge is based on allowing the land to gift you with what you need to survive.

Not only do we ask consent from the land when we are hunting and harvesting but we also communicate with the land through offerings and prayers when we receive consent from the land to inhabit it. During my time at Dechinta we did not have the opportunity to leave a prayer or acknowledge the spirit of the island during the first few days. This lack of recognition is what the Elders believed resulted in the freezing cold weather we experienced. The Elder took us to a memorial location on the island where the spirit of a young boy from the island was located. The Elder showed us how to leave an offering of tobacco and a spruce bough as a sign of respect and as a way for us to ask the land for permission to live and grow on it. Days after this offering, the weather changed for the better. To this day, I still believe the change in weather was from the offering and acknowledgement we communicated to the land through our ceremony.

These Dene teachings are solely based on experience and embodied practice. An experience that can be talked about through writing but only understood from physically witnessing and experiencing the action. This practice of acknowledging the land and receiving consent to occupy the island is embedded with in Dene Knowledge that reminds us to recognize the land as a body with agency and rights that can be equated to those of all living beings.

Consent is important in our interactions with each other around camp and in our lives at home. Thinking and practising consent enables us to respect the self-determination and body sovereignty of each other and helps us to grow strong and healthy communities. The practice of consent helps us keep each other safe. In Indigenous ways of living, this practice of consent extends far beyond humans to include plant life, water, land, animals, and all living things. This practice of consent and reciprocity is grounded in relationship with the land and everything she has to offer. In our day-to-day life we are constantly taking from the land without acknowledging the agency of the land. However, our ancestors and our Elders have lived with and on the land for time immemorial where they have practised reciprocity with the land and the animals, whether that be through laying tobacco or taking care of the land. Our Elders teach us to only take from the land what we need, to only hunt what we need to feed our family and our community, and to respect the land by taking care of it. I envision the Dene Laws that Elders pass on to us; share what you have, help each other, love each other, respect each other. These laws extend to our relationship with the land, water, and animals. These practices allow us to understand our relationship with Mother Earth while also teaching us to respect and care for it. Consent is a Western word that doesn't translate well with Indigenous languages so when reflecting on my experiences learning from Elders and the land I begin to realize that consent can look different and can be explained in different ways. To me consent is taking the time to understand our traditional practices and connect them with teachings I've learned from being on the land.

Mahsì Cho

I'd like to acknowledge and thank all of the Elders and teachers who have helped me think through my relationship with the land and influenced my understanding of consent, including Paul McKenzie, James Sangris, Maro Sundberg, and Leanne Betasamosake Simpson.

Our culture is a beating drum

Coleen Hardisty

When I am on the land in Denendeh, when I smell moose, when I hear my language spoken, I am instantly home. Land, culture, language, and Dene practices mean everything to my existence, my consciousness, my subconscious, and my body. The land is the provider of everything we need to live. Dene culture is a beating heart drum. Dene language holds the ultimate power of our teachings and understanding of what is. Dene practices are full of love, respect, and reciprocity. All these things overlap with one another. They cannot be separated into boxes, expressed in English, or on paper. Dene people know that the Universe or Creation and all its inhabitants are one and an expression of each other. More Dene people are waking up and remembering these facts, allowing them into their conscious mind, and realizing that they can make the changes our communities need to truly thrive once more. We can manifest our own beautiful, life-giving futures.

Our Creator gave us our Dene homeland to live in a way that promotes more life. This responsibility demands reciprocity in every way. We must respect, share with, and communicate with the land, or we perish. The land requires patience—take moose hunting, for example. You must call to the moose and let the echoes of your voice reach his ears. You must wait for him, and when he comes, you must be ready to receive the generous offering of his body so that you may survive another day. A moose will only be killed if he allows you to kill him, and consents to sacrificing himself for you and your family. The Dene Laws tell us that we must share this moose with our family and community. When we choose to distribute resources without judgment of who is worthy and who is not, we are remembering the true Dene ways—that everyone deserves to eat. We use tobacco, red willow, thanks, or things of value to us when giving an offering to something or someone we take from. Harvesting plants, like cranberries, is another example where we behave this way. When I pick cranberries, I leave tobacco at their feet, and thank them as I pick them. I spoke to their spirits while picking them at Dechinta and told them they are for Semo. I told them how she will make sauce with them, how happy she will be to eat them. Reciprocity is expressed when some berries fall from the plant or your hands while you are picking, planting themselves in anticipation of the following spring. That same reciprocity was expressed when we gathered fish from the nets and gave a couple to the eagles because as Archie Liske said, "They get hungry, too." What he did not say, but was implied, is that the eagles are sacred, and give their feathers to us for our prayers, ceremonies, and decorations. Giving back instead of taking and taking forever as the colonizers have done, will help us restore balance to land and waters that have been ravaged almost to death.

Our culture is a beating heart drum. Near the end of the first week at the Dechinta camp, we had a drum dance. During it, while I was dancing close to Randy Baillargeon, he let out a whoop, and then I did, and then someone in front of me did, all in quick succession. I felt this electric energy flow through me—our voices, set on the backdrop of the pounding caribou skin drums, beating with all our hearts, and lifting them to the sky. Drum dances show physically the magic that is Dene love, ceremony, and community. Everybody held hands and smiled as they danced together. When I saw this, I saw an ecosystem of inseparable community that creates and sustains positive energy. Singing and dancing are gifts that we can keep giving to ourselves and each other. We cannot stop doing those Dene things that bring us joy and shake off the sadness and threats of the world we live in. The things that keep us going when nothing else seems to be going right. We need to connect to each other in these visceral ways if we hope to keep Dene culture and individual Dene people alive. Our culture reflects the land, water, animals, plants, seasons—everything in existence that we can see and that we cannot see. One expression of this is fire, sometimes a sacred fire. As Leanne Betasamosake Simpson said in the first week at Dechinta, "Fire is a representation of community." Everyone takes turns watching the flames to make sure they do not extinguish. Everyone shares the labour of felling the trees, sawing the trunks, chopping the logs, and igniting the reaction supported by heat, oxygen, and fuel. Fire warms and dries us, cooks our food, smokes our hides, maintains our forests, provides light and place of ceremony. Fire is a little piece of the sun that we managed to harness, though it is still unruly if we are not responsible and watch it closely. Fire is an integral part of Dene life and we must not let it go out. Another Dene Law I have followed is to "always be happy." What I interpret this to mean is that we must do our best to be content and to carry positive energy into everything we do. One example of this at Dechinta was working on the muskox hides. So far, I have done this herculean task with a group of people, and there was always love, laughter, and sweat in the air. It is a Dene understanding that we need to do everything with a positive mind, heart, and soul. Otherwise, negative energy could find its way into whatever you are working on and impact the person that ends up using the objects that the hide gets turned into—like giant muskox hide mittens! The mindfulness and care we show for physical work can be adapted into everything we do, injecting love into all our relationships—personal, professional, and with strangers that we see throughout our days.

Dene language holds the ultimate power of Dene teachings and our understanding of the world, both tangible and spiritual. It is the key to deeper connections on the land, within our culture, and how we execute daily practices. I am, as Kristen Tanche said multiple times during her presentation, a "baby language speaker." I know very little about Dene Zhatie, and it breaks my heart that I am so far behind, but I am determined to learn my language in the next five years. In the meantime, I do not know what I do not know. This lack of knowledge leaves a huge gap in my grasp of Dene culture and practices, the land and water that we live on, and the plants and animals that I share this space with. Learning and using language at the Dechinta camp and with people from the Dehcho is priceless nourishment that I value and cherish with all my heart. It is a comfort that is matched by nothing else in this world. When I hear drum music and Dene Zhatie, my eyes well up with tears. I have been told that this is my soul grieving the disconnection and longing to be included in the Dene universe as those before me have been. This longing was expressed in a recent episode I had at the grocery store in Yellowknife, where I currently live. I was on the phone with Semo, and a personal topic came up during our conversation. I had this sudden, overwhelmingly strong urge to switch to Dene Zhatie. My mouth was paralyzed for a couple seconds, as I could feel my tongue trying to speak the language in vain. It was the first time that this had happened; I am convinced that my ancestors were trying to speak through me, that my mind was trying to access expression from my past life and from my Dene blood. The cultural secrets that have been kept from me through the interruptions of colonization come out of Elders without them noticing sometimes. Even though many people, Elders included, hold strict gender role beliefs, I hear language speakers betray themselves by interchanging pronouns without noticing. I have heard Elders talk about a man, yet calling him "she," and vice versa for women. I believe this is a result of Dene languages not specifying genders when referring to a person, but rather using the English equivalent of "they." This fluidity is everywhere in the language and is in direct conflict with the binary that some Dene people attempt to impose on individuals because of the influence from the church. I know that we could find freedom and harmony if we would let go of these rigid schools of thought (pun intended). Only when we collectively decide to stop oppressing ourselves and our own people will we start to see the full spectrum of Dene power, expression, and liberation. There are one million ways to be Dene, and we need all ways to build strong communities founded on acceptance and celebration. What is the point of calling our bodies of governance self-determining if our members are not encouraged to be their true, authentic selves and fully involved in decision-making?

Dene practices are devoid of strict instructions for learning or doing and assert teaching with love and patience. True love does not include violence or contempt. It is not controlling or abusive. These concepts are new to Dene People and have corrupted the way that we parent, treat our peers, and speak to ourselves. The trauma we have endured has been expressed by us sometimes hurting our loved ones, especially those most vulnerable, like our children, women, and Elders. But when another Dene person teaches me a certain drum dance, they do not give me steps or make me rehearse. There is no line dancing where I must dance in perfect synchronization with everyone else. There are a few suggestions given when learning new things, but there is room made for the individual and what works for them, what feels good to them. The first thing that comes to mind when I think of Dene practices is "giving without a second thought and without ulterior motives." I have seen many examples of this at camp, but my favourite example took place at the end of our first week. Tyra Moses brought a moose leg back from town, from her brother Morley. They gave the Dechinta community meat for everyone to eat instead of keeping it for themselves. Either person could have demanded something in return. They could have held it over our heads and insisted we were indebted to them. But they did not. This is the Dene way—sustainable, inventive, and practical, like rising and falling with the sun. We need to do it this way, or there will be nothing left for future generations and people will be no more.

All the answers for healthier, happier, communities are within us, on our land, in our culture and practices, and in our language. They are spelled out in our laws, and how we view the world. Coming to Dechinta has solidified my belief that we are the land and the land is us. If it is healthy, we are healthy. If we provide for it, it will provide for us. Dene ways have always been, and will always be, the best ways. As I continue to come out of the fog that is alcohol abuse and build up my confidence, the Dene way of life is allowing more truths to fall into place. I am seeing more connections and building them with others. The contacts that I have made so far are invaluable and I am so grateful for the resources that have been provided to me. I am so profoundly proud to be Dene.

Máhsı.

Finding Dendì, finding ourselves

Jasmine Vogt

Dechinta is a land-based university program that centres in a decolonial education system while focusing on self-determination and traditional land-based knowledge that takes place on Treaty 8 Chief Drygeese Territory (Yellowknives Dene First Nation). During each semester we respectfully live a traditional Dene lifestyle while also learning and harvesting from the land. Much of our studies are very Elder and community oriented while also allowing us to gain both Indigenous and non-Indigenous knowledge from our peers. Dechinta represents a community that is open to learn, explore and offers a teaching technique that you won't be able to find elsewhere.

Both my parents and myself were raised and have spent a good portion of our lives on the territory of the Yellowknives Dene First Nation (YKDFN). The majority of my family ties stem from the Sahtú and Delta regions of Denendeh, and while we have German and Scottish descents, *this* is the place my parents chose to call home. The stripping of our cultural identity started long before my parents' time, while growing up in a city and away from our roots was also a contributing factor. I was never able to experience ancestral practices of hunting, trapping, harvesting, or just simply living in the bush. I was never taught my language and was fairly distant from much of my family who still lived back home. Because of this disconnection I feel that it has been my own responsibility to find my way back to my culture and back to my roots. It is also my responsibility to find ways for my son to learn these teachings as well because he has no Father figure in his life. It is our

Dene self-determination that gives us this sense of personal freedom balanced with community accountability. And it is through my own self-determination that I have chosen to create a whole different lifestyle for us so that we don't have to see the repetitive cycle of identity loss that Residential Schools and colonialism have inflicted on our people. One of the colonizer's goals was to break the relationship that Indigenous people held with the land so that we would become solely dependent on all the Western luxuries that the land couldn't offer us.

During the final days before attending my first semester at Dechinta I remember thinking to myself: "What the hell am I doing? I've never spent a day of my life in the bush and here I am going to live out there for two months?!" Living a Dene lifestyle is a part of our cultural identity and the way our ancestors lived and it is something that was taken away from us long before we could even decide for ourselves. So naturally, I was scared and nervous for what was to come but I knew only good would come from this experience. I spent too many years disconnected from my culture and from myself because of addiction, so I felt that I owed it to myself and to my son, and that I needed to show us there was another way of life. It was far out of our comfort zone, but we adapted quickly and learned more than we ever would sitting in a desk. Having been taught self-determination and decolonization in practice, this left me with this sense of responsibility that I needed to keep learning as much as I could about our Dene ways so that I could reclaim what has been lost.

While using my knowledge from the spring semester, I came back with an open mind, an open heart, and my son in tow once again. We soon found out that, although there are similarities, this semester was far different from our last. With much repetition and similar lectures, I found different discussions and questions would often arise as if it was my first time hearing it all. With the change of season, I soon became aware that the land was about to teach us things in a different manner and that we had to do things a little faster as the sun began setting earlier as each day passed. We had been given a different set of students, staff, and Elders to learn from as they each brought knowledge from where they were at in life. But nevertheless, we still had our ever-present sense of community.

Dendì (Moose)

One thing that remained consistent with our second semester was the adventures we had with YKDFN Elder, Paul Mackenzie. Anyone who's ever been on a walk with him knows that you need to be fully prepared and to expect the unexpected, whether it be hopping on rocks and logs to cross a creek or bush whacking in the boreal forest while looking for medicine. After a busy couple day of crazy weather and getting settled into our camp, we all began getting sick with the flu. Of course, Dr. Paul (with his Bush PhD) decided it was time we go out to look for medicine. We had gathered enough spruce gum from the island alone but we were missing one thing—tamarack. There was no warning or time to get ready for this mission, so I grabbed whoever was in sight; Coya, Thumlee, and I scrambled to get all our gear then followed Paul and his trusty chauffeur, James Sangris, to the boat.

Prior to this day we had spent a few days out on the boats scoping around and calling for moose to feed our taste for Dene food. With Paul and James being the hunters that they are, they always have their eyes peeled for any wildlife they may see. We had been cruising in the boat when we came to an abrupt stop and Paul was grabbing his gun faster than I could even process what was happening. "Chıh" (duck). He was ready to go but not a shell in sight. "Darn, maybe next time," he laughed. We took off to our destination. During our boat ride Paul and James kept talking about visiting an old man. They said if we go visit the old man he'll give us moose. Our search for tamarack now had a much bigger purpose. As we pulled up to the island, there had been birch trees about ten inches wide freshly chewed down by tsa (beaver). Sure enough there were two of them just swimming around and this time James was quick to move. "Click, click, click," was all I heard from the gun. At the time, I kept thinking about what unfortunate luck we had and how devastating it would've been if we had wound up seeing a moose with no bullets. I realize now there was a reason this was happening to us at this time.

After a good twenty minutes of breaking trail and eyeing the birch trees for Chaga, we soon found out that the old man the guys had been talking about was the grave of a YKDFN Elder. I soon gained the understanding that it was protocol to stop by and pay your respects to the grave of this man and his loved ones that laid beside him. And thinking back on it now, I realize that it is Paul's responsibility to his people and to his land to stop here, to pay his respects, and to share these teachings. Our Elders don't recite the Dene Laws to us and tell us how to live our lives, they simply show us and give us these teachings by how they act, how they talk, and what they share with us. During this visit we made our offerings, prayed for moose to feed our camp, and headed back to the island with our tamarack in tow.

Within moments of getting back to our camp we got word that Gordie and Randy had shot a moose while they were on their way back from T'è?ehdaà (Dettah). Our prayers had been answered! Mahsì Cho! We gathered a boat full of people and we quickly went out to help with the harvesting process and what was soon to be our course work for the next two weeks. With Dechinta being so family oriented, we brought the kids out to the site without a second thought so that they were able to learn with us. Even though it had been the first time I've been able to be a part of this process I felt that it was essential to have my son beside me during this teaching lesson. I feel that it extends back to my previous thoughts on my purpose and my responsibility to find ways for him to learn these traditional ways and be a part of this intergenerational knowledge transmission. We take these things that Elders teach us and are basically being the transmission between them and the kids; we are showing and teaching them things that they can't get in colonial schools.

In the past, I was taught the importance of learning protocols from the people and Elders of whose territory you were on through a rather challenging incident. Although I appreciate the input and insight from other regions, I feel as if it's respectful toward the people and toward the animal to follow what has been taught on that land for so long. Having Paul with us during the harvesting of the moose made me even more eager to learn. He teaches us, he guides us, and he makes sure we are all included in the process.

When I spend time out on the land with Dechinta I am able to realize how crucial each person's role is within the community and how much we rely on each other to maintain that steady flow on a day-to-day basis. I found that it's very challenging to follow a detailed plan that one may have; the land is our teacher, and we have to work with whatever lesson it may hand us for the day. We all play a role within this community that we build, and we all have something to offer each other. The YKDFN offer us their land and their teachings. We have a responsibility to share our experiences and what we have taken from it. Each one of us has a reason behind our choice in coming to Dechinta; it is through our own self-determination that we decided to be here, and that is the spruce gum that binds us all together.

Mahsì Cho for being my sister, Miigwech for being my best friend

Jessica Sangris

I have been given an assignment from my Dechinta course. I have to write a letter to a leader in my life—to a strong, Indigenous, Queer woman. Is it really a surprise that I wouldn't choose anyone else but you?

I'd hate for this letter to be prim and proper, as that is the exact opposite of what both of us are. But I do want it to somewhat make sense and not be just me rambling on about how much I love you and look up to you. As much as you'd *love* to read about how awesome you are, suck it up and read this. Try not to cry, but let's face it, we both know you will cry reading it and I will cry writing it.

I want to start this letter off by saying thank you so much for being who you are. You are the strong, Indigenous woman in my life. You have been a huge influence on my life. Growing up with you as my bigger sister is the one thing that has kept me on a semi-straight path. You have always been my best friend and I've looked up to you in so many different ways. Knowing that I can count on you for every experience I go through whether it's good or bad is something I am very grateful for.

You are the most caring, selfless, and kindest souls I know. I can't remember a time when you didn't put someone else before yourself. I have so many memories of you bailing me out in times of need, or being the shoulder I needed to cry on when things got too heavy for me, or telling me to calm down when I was on the brink of doing something harmful to myself or others. Or being the judgmental ass, eyeballs looking sideways at me for some of my RIDICULOUS fashion choices I made in my youth. What can I say—2000s hip hop/ gangster rap raised me? Ha! Thank you for bringing up these fashion choices to me every now and then. I truly appreciate the reminders of me trying to wear a baby pink velour track suit all the time.

I was so scared when you left to go to Trent University and I was going into grade ten and was going to be left alone with Mom. She was going through her own hardships and was in no way capable to help me deal with growing up. It was so hard when you left and I was stuck to deal with my own demons and help Mom with hers. It was a bad mix. I couldn't wait for you to come home during holidays and summer breaks and help me get back to a good state of mind. Your visits started spacing out and happening less frequently. I selfishly wanted you home to help fix our broken home and help me put the pieces of our Mom back together again. But we were just kids and it wasn't our responsibility to do that.

I understand now why you couldn't come home. There was so much hurt and pain in that home that it wasn't a healthy environment for anyone to be in anymore. I don't and have never blamed you for staying away for the long periods of time.

It was during this time that you blossomed into this amazing person that I absolutely adore and admire so much. You found your true self and came to terms with who you really are. You found the courage and strength to come out to us as a lesbian. You found the spirit and bravery that I wish I had during those years. You were the cowardly lion who went to Oz and found your courage. I have never been more proud of you.

Since then you have built this beautiful network of friends, from the LGBTQ+ community, the high school friends who have stuck through the times with you, randoms you have picked up along the way, and the wide array of Indigenous families who gathered in Ottawa and Toronto. I've been lucky enough to have been let into this group of friends. This group of friends had become your own chosen family in times when we couldn't be there for you.

This group of friends helped bring you to meeting your wife. I love hearing the story of how you two met. Both working for the Assembly of First Nations in Ottawa as summer students. You swooped in and stole her from her long-time boyfriend and won her over with all your lesbian charm. She was hooked and the rest is history. I am so grateful that she came into your life when she did and helped break down the wall you had built up around yourself and your heart for so long. You two have built this amazing life together. When you guys got married, I knew that as long as she was by your side, you would be all right and would always have someone to walk this crazy world with and keep you grounded.

When our young cousin was pregnant, she called you two and asked if you two were interested in adopting her baby—she was due to give birth in less than a month. There was barely a second thought; you and Mir jumped into action mode and started getting all the arrangements in place for the arrival of your new baby. This was when your generosity really shone through. You went from a young, fun, carefree married couple with your simple routine between the two of you, to being thrown into a whirlwind of planning and rushing to get ready for a new baby being thrown into the mix. You two quickly found a new house to live in to accommodate your growing family, you got a bunch of the legal stuff prepped, you guys made tentative travel arrangements to get here a week before her due date so that you could be here when the baby arrived.

Little did you know that I would be calling you two to let you know that I was in the hospital with our cousin because she was in labour. You immediately put everything on hold and caught the next flight out of Toronto and made it to Yellowknife in eighteen hours to meet your brand new baby GIRL!

Watching you meet your daughter for the first time was one of the greatest things I was able to witness. I knew that this was what you were meant for; she was your daughter right from the beginning. She belonged to you and there was no one better in this world to look after her than you and Mir.

Maggie is the luckiest girl in the world to have you two as her parents—two of the most strongest women I know. She is growing up with your sensitive side, and Mir's sassy attitude. I know that she will be raised with an amazing wit, a keen fashion sense, and she will not take any shit from anyone. She has so much of your personality; she is so kind, so full of love, and an absolute joy to be around. A crazy mixture of DeLeary and Giroux though.

188 Ndè Sìì Wet'a?à

I want to thank you for always being by my side and teaching me without the lessons, how to be resilient, generous, loving, kind, and independent, and how to be a strong female. It's hard for me to think of strong, independent women in my life, because I'm surrounded by men at home, at work, in my community, in my councillor role—it's all very male driven. I just need to look at the strong, resilient, Indigenous women in my life and I am comforted. You have helped me overcome this obstacle by showing me that I had to fight a little bit harder to get where I am today. It's all been worth it.

When I feel like giving up, I always think about what you would do and how you would handle the situation. I'm confident that you would have a good cry, or two (or even maybe three really good cries), but after that, you'd pull it all together and get whatever needed to get done, done. I can't imagine not having you in my life. In all honesty, I doubt I would have made it this far, accomplished what I have, without you.

Mahsì Cho for being my sister. Miigwech for being my best friend.

I love you always, my love.

Life along the Arctic Ocean

Noel-Leigh Cockney

Living along the Arctic Ocean you have to grow up quickly, which was especially so for my ancestors. I grew up in as close to a traditional Inuvialuit lifestyle as one can. Our connection to the land is what has allowed us to live up here for so long. Without the Arctic providing us with shelter, water, and food, it wouldn't be possible for anyone to survive in a place like this.

The importance of showing respect to what we gather is what allows the land the ability to provide for us. It is the land that we have to listen to so that we can learn the lessons needed to survive. As Inuvialuit People, who live on the coast of the Arctic Ocean, we respect every aspect of the land.

We respect the land by listening to the natural forces upon it. We understand the strength and unpredictability of weather, particularly on the ocean. There weren't many people long ago who knew how to swim, because they didn't have the luxury of a continuously heated, solid walled home to get back to from the freezing Arctic Ocean. Our ancestors had to be patient, waiting and finding the appropriate opportunities to get out to gather what they needed to live. When those opportunities came up, our work ethic had to be strong and persistent. When we were going, we went until the weather turned since we didn't know how long the next bad weather would last.

We respect the land by being appreciative for all that we gather. Without the appreciation for something's life, those lives wouldn't see that we are in need of them. They know that, despite us taking them for our use, we will use them to all of our ability. There will be no waste of their lives.

If there was a waste of their lives, we would quickly find out what we did wrong. That's what all of our mistakes accumulate to. That knowledge is passed down from generation to generation. That's why stories are so important to our culture, so important to our lives. Our lessons on how to travel, how to navigate, how to know where to harvest plants, how to hunt, trap and fish, how to process the animals we catch, is everything about the way we live our lives.

Without those stories from the people who have lived their lives, we would have continued to make those mistakes over and over again. If that was to happen in a place like the Arctic, we wouldn't have survived very long. The stories are the things that we have to continue to listen to—to listen to so that we can advance our culture and our lives. In today's world, advancement doesn't mean changing the way that we do things, rather the advancement of our education to the next generations.

The passing of our culture to the next generation seems in dire need in today's society. It is needed because you cannot learn the skills through a screen. You cannot understand the anatomy of our food without going through the motions of the harvest. You cannot understand how to travel through your land without walking, drive a boat or snowmobile, or navigate your terrain from your bed or couch.

When I was growing up, my family and I were out at our camps as much as we could. We were lucky with having two other families that I grew up with along the coast. Not only did I learn how to hunt and fish and gather firewood from my family, but I had the pleasure from learning from two very well-versed families along the coast. In my very early years, I only went out with my grandparents and my Mom, learning how to travel throughout the tundra, learning how to hunt geese, caribou, and whales. As I grew up with the other families' kids, we were able to go out, not too far from home, to hunt geese on our own. This is what has allowed me to not only learn from people outside of my family, but also take some leadership in some tasks that we did.

Growing up with many generations around me, I've been able to learn from, and observe, the way that each generation teaches, learns, and interacts with each other. The lessons in my life provided me with a great base to understand a lot about life. Today, I hope for this kind of interaction for all generations.

We are a species that needs to comprehend how to go through this journey we call life. It is not going to be the same for everyone, but the lessons are the same. We learn how to take care of ourselves so that we don't kill ourselves. We learn how to interact with others, regardless of where we come from or how we look.

I do not have a family of my own, but seeing how protected the children are today, I'm sure that my Mom and grandparents could have been heavily judged by today's standards. I love that they allowed us as children to explore and experience things on our own and I think more of that is needed today. At points in our life, we need different things. Sometimes we need structure to know what we need to survive. We also need the freedom to experiment. We need mentors in our life to understand how we learn. We need to learn lessons the hard way.

Estu Nátse

(My grandma is strong)

Taylor Behn-Tsakoza

Dear Grandma,

I miss you. In the time you've been gone I have done a lot of reflecting and appreciating of all that you taught in our time together. I wish I would've done more of that when you were here, but I can't dwell on the past. There are so many memories that I hold close to my heart like our time at the cabin skinning beavers or in the smoke shack making dry meat. Though there are skills that I wish I could've learned from you. There are too many times to count when I watched you bead but I never picked up a needle. Numerous times throughout the day where I would listen to you and grandpa speak Slavey to each other, but I never asked, "What are you saying?" You never did push anything onto your kids or grandchildren, you always showed love and kindness for our decisions even if they weren't the greatest ones. I think that's what I have taken most from your teachings and guidance is that we all deserve love and acceptance no matter what direction we choose to go in life.

I am currently exploring the complex topic of gender and although we never talked specifically on this topic, I like to think you taught me indirectly about it. As a little girl I always thought it was normal for Aunty to have a girlfriend and for Uncle to be a little feminine because no one ever said different. You always lead by example, and I think everyone around you followed your lead when it came to the matter; you didn't treat them any different, you didn't love them any less and you certainly didn't exclude them from our culture. As I actively try to learn more about queerness and Two-Spirit people, I choose to be the example for others that you were for me.

I graduated from university this past spring and I can't put into words how I felt when I held my degree in my hands for the first time. It's hard to fathom what your life could've been like if you had the chance to go. Nonetheless, I always tell people you and my grandma Rosie were the smartest people I knew even though neither of you could read or write. Your fluency in our language, knowledge of our traditions and culture has proven to be far more valuable than anything I learned in the six years I was in the city. Not being able to read or write must have been a challenge in this modern world. I had the privilege and resources to go and you didn't; there truly leaves no room to compare. You had to fulfill your role as a wife and a Mother here at home and I applaud you for that. I always wondered if grandpa had been less strict on imposing the colonizers ideas and beliefs of what being a woman meant and if he had kept our Dene Laws and governance structures strong and prevalent in his life, would he have given you the freedom to pursue the things you wanted? I have noticed grandpa's tendency to control the women in his life since he can no longer boss you around. Some days it can be hard for me to hold back my feminist, radical attitude but I have too much respect for that man to not do as he says.

Growing up under the guidance of you I always felt compelled to push the boundaries of any box people tried to place me in. My physical build and confidence allowed me to compete in activities that perhaps my smaller, more reserved twin sister couldn't. I was one of three girls on the local boy's hockey team right from age seven to eighteen, and you were at every game cheering me on. Remember when I was ten and me, you and grandpa went for that ride in the bush and I shot my first moose? I am thankful for my good aim and that grandpa accepted my eagerness to learn how to provide for our family. After my brother passed, I felt that subconsciously I was training to fill the duty he had as a male to provide. But why was it left up to the boys to learn these skills? I was just as good as them, and at times, better. These are the questions I wish I could ask you. I want to know more about how Dene people viewed Two-Spirit people in our community. I know they had a place in our society but to hear the stories and the language used to describe them would be helpful right now in navigating and understanding the roles in which they held in the community. I dedicate my work and time to bettering our communities for everyone and I think if I had the knowledge that our ancestors did then maybe I would be able to fulfill my purpose of doing that.

As I continue to learn how to live without you, I want to remain committed to learning our language and challenging outdated and Christianized views of what settler society thinks our people should be like. With the tools I've been armed with, Western education and Dene teachings, I know I have a chance at making a difference in the way non-Indigenous people view and understand us. As I move through this world as a strong, brilliant, and resilient Dene woman, I want to make space for the teachings that were ripped from you and our people at the hands of colonialism and instill into our community that they have a right to embrace the fluidity of their identities and spirits. I will continue to honour your legacy of treating everyone with love and kindness.

The Dene Laws

Indigenous culture is wellness

Jennie Vandermeer

As is customary in Dene culture, it's important to tell you that what I'm sharing in this article is not my knowledge. This is ancestral knowledge gifted to us by Newehstįnę (Creator) and passed down by ʔǫhda ke (Elders). I'm sharing practical ways in which I try to live by the Dene Laws. It's also important to note that while I'm bringing you a Dene perspective, these teachings can apply to anyone.

I especially want to thank setsį (my grandmother), Cecile Modeste. She passed away when I was a teenager and, sadly, I was not able to fully grasp her teachings at the time. But I was gifted several of her recordings a few years ago and have learned so much about our language, spirituality, and how to live a good life. I also want to thank senǫ (my Mother), Jane Modeste, for being patient while I ask endless questions on how to pronounce or spell a word in Dene kədə́ (North Slavey) or explain a spiritual concept.

Being Dene and becoming a capable person

It is said that the (nǫbálewá) tipi is like the education that is given to our children. The poles represent the basic Dene perspectives lived around the children. Each of the poles is firmly grounded in the land which nurtures life. The poles hold the child close to family until the child is ready to fly. The poles must guide the education of the Dene children. The mowa (opening on top of tipi) is the passage into life as a capable adult. The child that is respected will eventually come to the mowa. When all of the perspectives come together in one place and become alive in the child, the child can fly off to be on its own.[24]

---

24 *Dene kede Education: A Dene perspective* (1993), https://www.ece.gov.nt.ca/sites/ece/files/resources/dene_kede_k-6_teacher_resource_manual.pdf.

I included this excerpt as I'm still learning what it means to be Dene and what it means to be a capable person. The Elders presented us with the knowledge, skills, and attitudes that Dene should strive toward in order to become "capable." Capable people, are ones who had integrity in their relationships with the spiritual world, the land, other people, and themselves.[25] It's important to keep an open mind and have childlike curiosity regarding our culture. ʔǫhda ke teach us that being willing to learn and taking initiative are admirable traits to have.

I grew up in Délı̨nę, Northwest Territories (NWT) and speak Dene kədǝ́, but I left for school when I was a teenager and did not learn many of the traditional teachings. I'm now learning or relearning many things as an adult. It can be frustrating and humbling but I welcome the challenge as I know that being connected to my culture will contribute to my healing.

Due to impacts beyond our control, what was common knowledge among our people several decades (or years) ago isn't common knowledge now. My Mom's generation grew up on the land and are strongly rooted in their culture. I, however, grew up in town and had a much different upbringing, where I was more heavily influenced by white culture. I often feel shame that I don't have a lot of the traditional knowledge and skills, or when I stumble on my words when I speak Dene kədǝ́. For a long time, I was scared to ask questions for fear of being ridiculed or scorned. Now, I'm constantly asking questions and seeking cultural knowledge. Learning about our culture is healing and helps us to become capable people.

Several years ago, I started sharing my personal journey in a Facebook group that I named Everrrr Sexy Health and Wellness. I also provided wellness advice and had clients across NWT, Canada, and the United States. Although I no longer use that platform or provide coaching services, I continue to use social media for discussing addictions and mental illness while offering advice and suggestions on how to deal with these challenges. I also provide presentations and workshops throughout NWT on nutrition, exercise, mental health, addictions, intergenerational trauma, domestic violence and, most importantly, resiliency. This has

25   Dene kede Education: A Dene perspective (1993), https://www.ece.gov.nt.ca/sites/ece/files/resources/dene_kede_k-6_teacher_resource_manual.pdf.

helped me to heal and has provided inspiration for many others to do the same. Ultimately, the purpose of this is to be the best version of yourself in all aspects of your life.

What does wellness mean to you?

Let's get something straight; Indigenous culture is wellness. Traditionally, our people knew (and still know) how to take care of themselves. We had to be healthy and balanced; this was a matter of survival. Although I have certifications in nutrition, resistance training, and yoga, I'm not going to tell you to lose weight or exercise. This is beyond the aesthetics; this is beyond looking good. It's about honouring our ancestors' teachings and carrying them on.

I consistently receive different answers when I ask, "What does wellness mean to you?" To some, it means living a sober life, or getting fit, or addressing trauma. There's a whole spectrum of answers and they're all valid. I've found, though, that in regard to wellness, there is a distinct difference between Western/white views and Indigenous views.

Again, this is my opinion, but I've found that Western/white society is very focused on looking good. There is a billion-dollar industry that's entirely centred on appearing thin and young. We're bombarded by messages on television, social media, and magazines telling us that we're not good enough as we are and that we need to look or behave a certain way. Because we're being inundated with these types of messages (on top of the trauma we've experienced as Indigenous Peoples), many get swept up in that type of negative thinking and we become conditioned to overlook our own beauty. It is no wonder that so many of us are in pain. There's nothing wrong with wanting to look our best but there's much more to experience in life.

When you compare this viewpoint to those of our Indigenous ancestors, you'll see that there's quite a difference. Our Indigenous cultures are quite diverse but many of our beliefs and core values are similar, including our definitions of wellness. For Indigenous Peoples, wellness is rooted in our knowledge and value systems. Indigenous language, spirituality, culture, land, physical health, mental health, emotional health, and community (people) are all parts of a system. Every part of that system needs to work together in unison and in balance for a person (and community) to be healthy and whole. As mentioned above, our ancestral teachings are designed to teach us how to become capable. We need to be healthy and whole to become capable; our communities need us to be well so that we can carry on our customs, cultures, and languages.

Trauma in our communities

The Creation Story is fundamental for the Dene, for in it, the order of our universe is laid out. The order enables us to see ourselves as a people in relationship to the world. This is our world view—our perspective, the perspective from which we see life and all things around us. In the Creation Story, people are the last to be made. The land and the animals made before us did not really need people and therefore people had no reason to exist. When Dene were created, they were the only people that relied upon everyone else for their survival. They were the weakest of all creatures: hence, the Dene perspective is that survival would be difficult and people, in their relationship to the land, would have to be humble and respectful.[26]

Indigenous Peoples are strong, resilient, and adaptive. But we're also dealing with a lot of hardship and challenges. Our communities are deeply traumatized by the effects of colonialism and racism. In order to access our natural resources, government policies were established to either assimilate or destroy us. These policies forced our families into Residential Schools where many faced extreme abuse and/or neglect. It makes sense; if we're weak, then it's easier to exploit our lands. The effects of this trauma are intergenerational and have devastated our communities. Now, many of our people are disconnected from our culture, language, and the land. Due to this disconnection, too many of us struggle with addictions, mental illness, and poor health due to lifestyle choices. I know this because I'm one of those people. I'm grateful that I've been sober since 2016; it's been very positive and changed my life dramatically in all aspects.

Definition of trauma is a severe emotional shock and pain caused by an extremely upsetting experience.[27] A study called the Adverse

---

26   Dene kede Education: A Dene perspective (1993), https://www.ece.gov.nt.ca/sites/ece/files/resources/dene_kede_k-6_teacher_resource_manual.pdf.

27   "Trauma," Cambridge Dictionary, accessed July 25, 2020, https://dictionary.cambridge.org/dictionary/english/trauma.

Childhood Effects (ACE) study was conducted in the 1990s. Over 17,000 participants from California completed confidential surveys regarding their childhood experiences and current health status and behaviours. Examples of trauma (or ACEs) can include: abuse, neglect, divorce, death in family, and so on. The results of the study found that ACEs are linked to risky health behaviours, chronic health conditions, low life potential, and early death. As the number of ACEs increases, so does the risk for these outcomes.[28] Meaning if you've had more traumatic experiences in your life, you're more susceptible to these challenges.

Although this study was not done with Indigenous Peoples (the participants were primarily white), I'm certain that it still applies to our people. Trauma is trauma; it impacts everyone. Indigenous Peoples face high rates of chronic illness (for example, diabetes, heart disease), mental illness (for example, depression, anxiety, suicide), incarnation, and domestic violence. Many of our people are vulnerable and are never heard from again (as seen with the National Inquiry into Missing and Murdered Indigenous Women and Girls). Please know that we're facing these issues not because we're bad, lazy, or ignorant. This is a social injustice issue. Many of our people are dealing with these issues due to trauma caused by colonization: abuse, forced removal from traditional lands, and disconnection from cultural practices. The colonial system is so destructive that our planet and everyone on it (including non-Indigenous people) are suffering from it.

The colonial system has attempted to brainwash us into thinking that our Indigenous knowledge is inferior, that we as a people are inferior. But they're wrong. This system has tried to separate us through addictions, violence, land claim negotiations, resource development exploitation, but we're still here. And we still need each other. Healthy people create healthy families and healthy communities. It's our culture to serve our community. We are meant to help each other to survive and thrive. It was true in the past and it's still true today. We need to be strong for each other.

28   "Preventing Adverse Childhood Experiences," Centers for Disease Control and Prevention, accessed July 25, 2020, https://www.cdc.gov/violenceprevention/acestudy/fastfact.html?CDC_AA_refVal=https%3A%2F%2Fwww.cdc.gov%2Fviolenceprevention%2Fchildabuseandneglect%2Faces%2Ffastfact.html.

Gifts from Newehstı̨nę: Methods of resiliency and healing

The good news is, with proper supports, we can let go of the shame because we know **why** our communities are facing these issues. Now we can focus on **how** we're going to heal so that we can become capable people, who then serve our communities.

So, you may be asking how am I supposed to deal with stress and take care of myself? Particularly when the system continues to be designed to tear us down? I don't have all the answers, but I will share how the Dene Laws have helped guide how I live my life. I struggle some days but following the guidance of our ancestors is helping me get through it.

It's important to keep a perspective of humility and respect in mind with regard to the Dene Laws. These laws were created to guide us and help instill self-discipline so that we could become capable people. I've heard and seen slight variations of the Dene Laws but based on the conversations I've had with ?ǫhda ke, love and respect are at the core our Laws. The Dene Laws below have been taken from the Dehcho First Nation's website. I'm grateful to them for sharing these widely.[29]

The Dene Laws:
Share what you have
Help each other
Love each other as much as possible
Be respectful of Elders and everything around you
Sleep at night and work during the day
Be polite and don't argue with anyone
Young people should act respectfully[30]
Pass on the teachings
Be happy at all times

I was taught by an Elder that it's not our way to tell people how to live their lives. All we can do is live by example and share knowledge with those who seek it out. I hope that others will look to the Dene Laws

29   "Dene Laws," Dehcho First Nations, accessed July 25, 2020 https://dehcho.org/ government/about-us/dene-laws/.

30   The Dene Laws are not meant to exclude anyone, but the language may not be reflective of the growing number of 2SLGBTQIIA people in the North. Please know that you're loved and supported.

to see how to live a good life. That's what they're there for. Please keep in mind that what works for me may not work for you; we're all individuals with different experiences. Create the life you want with the tools Newehstı̨nę gifted us. This knowledge was given to our ancestors and ʔǫhda ke by Newehstı̨nę; it's a gift so that we can thrive while we're here for this short time. We all know the benefits of self-care (for example, eating nutritious food, reducing or eliminating consumption of alcohol and drugs, exercising, sleeping, reducing stress). I'm hoping that if you understand that Indigenous culture is wellness then you might be more open and willing to incorporate some of these practices into your everyday life.

Share what you have

Sharing is very important in our culture, especially sharing food. When our hunters are blessed with a successful hunt, it's customary to share with Elders and single mothers. We are thankful and provide an offering to the land and the animal for the gift. A successful harvest in the community is a good opportunity to reclaim traditional food practices: learning to hunt, fish, and process traditional food (for example, make dry meat, dry fish).

Our ancestors knew the value of watching what we eat and had rules for what types of food to avoid at certain times in our lives. They knew that what we eat affects our mental health; when we choose foods that are nutritious and satiating then we feel better mentally and physically. They also knew that cooking and preparing food are considered "ceremony"; it's important to have good thoughts and words when preparing food, especially traditional foods. I enjoy going to restaurants, but I mostly eat at home. Dining at restaurants gives power to others and cooking for yourself takes it back. I encourage you to learn to cook.

Again, I'm not going to give you a meal plan or tell you to follow a particular diet. It's up to you to make smart choices for optimal health. Also remember that food is meant to be enjoyed and you shouldn't feel restricted in any way. I will, however, share my approach to nutrition:

I try to eat traditional foods when I can (meat, fish, berries, and so on). I'm very grateful when I do get these foods and consider it a blessing. But I don't always have access to traditional foods or sometimes I want greater variety. In that case, I mostly eat whole foods in their natural state; I eat foods that are as close to their whole state as possible (for example, fresh fish versus processed fish sticks).

I drink lots of water and rarely have sugary drinks such as juice and pop. I limit coffee to two cups a day and don't add sugar. I also avoid artificial sweeteners.

I try to eat vegetables with two meals a day (minimum). I realize that food security is an issue in the North and not every community has access to fresh produce. Frozen fruits and vegetables are just as nutritious as fresh and can easily be added to meals. I like to add frozen kale or cauliflower to smoothies, veggies to a stir-fry or roast them in the oven with some olive oil and spices.

I read food labels and try to buy foods that have fewer ingredients. Foods that have a long ingredient list usually have lots of added sugar and preservatives.

I try to avoid sugar. The food industry adds sugar to so many foods that you wouldn't think of (for example, pasta sauce, soup). There are also many names for sugar; look for ingredients that end in "ose" (for example, fructose).

I enjoy treats in moderation (for example, junk food, chocolate) but don't make it a daily thing. I eat it, enjoy it, then move on.

When I'm craving something, I ask if I'm truly hungry or if I'm just bored or sad. Emotional eating is a huge issue for some. If you're eating to comfort yourself and numb out rather than deal with your emotions, then you may want to pay attention to that.

Help each other

It's important to help others in our community, this includes helping others to acquire new knowledge and skills. You never know the impact you'll have on someone who may be struggling to learn their language or how to tan moose hides. Trying to learn traditional skills makes people feel connected with their communities. We need to have a sense of community and belonging for our mental health. We need to feel connected to others.

Love each other as much as possible

We need healthy relationships (family, community, and intimate) to continue our culture. Unhealthy relationships (for example, domestic violence and lateral violence) are a direct result of historical trauma. Some great advice that I've received from Elders includes: the importance of working on yourself before you start intimate relationships and setting healthy boundaries to protect yourself and your family. Lateral violence (for example, bullying, gossip) is also prevalent in our communities; we need to support each other instead of tearing each other down.

Be respectful of Elders and everything around you

Respect and honour your Elders. Spend time with them; they have so much knowledge to give and are happy to share. When travelling, pray and ask for safe passage and provide an offering—anything of value to you. It could be shells (if you're a hunter) or small amounts of tobacco, food, and so on. Try to establish a respectful connection to land and water. The land is a source of renewal, strength, and healing. Everyone feels better out on the land. We need to take care of the land so that it'll take care of us.

Sleep at night and work during the day

Sleep is important for all aspects of health. For Indigenous Peoples, we believe in the power of dreams and see them as messages from the spiritual world. If we don't prioritize sleep and get into that deep sleep (REM cycle), we can't get those messages. Traditionally, our people passed down knowledge orally. Memory consolidation is needed to remember oral histories. Sleeping helps with memory consolidation.

Be polite and don't argue with anyone

Emotional intelligence: we need to learn how to experience and process anger and pain in healthy ways. We need to learn to practice emotional regulation by not acting out and hurting yourself or others when you are in an emotional state. Learning meditation/breathing exercises and clearly communicating your needs can help.

Young boys and girls should act respectfully

There are many rules set for when girls and boys become women and men; they are typically taught by the family. Examples include not eating certain foods, fasting for certain periods, and specifically for women, it includes not walking over men's possessions (especially hunters), an animal carcass or animal blood, and so on. At first, these rules may seem restrictive, but they are meant to empower and instill self-respect and self-discipline.

Pass on the teachings

Prayer is ceremony. Everyone should be able to worship in their own way; it may mean going to church for some, and for others it could be more spiritual. Regardless, prayer is about showing gratitude and having a relationship with Newehstįnę. For many Indigenous Peoples, prayer includes smudging, drumming songs, drum dances, fire feeding, and offerings to land and water. Prayer could also be as simple as saying, "máhsı."

Meditation is also ceremony. I remember when my grandparents would take us out in the bush and setsée (my grandfather), Isidore Modeste, would wake up really early to start the fire. I'd watch him as he sat by the fire in quiet contemplation. It wasn't until a few years ago that I realized he was essentially meditating. Tsįnę ékanet'e means to "quiet your mind." I meditate for a few minutes each day to make sure I'm in the right mindset to start my day. It's helped me dramatically in my relationships and ability to handle my stress and anxiety.

I read somewhere that prayer is when you talk to Newehstįnę, and meditation is when Newehstįnę talks back to you. I think that's beautiful.

Be happy at all times

Stress and trauma cause profound negative impacts on health. A solid self-care plan can help you to be a happier, calmer, more capable person.

Traditionally our people were always moving. They had to so that they could survive on the land; being active was an everyday thing but that's not the case these days. Years ago (when I was still drinking, smoking, and not taking care of myself), I went berry picking with my Mom, aunt, and uncle. I was embarrassed that I struggled to keep up with them because I was so out of shape. I saw my family walking confidently and effortlessly in the muskeg and saw how healthy and strong they were. They were raised on the land and the importance of staying active was instilled in them from a young age. It's not very often that I see them sitting around, doing nothing. I asked my Mom about this and she said that you needed to move out on the land to be independent (plus it helped them to stay warm).

I've lived with depression and anxiety since my teens and I know that when I'm not active, my depression and anxiety will surface. To avoid this, I try to do some form of movement everyday (walking, yoga, weightlifting, paddling, and so on). Movement helps decrease feelings of depression and anxiety. Sitting around all day encourages laziness and depression. Movement is critical to all aspects of health; it helps to process emotions and trauma (otherwise it stays in body and shows up later as sickness and/or physical pain).

An excess of alcohol and drugs are detrimental to all aspects of your health. Many people can partake responsibility, but many others can't. I won't tell people not to drink or do drugs because I know they won't listen if they're not ready. I didn't listen when people talked to me about it—I didn't hear them until was ready. I don't drink because I had a problem with alcohol. Alcohol took up a lot of space and it didn't bring anything positive into my life. I'm happier and healthier without it, my relationships have improved, and so many amazing opportunities have come into my life since I created the space for them. If you find that you're struggling with this, there's help out there. The decision is yours to make.

Traditionally, Elders played a large role in counselling those who were troubled and seeking guidance. I remember setsį (my grandmother) would often have visitors that came to her for a cup of tea, a listening ear, and counsel. If talking with an Elder is not an option, I highly recommend getting a professional counsellor; there are currently many affordable or even free options for Indigenous Peoples. I always say that finding the right counsellor is like dating: you need to spend some time with a few before you settle on one.

Wellness and the warrior path
To become an Elder in the Dene community, one must earn the right. The Elders are those who possess Dene knowledge. They are the primary source of all knowledge which has been accumulated by the Dene, generation after generation. Because of their life experience, they have the wisdom to advise new generations as to how to deal with life and its problems. It is hoped that [Indigenous Peoples] will become aware of their role or responsibility in ensuring the succession of knowledge and therefore the culture. Whatever is not obtained from our Elders is

gone forever. This is the only way to ensure that the culture continues to exist and the connection with the past can be maintained.[31]

In our culture, we're taught to respect ʔǫhda ke (Elders) as they have so much knowledge. An Elder once told me that there's a difference between Elders and old people. ʔǫhda ke are compassionate, kind, patient, and wise. Old people are those who've missed the opportunity to become Elders. In my opinion, ʔǫhda ke are the ultimate warriors as it's a difficult path. You don't become an Elder by having had an easy life. You become a compassionate and kind person because you've experienced the opposite and don't want to inflict that on another. You become patient because you've experienced impatience. You become wise by making mistakes and learning from them.

I would be honoured to be an Elder; I have a small circle of friends who are on similar journeys and we use the phrase "Elders in training" to describe the path we're on. I believe that you become an Elder in training from the day you're born. All of our life experiences are meant to help form and guide us into this role that's vital to the continuation of our communities and culture. But how can we become Elders who pass on our ancestral knowledge if we're not well? We need to be well to live long, healthy lives to become an Elder. Many are passing away too quickly and we're losing that knowledge.

I don't want to deter someone from going down this warrior path but dealing with trauma and breaking intergenerational cycles is extremely challenging. It'll probably be one of the hardest things you'll do in your life. If it was easy, everybody would do it. But that's how we become amazing Warriors/Elders! We need warriors to help us in our communities. We need healthy role models and leaders that can continue our teachings. The good thing about this life-long path is that it's a marathon, not a sprint. Take your time and put one foot in front of the other. Any movement forward is progress.

The beginning of a healing journey can be lonely and you'll need to conserve all your energy for your healing. You'll need a good support system; remember that you become like those you spend time with so

---

31   *Dene kede Education: A Dene perspective* (1993), https://www.ece.gov.nt.ca/sites/ece/files/resources/dene_kede_k-6_teacher_resource_manual.pdf.

choose your friends wisely. The ʔexele (drum) is significant in our culture and when we drum dance, we dance in a circle. The more people that join, the bigger that circle gets. We start forming circles within those circles and thus, strength and power together.

We all have strength and resiliency in our blood. It was passed down from our ancestors but we forgot it for a while. Despite cultural genocide, disease, and starvation, we are still here. We have a responsibility to be healthy and strong. We need to take better care of ourselves to honour our ancestors and the struggles they faced so that we could be here today. We build resilience through reconnection with culture and land and knowing who we are as Indigenous Peoples.

As I write this article, it's the summer of 2020 and it's been a few months since the COVID-19 pandemic was declared. There are rallies and protests going on across Canada and the United States for the Black Lives Matter movement. I'm feeling a roller coaster of emotions. I feel sad, helpless, and angry some days, then I'm happy and grateful on others. Many are feeling this way. Newehstįnę is forcing us to practise stillness—physically and mentally—so we can look at our feelings and thoughts, some of which we ignore with work, sex, drugs, drinking, and so on. Since I quit drinking, I've been ignoring the feelings and thoughts by working non-stop. I didn't realize it at the time, but my desire to keep busy and be productive was actually my avoidance of sitting still with my thoughts and feelings. Tsįnę ékanet'e means to "quiet your mind." It's important to have time for self-reflection to know if we're still on the right path in our lives. Now's our opportunity.

In my journey, I've found that returning to my Dene roots has provided me with the knowledge and strength to become a healthier person. Denenį nátse, means to have a strong mind. Basically, it means to be resilient. We must remember the strength and resiliency of our ancestors in our blood. With that, we can get through whatever challenges we're facing.

Máhsı (thank you) for this opportunity. I hope you use some of these gifts in your wellness journey and find them as helpful as I have.

Resources:

Meditation and home workouts:
https://www.youtube.com/channel/UCn1TEgoB1R6Anjre
OeIMWvA?view_as=subscriber

Yoga:
https://nativestrengthrevolution.org/

General wellness:
https://www.wellforculture.com/

General wellness:
https://www.nativewellness.com/

Indigenous health and research:
https://nwtspor.ca/

Indigenous Leadership:
https://www.denenahjo.com/

Aboriginal Sports Circle:
https://ascnwt.ca/

Counselling:
https://www.sac-isc.gc.ca/eng/1581971225188/1581971250953

NWT Help Lines:
https://www.hss.gov.nt.ca/en/contact/help-lines

Arctic Indigenous Wellness Foundation:
https://arcticIndigenouswellness.org/

Dene Nation strong

Tyra Moses

This land belongs to the Dene, our ancestors have always told us so. The Mountain Shehtah Dene lived a seasonal transhumance existence meaning that they lived in massive land use areas in accordance with the animals, plants, or fish available to them at that time of year. During the summer, they commonly lived around lakes that supplied them and their sled dogs with massive amounts of fish; in the old days it was common for families to set fishnets and check them each day. In the summer months, they would also edge around the lake shores quietly by canoe in the morning to capture duck eggs to boil for breakfast. In the winter months, they could be found in the mountains near the bountiful forest full of rabbits and moose.

My great-grandfather, Philip Moses, was a great provider for his family; it was said if he got on the trail of the moose, the moose was as good as harvested. It was common for a moose to be immediately skinned, smoked, and then made into dry meat. It was dried by the smoke of the fire, which also helped to keep the bugs away as the meat was cured into thin strips of dried meat. My Father, Floyd Moses, had his own dog sled team growing up—then he would eventually adopt the modern snowmobile. His grandfather, Philip Moses, learned to harvest animals with finely crafted bows and arrows. Then he eventually adopted the modern rifle for harvesting especially larger game animals like the moose.

Indigenous nations have always easily adapted to new living conditions. With innovation and determination, they survived on this Dene land since time immemorial. Our oral histories remind us of the times when ancient mega animals roamed the earth like the Giant Beaver. Throughout my life I thought the stories of Yamoria and the large beavers were untrue until I visited the Royal Ontario Museum in Toronto,

Ontario, and saw a mega beaver head skull on display. They mentioned large animals were once able to survive on the land with massive fauna and flora vegetation surrounding the earth.

Dene Peoples were always very hardworking; we survived in the Boreal Forest with the extreme weather temperatures because of our incredible knowledge of the land, animals, waters, plants, and medicines available. We were never nomadic, but we lived a seasonal transhumance lifestyle that included maintaining large land use areas while harvesting with the seasons and our agricultural endeavours were completed on a massive scale unknown to people today. We were inventors, craftsmen, doctors, engineers, lawyers, and we lived as part of the lands, waters, animals, and fire. Our berry patches in the North are large because our ancestors have harvested from them; when you harvest berries they tend to fall off the vine when they are too ripe and this plants their seeds. Each season the berry patch grows larger and larger.

This summer, I went home to Liidlii Kue and then Pehdzeh Ki and I was warmly welcome with coffee, tea, and food. I travelled to Pehdzeh Ki on a dirt road three hours from Liidlii Kue so that I can connect with family, take pictures and videos, and also develop my Indigenous knowledge through oral and intergenerational transmission. In Pehdzeh Ki, I stopped by my cousin's house after taking pictures and videos and immediately after jumping out of the vehicle I was offered coffee. Then when I saw my cousin I was once again offered coffee. I entered the house and boldly introduced myself to the Andrew family stating, "Tyra Moses suzhe. Floyd Moses Seta. My name is Tyra Moses and Floyd Moses is my Father," and they replied, "Come in and have some coffee." Once I had my coffee and sat down, Marlene quickly told me to eat some breakfast and I kindly accepted. I told them about myself and who I am from.

Immediately upon meeting someone new in the North, they always ask, "Who are your parents?" As always, I proudly reply, "Floyd Moses and Lorayne Menicoche-Moses," and then most of the time they reply, "Oh, you look like your Mom," and the bond grows as we understand our connections. This is northern hospitality at its finest and I am so grateful to be Dene.

I sat with them most of the morning and through photography I captured my cousin Jamie Moses, along with Ricki Andrew and Carl

Yakelaya harvesting the moose Jamie shot the night before. The movements of the skilled hunters with their tools like the knife, saw, machete, and axe were surprisingly graceful as they respectfully harvested the moose; I was in awe of the sense of community.

Dene means people as part of the land. Without the land, the Dene are nothing. With the land, the Dene will always survive and thrive. The Dene tended large berry gardens. We harvested on a large scale from the forest—berries, edible plants, teas, medicines—and developed Indigenous knowledge systems that worked within our territories. We knew the medicinal properties of plants; our medicine peoples had a large collective knowledge of plants and how best to use them, including ensuring proper vitamins needed to survive were consumed. Dene Peoples used each part of the animal and gave thanks for each element harvested. Dene Peoples had treaties with the land, water, and animals long before we had treaties with other nations. They knew that Dene Peoples had to live in harmony with the land and seasons so that they could survive on the land.

My Father tells me a story about his trapping days and growing up in Pehdzeh Ki with George Blondin. For parts of George's life he was raised by my great-grandparents Philip and Mary-Louise Moses. My Father tells me he was very fond of my grandparents. Each summer when he returned to Pehdzeh Ki for his summer stay, George would travel from Tulita to Pehdzeh Ki on a scow with his kids and even his dogs and he would always bring Grandfather smoked geese upon his return. My Father recalls how much Grandfather and George loved to geese hunt together. My Father was a trapper and he covered over two thousand kilometres of land-use area, from close to Berry Lake, next to Spruce Lake and Bulmer Lake—not too far from Liidlii Kue (Fort Simpson)—all the way to the Shehtah Mountains to the Johnson River and Keel River. Also, he would harvest at Blackwater Lake and Fish Lake, which were way past Pehdzeh Ki. It was important for them to continue the seasonally transhumance movements each winter and find a new territory within this large territory they knew and stewarded so well. They ensured they would respectfully trap so they would not deplete the resources in the area, and they always respected the animals.

My Father was a successful trapper and worked incredibly hard in the bush to provide for his family. My Father and his uncles, Leon

(Leo) Moses and James (Jim) Moses, were so successful at trapping that at one point after harvesting for the season at Berry Lake, my Father chartered a helicopter for their bounty of Martin fur from Berry Lake to Liidlii Kue. He requested it through the old, orange bush radio that was the northern communication venue of the past. After returning to Liidlii Kue, my Father flew to Sambah Ke (Yellowknife) to stock up on supplies they needed, and he then returned to Liidlii Kue where he bought a brand new snowmobile that would be airlifted back to their camp with the helicopter that helped him arrive in Liidlii Kue. After his return to the camp and on their way back to one of their homesteads in Pehdzeh Ki, they would unknowingly forever abandon their previous snowmobile at their camp at Berry Lake because my Father's uncles refused to drive snowmobiles. With my Father being the only one to drive and maintain the snowmobile equipment, he brought the new machine back while he resolved to go back to get the other one. He would start work the next year and his trapping life would never be the same.

My Father and his uncles trapped with ease together for many wonderful years. They passed on their knowledge with strength and in the Dene ways of knowing. My Father would break trail with his Elan while one of his two uncles would follow behind him on the dog sled team. In those days, it was common for most people to have dog sled teams, and this was no different from my family's experience. A good dog was better than cash and it was often found to be a source of wealth for the Dene. A good dog could bring a lot in trade if needed.

My Father Floyd Moses is a Dene Indigenous knowledge keeper. He is incredibly smart and has tremendous knowledge of the land and the Dene Peoples history. The reason that I know the stories I know is because he and other Indigenous knowledge keepers told me. I have learned more knowledge from the Dene Peoples than any education institutions that I have attended, and I am a Red Seal Electrician by trade and an A-average university student at the University of Lethbridge. I work within anthropology and I am working on Dene Media, which is a business venture that I am currently pursuing to help capture the Dene culture, language, and traditions. The best part of my work is the stories that are told to me.

Mahsi.

Sacrifice

Jamesie Fournier

Arctic wind curled off the ocean and swept across his face. "Ataata, what were they like?" the boy asked.

"Quiet..." his Father whispered as he stared down the shore. Spring break-up had come, and large floes of ice drifted across the ocean. Inshore, Father and son hid behind a large block of snow which blended them seamlessly into the land. The Father's rifle leaned against the snow blind while his son sculpted his own snow block into a misshapen inuksuk. Queerly lopsided, it leaned mockingly, its blank face cold and sightless. The boy stepped back and studied his statue for a moment before raising an invisible gun to his eye. Silently, he jerked his shoulders back. Bang. He lifted his head and stared at his target before he spoke over his shoulder.

"The Tuniit, the strong people you told me about."

"Not now, Tal. Shhhh..." the Father hushed. In the distance, a small, dark head bobbed out of the water. Slowly, the Father picked up the rifle and pressed it into his shoulder. His palm locked the firing bolt tight as the head slipped back underneath the waves. He levelled his sight to the horizon and inhaled. The scent of rotten ice filled his nostrils. Suddenly, to his right, the head slipped up and out of the water. The Father quickly pivoted as it disappeared behind a snowbank. He raised his head and scanned the shore, gauging where it would reappear. He looked down the barrel and tightened his grip. Slowly, the creature's head crept into the open.

"KEEYAH!" the boy screamed from behind. The Father snapped his head, his face blank with surprise. Standing over his broken inuksuk with his fists raised, his son twisted back and forth in victory. The boy finally met his Father's gaze and immediately lowered his arms and stepped back. The Father quickly looked back to the shore just in time to see a tail slip back into the water. He closed his eyes and sighed in frustration.

"My boy, this is important. You have to stay quiet!"

"But it's so borrring!" The boy kicked the snow and pouted. The Father stood, scanned the shore, put his palms to his back and stretched. He turned to his son.

"All right, I tell you about Tuniit, but then we're quiet again, okay?"

"Okay!" the boy exclaimed. He sat down and his Father leaned over with his hands on his knees.

"The Tuniit were here first. Before Inuit. First, first peoples, eh?" he smiled, missing teeth. "They made the first Inuksuit. Broke in the land, y'know? Showed us Inuit how to live way back then. They were strong! Huge! Much bigger than Inuit. They could throw a whole walrus over their shoulder! Carry it home like fish!" The boy smiled as his Father mimed carrying an enormous weight on his back before finally falling down. The boy laughed into his mitten as his Father groaned in the snow. Hearing this, the Father quickly stood and brushed the snow off his furred pants as if nothing had happened. He continued without missing a beat. "But then, one day, they vanished, eh? Poof! Disappeared! No one knows why!" The Father stopped and studied the shore before moving on. "They kept to themselves, y'know? Quiet. Shy! Very shy people." He paused and his face grew dim. "Some people say that when they disappeared, the strength of the land went with them. That it just drifted away like low tide..." He swept a hand toward the ocean as if to push back the waves. A cold wind blew from the shore. "Lots of bad things happened then, those times there..." he trailed off, quietly staring into a blaze of sun. The son watched as his Father searched the shore, swallowed deeply, and breathed out. He turned back to his son and smiled. "But you know the thing about tides, my boy?"

"They come back!" the boy brightened.

"That's right! Things, people, places. They come. They go. They live. They die. It's a wheel, my boy. It turns." He twirled a finger in the air and looked out across the ocean. He watched the sunlight glint darkly between the waves and sighed. "Some people think we killed them, you know? The Tuniit, I mean. Wars. Fighting. That we hunted them for being so different. Just because we could." His gaze fell to the broken inuksuk. "Guess they were right to keep to themselves, eh?" The Father smiled and then raised his eyebrows struck with recollection.

"That's where your name comes from! Tal! Taligvat. Long Arm!" He stretched his arm out and flexed exaggeratedly, smiling. "Like Tuniit! It was your Mother's name before yours and her auntie's before that. That's why Mom calls you auntie! It keeps them alive, with us. Keeps our family together. Strong. Going way back to when Tuniit and Inuit lived together; to honour them and their sacrifice for us." He stepped toward his son and crunched snow underfoot. "What goes around comes around, my boy. That's why it's important we show respect. We share this world. We don't own it." He pointed toward the ocean. "That's why nattiquna! This seal is important. It's giving its life to us. Offering itself so that we may carry on. We must be thankful." The Father kneeled down to the boy. "One way we show respect is that Nattiit live in the ocean, yes?" The boy smiled and nodded. "Yes, and the ocean is salty. So, when they die we give their spirit water to drink because they are so thirsty. We thank them for their sacrifice." The Father reached out and pinched his boy's cheek. "From his skin we will make clothes. His meat we will share and his fat we'll use in our qulliq, our lamp, to bring us light and warmth."

"Yuck!" the boy groaned and held his stomach. "I don't like qulliq. It smells..." His Father laughed out loud and then quickly covered his mouth and smiled.

"It does, doesn't it!" the Father hushed mid-laugh. A black dot bobbed in the distance once more. The Father fell to his knees and nuzzled the rifle into his shoulder again. He sighted and waited for nattiq to reappear. As he scanned his thoughts drifted with the waves. In his mind, he saw the seal swimming lithely in the dark. He thought of Tuniit, ancient and stronger than any Inuk had ever been, dying scared and alone. He thought of surviving. Of the choices we make and the ones that are made for us. He looked up and saw his son breathlessly watching the shore.

The Father pulled his son close. He seated the rifle into the boy's shoulder and watched as the boy's eyes lit with surprise. The Father smiled and tilted his head toward the shore. Nattiq flopped out of the water and hid behind the snowbank once more. The boy closed one eye and peered down the sight. His Father watched and slowly traced the barrel along the seal's unseen path. "Walk with him, my boy," he whispered. "Know him. Feel his next step ... Take a deep breath and when you're ready—let go." The boy drew in a slow breath and watched the shore. The seal waded out into the open and stopped. Its large black eyes scanned the horizon before finally meeting the boy's gaze.

"Thank you," the boy whispered and his Father's rifle cracked and thundered down the shore.

Taima

Caribou, wolverines, and spruce gum

Thumlee Drybones-Foliot

This is a story of an encounter between the Dene and the Wolverine. It is my understanding that Dene stories hold the core values of our people. As a Dene woman, these stories help me to understand who I am and my place in the world. One story can reveal many core values—some are obvious and some are more subtly woven in the same way as Ama weaves a spruce bough floor. I come to a new awareness of these values the more I work with a story. Though I may use the same boughs to weave a floor, Ama's hands in her old age are still more skilled; her weave is tighter and stays in place better because she knows where best to place each bough. This story was told to me by my Mother, my Ama, Aileen Drybones who received it from her Ama, Madeline Drybones. Now, I have my Mother's permission to continue to share this story, which I have been working with since I was young. It is a story of how the Dene people received the gift of spruce gum. It happened when the world was young and some of the animals we know today, were giant.

A camp of Dene are waiting for caribou. The caribou never come and the camp begins to starve. They decide to send their strongest and best hunters to search. No one returns. In desperation, they send one more who also never returns. Then another Dene, who is clever, sets off to find caribou.

This one clever Dene follows the trail of the others up a big mountain. At the top, they can see all the Land. It all looks beautiful, but down the mountain they see a dark area. Like the others, they slide down the mountain until they find themselves trapped. Looking around they don't see what has caught them. Confused, the Dene sits and as they do, they come to remember Elders once speaking of the medicine of the sun snare. This Dene doesn't have medicine powers of their own and they know they are no match for ones with such strong medicine. Sitting there, the Dene decides that the best choice is to be clever; to sit and wait and see who comes to check the snare.

Before too long, the Dene starts to feel the earth rumble. Looking up into the distance they can see a small black dot moving across the Land. Boom. Boom. Boom. With each advancing step, the ground quakes and the Dene sees a giant Wolverine. The Dene knows Wolverine is strong and smart and vicious. Wolverine has used the sun snare to catch all the caribou. The Dene thinks, "I am no match for Wolverine, but I am clever and I can outsmart Wolverine. I will lay here in the snare and pretend to be dead."

The Wolverine comes over and looks at the Dene and says, "Hey this person is already dead." Wolverine un-snares the Dene, picks them up, and puts them in a bag. Off they go back to the Wolverine camp. Boom. Boom. Boom. That Dene is scared and now their belly begins to turn and rumble. Before they know it, out comes a big fart. Wolverine jumps, grabs that Dene out of the bag and lays them out on the ground. Poking the Dene's belly Wolverine says, "I guess my meat isn't that fresh. It has started decomposing." That Dene doesn't say a word. Wolverine puts that farting Dene back in the bag and keeps walking. Boom. Boom. Boom. Before too long, the Dene's stomach begins to turn and rumble and before they know it, they let out another big fart. This time Wolverine says, "Hey, if you are trying to be clever I will catch you." Still that Dene doesn't say a word. Now Wolverine is suspicious as they continue to his camp. Boom. Boom. Boom. Again, that Dene's stomach turns and rumbles and out comes a really big fart. Wolverine throws that Dene down and this time says, "Hey, are you still alive?" The Dene still says nothing. Without warning Wolverine lifts up that Dene's arm and he tickles their armpit, he tickles their toes, and he even tickles their belly, but that Dene doesn't laugh. Wolverine says, "I guess you really are dead and you just have some last gas leaving the body." Deciding that Dene really was dead all along, he slips the body back in the bag and they continue to Wolverine's camp.

Wolverine is giant and can travel fast, so in no time at all they get to Wolverine's camp. The Dene can smell something so horrific. The Dene gently opens their eyes and sees they have arrived at a giant tree hut with a Mother wolverine, two teenage wolverines, and a baby. By the fire the Dene can see the body of one of the hunters cut down the centre with his guts spilling out. Mother wolverine has already finished cooking one big chunk of the hunter on the fire. Baby wolverine, sitting on the steps, complains, "I don't like this meat. Why do we have to eat it? It's so disgusting." Mother wolverine says, "Quiet now we are grateful your Father has brought us this meat." Looking at the Father wolverine she says, "Put that away and come eat now."

The Dene is laid on fresh spruce boughs by the bodies of the other hunters. After the Wolverine's belly is full he lays down to have a nap. That Dene, getting restless laying on the spruce boughs, opens their eyes. Baby wolverine is looking so that Dene gives him a wink. Baby wolverine says, "Look, look he's alive." Mother wolverine scolds baby wolverine saying, "That's enough now, leave the food alone." Baby wolverine sulks off. With a big yawn Wolverine wakes up, looks around and goes back to sleep for a few hours. All the while that poor Dene has been laying on the boughs. Mother wolverine builds up the fire again. Wolverine wakes up, takes his birch knife, goes over to that Dene and tries to cut into the Dene but the knife is dull. Wolverine says, "My wife, my wife, pass me that stone knife. This one is dull." Next, he uses the stone knife and again the knife is too dull. Wolverine, annoyed, says, "My wife, my wife, you didn't sharpen any of these knives. Pass me the bone knife. That one can cut through anything." Wolverine takes the bone knife, first cutting through the Dene's caribou hide jacket. Next is the rabbit skin. The Dene carefully slips his leg up and throws Wolverine off balance. The Dene jumps up and throws him into the fire. One by one he throws them all into the fire. All but baby wolverine, who was at a safe distance. The baby wolverine climbs into a spruce tree, but that Dene is coming after it. Baby wolverine says, "Stop! Wait! I have something for you. Take that rock in the ground there and smash my paw on the side of this tree." The Dene does this and from the paw runs fat and blood onto the tree. "You see, this is medicine. From this day forward it will heal your people and we will leave you alone."

To this day Dene use spruce gum as medicine.

To this day, wolverines are not giant—they are size of baby Wolverine because they continued to steal from the traps of the Dene when they were giant.

In my youth it was easiest to comprehend the literal meanings of a story. Just as children laying spruce boughs on the ground doesn't yet make a full woven floor, I didn't understand the full meaning. Walking in the bush collecting spruce gum, I marvelled at the beauty of Wolverine's medicine power. Out of the spruce tree runs the blood and fat of the baby Wolverine's paw, and just as the baby promised the Dene so long ago, spruce trees will always carry Wolverine medicine as a gift. This story explains how we received the gift of spruce gum medicine and how wolverines became the size they are today. The wolverines were greedy for the caribou and disrupted others and hurt the Dene. The baby that survived did not grow any further and wolverines are no longer giant. The way Dene come to agreements is to make verbal treaties. The result of this treaty is still seen today on the trees dripping with gum. This is the story of how the Dene received the powerful medicine of spruce gum, known for its healing properties.

Since I was young, I've grown a new understanding of the Dene Laws. This is how a new awareness of Dene Law is transmitted through a story and it demonstrates how to interact with the world in a good way. We are taught to share what you have and take only what you need. Wolverines got very busy trapping all day and eating up all the caribou, leaving nothing for the Dene. Because of their greed they lost their ability to be giants.

We also see that our communities are consent based: the Dene who is successful in finding out where the caribou have gone is the one who chooses to go in search of them. No one demanded this Dene go; they go of their own will, inspired to save their people as an act of service.

Today, trappers still have trouble with wolverines stealing from them and stealing from their traps. I think about the treaty the Dene and Wolverine made and how, just as in life, things don't always work out as we want them to. Wolverines stay true to their nature and continue to steal, though we still get their medicine. Just as in my life when things seem the hardest or darkest, there is still a silver lining as long as I choose to find it. Sometimes it's easier to see it looking back, but there is always one there. This is one way to choose to live in a good way. Just as Wolverine trapped Dene, sometimes we are the trapper and sometimes we are the trapped. The balance reminds me to be respectful because we all have times of hardship and times of plenty.

In a spring semester at Dechinta, during a governance meeting Elder-professor Paul Mackenzie started speaking about a bushman near our camp. The bushman is a malicious creature who is largely undetected but has a great medicine power. It is well known in Dene communities that we do not speak of the bushman because doing so might draw it closer. I was terrified and extremely cautious of my actions around camp. I talked to another instructor about my fear. Dr. Leanne Betasamosake Simpson said the shift of season brought many changes, challenges, and gifts. The snow and ice melts in spring and the bears wake up, so as a group we needed to be aware and prepared for these changes. She asked if this is what Paul could be reminding us of with his bushman story: the changes and dangers that our group might face, and how we as a group could protect and support each other. I began to realize that our Elders are vigilant in assessing us as individuals and as a group. They look at our skills and needs and know how to present stories to us that guide our activities to both safety and deeper understanding of the world around us.

None of the semesters I attended at Dechinta have been the same. The Elders' teachings unfold in the same way our environment changes with the seasons. The lens that Simpson gave us to look at the teachings of the bushman changes the fear-based listening to a powerful teaching rooted in love—one that reminds us to be careful and mindful. Not only did this help me sleep again at night and even gave me the courage to step out of the tent to pee at night, this teaching forced us to pay close attention to the Land, to see its dangers, and to travel safely through it.

Storytelling has deepened my knowledge of the Land and Dene communities by being examples of how to live in a good way. In community, stories connect people to each other: when we share personal stories, we learn how to be gentle with one another. This creates supportive communities. I have known and been working with the Wolverine story for many years, yet I can see the progression of what new teachings I learn each time I revisit it. During my time at Dechinta I have noticed storytelling always seems to happen at the exact moment it is needed. Elders don't usually gather everyone around and tell a big story; most of them happen in a casual way. I have heard many other stories at Dechinta and for most of them I happened to be in the right place at the right time. Oral stories are never told in exactly the same way and different people may receive very different lessons—lessons that are intimate and personal. There are many ways to tell stories, and stories are meant to have intentional outcomes for the listeners. Elders are very deliberate in their actions and words and when they choose to tell stories they are interwoven with values and lessons. This represents how we value non-interference, self-determination, and how we are all in charge of our own personal growth. This is then reflected in our communities. This is my understanding; I know that I have the boughs and I am starting to weave. I will continue to work alongside my Elders who have expertly woven the values of Dene Laws into their lives and in so many ways encourage us to live a good way. The themes, bones, structure, base, or boughs, if you will, of the story are always the same. The caribou go missing; the Dene go in search of them; the Wolverine and the Dene battle; and in the end the Dene receive spruce gum. The story changes from one storyteller to the next, just as the same storyteller can tell the same story multiple times and each time it changes. Repeating a story verbatim is a safe place to start storytelling. Just as children know to put the spruce boughs on the ground, it doesn't yet make a full woven floor. It's my belief that I should stay true to my nature and let the story come as it feels right to me. Elders have the knowledge to use stories to help deepen awareness within ourselves. Understanding our stories helps us find our voices. When we use our voice to weave our own stories, we are building spruce bough foundations our ancestors would be proud of.

I also know that I am just one voice with my own narrow view of the world. My hope is that by sharing this story, it encourages others to share their own stories.

Pluck me softly from the sky

Megan Samms

Kwe' kwe' kiju',

Remember how you, Dad,[32] and Gordon[33] used to call me a boy? "My boy, how is your day going?"
It was meant to be funny then, but over time, this turned into a part of myself that I love. I carry the energy of e'pit and ji'nm, sometimes more of one or another but still, I am comfortably positioned in the in-between. I learned how to be human from you—watching you do hard physical work that is often gendered and called "man's work" (but rarely without your ceremonial markings): bucking, splitting and piling fire wood, working the garden, always smelling real good, skipping on a mussel boat, sewing our clothes and watching you hand stitch the binding on countless quilts, not to mention all of the pla'kit you made for each new baby in the family. These, and the way you made good food for people grieving showed me how to take care and in the very same moment, be

32 Consent has been granted from individuals considered in this piece.
33 Names of those that I have not been able to gain consent from have been changed. I write to nkij. I was in conversation with her during my writing of this piece. (Thanks to imessage.) We have been engaging in dialogue about this and related topics, emotions, and experiences for a number of years. Where I make statements in this writing, they are my own perspective. When I needed clarity while processing and writing I had the opportunity to ask her for her help or opinion. Before I began writing and before I decided to share this writing and our process, I asked if she was comfortable and if she consented to me doing so. She gave me her permission to do this. She has read everything I am about to share with you. Certain (crucial) pieces of our relationship, my experience, family history, further familial connections, events, and dynamics have been omitted in order to respect the emotions, traumas, and identities of those involved who I have not been able to connect with; to this, some names have been changed. It has not been easy to arrive where we are now, although sometimes, it has.

taken care of. When you showed your grief, your anger, and your intense excitement and happiness I learned to let each of my various emotions hold equal agency; at the same time, I learned to take responsibility for them. The actions you made/make in your day-to-day life were/are not gendered. You taught me how to run a rototiller *and* pluck my eyebrows.

Remember how I used to lay in bed with you for hours before sleep and pet the skin of your arm?
You didn't come to motherhood easily, I know that. I know that your central example of how to Mother was misshapen. Nkwe'ji'j and I know that your Mother likely did the best she could and that she came from a really, really fucking hard place. You had to/still are learn(ing) mothering much on your own as you went/go along. More often than not, you did the parenting for two. I see this, mum. You are warm, soft, intentional, kind, firm, big (in that reside-in-a-huge-part-of-my-heart kind of way), generous, fair, wild, and engaged. I didn't know until I reached later tapuiskikipuna't that the hours of tiny, sticky ti'ti fingers stroking the soft skin on your forearm drove you crazy. Learn me patience.

How many cups of tea do you think we can drink in a day?
You've been a Mother for over thirty years. I see more and more of you in myself. In four more years I'll be the age you were when you became nkij. I like my pitewey reeaal barky, with milk and honey—and approximately five times a day please. Give me a twenty-minute nap, let me file my own tools, let me be ready, show me and then let me try, take me to samquan every day, make time for quiet spaces and places, see your work through well, give everything away. I learned from you that what we create with our hands holds equal power to what else we do with our bodies and what we say with our words. You taught me that any action I choose to make and words I choose to use are for me to decide on and that I can architect my world with those small and simple, yet enormous, things.

What is it that you do?
I bet you remember this ... Remember the time that you helped to form a committee to put the school that first nujj and then nkwe'ji'j and I went to into the public school board's hands, instead of in the hands of

the Catholic Church? I was only eleven or so, but I certainly remember the changes and the impact. I remember the sense of relief that came with the new school. I remember shedding much of the fear and anxiety that I associated with the old school. I remember feeling somewhat freer to move. But I also remember tension. And although the public school system still wasn't necessarily the safest place for me, it felt better than the previous one. I got to see your priorities and see you and your body as a political order. I learned that what we do *is* our politics. How we take action is more important than what we speak.

Are you or aren't you?
I have, on multiple occasions, received the question(s) from a particular gaze in terms of my ancestry, sexuality, and gender (me, already knowing why they want to know): *"What* are you?" "Are you or aren't you straight/queer/status/non-status/native/non-native?" As in, what kind of box can we push you into?

You told me when I was very young—"You're Native. But I don't know how to guide you there." You didn't know what else to show me at the time, but you taught me that we needed to continue some sort of relationship with what we're made of. That maybe we could learn and un-learn and build ways and worlds; we could continue despite everything that was against us. Despite a certain inner misery, I could possibly craft newness, make the way I wanted to be in the world, and simultaneously, make my world. It's possible that movements and actions that I *can* make/do aren't so far from the edge of my fingertips; it is possible that this knowing changes everything.

When your Mother scoured the brown off the back of your neck, you somehow didn't lose the wanting/needing of your Indigeneity, your Nlaka'pamux and Mi'kmaq world; you kept going back to it even though the promise of that world you wanted was still a long way away. And so, you did all you could to guide me to our place. When you brought me out on the land, we picked atuomkomin, fished, walked and swam, dug e'sɨk and ran, we leaned deep into the salty wind, collected firewood, lay in the bog cotton, worked the garden and sometimes simply watched samquan move and puktew snap. Sometimes we watched too much TV and ate all the food that today they say wrecks a person from the inside out. But I felt like we got to do it all.

You and I, we didn't get the opportunity to know our grandmothers before they were removed from our lives. Potential lost before it was even a possibility; a jagged Mother-line. You told me today that you have felt genderless for most of your life—removed from women. You felt like e'pit when you gave birth, twice. But mostly, genderless. I think that you didn't have the space and safety to have conversations or expressions about gender and your identity as a younger woman. Teliaq. You told me that this is the truth. But the ungendered way that you raised up nkwe'ji'j and I, paired with your openness to dialogue, has given me a sense of autonomy to present myself however I feel at any given time and it felt/feels very natural. Your way of raising us up without particular narrows did not appear to me to be outside of any ordinary. I am fortunate—the experience of freedom and comfort I feel in my body is a gift, from you. I know that I am loved by you. I want you to know that I know this. I offer the same gift to you.

I say Wela'lin to you, my Mother. I thank you for making the space and time for me, for choosing me, and loving me; I'm grateful that it was you that carefully and diligently and softly plucked me out of the sky and held me in your body and today, holds me close day to day.

Kesalul,
M.

Notes
Pluck me softly from the sky is a title given to this writing that my Mother, sister, and myself decided on in a collaborative way.

Dënesųłiné teaching and parenting

Brenda Dragon in conversation with Chloe Dragon Smith

The following contains excerpts from a conversation between myself and my Mother, Brenda Dragon. This is a small window into our relationship and our (very) continuous dialogue about how to live our lives and affect change in the world. My Mom grew up in Fort Smith. Her Mother is Jane Dragon and her Father was David Dragon. Among many other accomplishments, she is now the founder and owner of her northern Indigenous business, Aurora Heat, where she sells sheared beaver fur for warmth. She is 58 years old and is my biggest mentor and idol. My Mom gave me a strong foundation for understanding the world, working with me over my life, always encouraging me to develop my confidence and take opportunities. She has been a pillar that set me up to be able to take guidance and understanding from others, too. She shared and taught without judgment, pushiness, or precedence. My Mom has a strength and confidence within her that shines brightly for all to see. She affects the world just by being herself and I am always grateful to be her daughter.

Through our conversation, I wanted to share a bit of our story and also try to interpret some of the ways we are. My Mom and I both have rejected many Euro-Western mainstream norms in favour of finding our own unique and innovative paths. As I have grown older, I've begun to explore the complexities behind Indigenous worldviews, and I find that a lot of how we think aligns with other Indigenous Peoples in the North and in Canada. Much of our work has been within the realm of education and learning. My Mom chose to homeschool me and my brother up until grade four. From grade four on, I still missed a lot of school, and she always seemed to have the confidence to know it was ok. While she was homeschooling me, she also brought a lot of change to the public school system, where my peers were. She worked with my teachers, but I noticed she worked with other teachers and staff as well. For example, she would bring in ducks to pluck and make soup. Patiently, steadfastly, and with humour, she would share her values and strengths with those around her. In this way, I realize, my Mom has left a legacy—certainly in Yellowknife—but also across the Northwest Territories. She has been a changemaker in a system that did not fit her well. Today, I am working on changing the same systems, and I still look to her for advice and guidance often.

Chloe: When I read about Indigenous worldviews and parenting and learning, I feel like you embodied a lot of it during my childhood. Was that a conscious choice, or were you following your intuition?

Brenda: My intuition mostly. I recalled how school was ineffective for me. I excelled when I was young, but I didn't particularly like school, and I didn't care much for excelling. Class was uninteresting for the most part, and it just felt like memorization. More than anything, I like to help people—I ended up being more of a classroom assistant. The other thing was, it seems every time I was interested in something, I would be stopped. We would have to open our math books and then go to gym. If I was doing something that I liked, like reading, I always was forced to stop. We did not have books at home, and I wanted them. I was the type of kid who didn't like being interrupted! I wanted to give'er.

When it came time for you to go to school, all those feelings came back—the constraining rules and ways of the system. I just didn't want that for you, so I went about finding another way. I met and became friends with the principal of the school you would go to. I knew I wanted to homeschool, but I couldn't find a curriculum that wasn't religion-based. The principal really encouraged me, and because I had taken an early childhood course when I got pregnant, I was confident I could do it my own way. I was very committed to be the best parent I could be.

After some basic searching, I decided that above all, I was going to let you follow your interests, and to try to do it without judgment. I saw early on that if I put something in front of you, you were curious. There was little complaining, you enjoyed playing (learning), and there was little conflict. It didn't bother me that you took off and did your own thing—I wanted that. I wanted you to be free.

Chloe: Do you think freedom is an Indigenous value?

Brenda: Absolutely. However, I think it does run awry if you don't pay attention. Freedom is not just ignoring; it's a controlled state, a caring space. It's exercising your ability to resist overcontrol. And it IS an ability. That Indigenous view of taking little if any space for people to learn is really important.

In grade seven, I remember asking to do what was essentially independent learning, and my main teachers allowed me to do it. I scored high enough on some tests and they agreed. I loved it! Then in grade eight they made me go back to regular scheduled school ... It wasn't long before I was skipping school. There I excelled, sometimes I would miss upwards of forty days. Our family started the school year by going into the bush every year. We would be gone for the first few weeks—and yeah, we brought our books but I never even cracked them while we were out there. I realized I was able to catch up really fast and what that taught me was that I didn't have to be present to pass school. And because I did do well, no one really gave me a hard time. I'd just read other people's notes, go in, do the test, and try to appear as all was fine. It kinda was.

Chloe: Sounds actually pretty similar to me. I skipped school a lot. I don't know if you knew that!

Brenda: Yes, I was completely aware of that...

Chloe: Really? How did you know?

Brenda: The teachers told me.

Chloe: You knew in high school? Really?

Brenda: I went to parent teacher interviews, Chloe.

Chloe: All the way through high school? Really? They do parent teacher interviews that long?

Brenda: Yes, and I always went.

Chloe: I never knew that!!!

Brenda: Yes, my dear.

Chloe: Okay ... switching gears ... so, at what point in homeschooling did you feel like an educator? Or did you ever? Lately, I've been calling myself an educator (even though I don't have a degree) to ensure I recognize the credentials I've learned from the land and from family.

Brenda: Yes, never discount the knowledge you come with. I wasn't a formally trained educator either, but I had the confidence that I knew enough. I focused on feelings and thoughts as opposed to questions to answer. I didn't call myself an educator then, but I certainly would now.

Chloe: How could we recognize Indigenous educators without having to put them through a system of Western education?

Brenda: I think you have to help people trust their gut and their intuition. They need to be affirmed to trust their natural ways. It was my job at one time to teach Elders to teach kids for culture camps I organized for the district. They were to fix the muskrats and beavers and share other on-the-land skills.

What I had to do for them was teach some basic tips for (essentially) crowd management because the groups were always too big. Then show them how to describe what they are doing and to watch for kids' reactions. That goes a long way because kids are curious and if you pay attention, sharing knowledge can be a natural flow.

Chloe: I wonder if there is a way to formalize that, what you did back then as part of the public school system. Sounds like teaching tools, but not content or direction. Do you think it's possible to merge worldviews and create proper space for Indigenous education in the public system, or is it too much to overcome? For instance, power balance, boundaries around time and space, and rules? Do we need to let the school be the school, and do our own thing?

Brenda: Depends what outcomes you are looking for. You have to "de-school" kids to be open to a different way. This is almost like decompression. At the beginning, I found they were often waiting for something to happen, waiting to be directed.

Back then many of us thought the answer was to teach the teachers, or "de-school the teachers." It turned out that most teachers were not very settled because they were used to structure. They had a great time, but they didn't think this way of being counted as learning. They would come with us, pick berries, hang out, and eat food. But I can't say they saw a lot of the value of destructuring.

I think, ultimately, we need bridge builders. Facilitators with kind hearts and patience to help people work through their biases and notions about these foreign concepts.

It was phenomenal for me to see the work you were doing at your courses for teachers last year. We had tried that fifteen years before and almost no one was open to changing the way they did things. At your course, I was seeing people really open to it. And you ran the whole thing in a very Indigenous way [laughs]—everything ran out of time, there wasn't enough time for anything, because you let them finish what they were doing before you moved on. You chose to let things go with the flow. That's something many teachers are not used to. And they loved it! It was great to see forward movement and changes happening. I think we need to keep at it, relentlessly—we need to be together and the system needs change at almost every level.

Chloe: Were there some examples of things that you saw that worked during your time with the schools?

Brenda: Where to start? There was a time I was loving a program they called "Restitution" and what it had to offer. There were many problems with the delivery though. I know you didn't like it! The school stuffed it down people's throats, and insisted on labelling it "Restitution," as though it was something so foreign and not natural—that was the wrong way.

But the way it was right, was that it was about love, caring, really seeing a kid, looking at their feelings, and self-actualizing for both the teacher and the child.

We can do this in so many ways; it comes down to focusing on empathy, self-awareness, and love. More on coping tools and foundational skills and less on content. A kid has to feel accepted and loved to learn. There is an analogy I like: raising a child (or teaching a child) is like a plant. Give it what it needs to keep it growing straight and support it so it doesn't fall over. Acceptance and love will keep that plant upright! When I think about love, I think of a healthy state. Without love we are not healthy, mentally or emotionally.

Chloe: Do you think we can access love and empathy better on the land?

Brenda: Yes, 100 percent. Because we're calmer. People have room. We learn about what's around us and what's in our lives. There aren't too many rules to stifle and contain. Love flows more freely.

Chloe: Did you have any mentors?

Brenda: Not really, but I do learn from everyone. My passion was coming from within me, but I filtered it through a lot of people's thoughts and actions. I synthesized, affirmed, and kicked out a lot, too. The main thing I kept was that my way was going to be freer.

Chloe: We're both mixed blood, but our Indigenous heritage is continually on the maternal side. Do you think that makes a difference?

Brenda: Women almost always made the decisions around children and families. My Mom raised me very free and I didn't feel judged. I'm a very observant person. Is that an Indigenous thing? I'm not sure. What I am sure of is that inquisitiveness comes from acceptance and love, and that gives rise to confidence.

Chloe: Where does that deep acceptance and love come from, and do you feel like we're losing it in society? How could you tap into these understandings of Indigenous learning and teaching, even though you weren't really conscious of it and were just doing your own thing?

Brenda: Well, I always gave back. I didn't just take. When I started homeschooling, there were other parents that wanted to do it. I was used to having my brain picked about what I was doing, and I'd answer as best I could. I think if there was a measuring stick, I would come out as giving more than taking. A lot of kids spent a lot of time at our house with me and you guys. I was aware that was happening, but I wanted that. I wanted you to be home so that made sense to me.

That innate system of reciprocity runs very deep inside of me. There were things inside me that guided me toward that way of thinking. I think I had to give back to feel good about myself. As a parent, I took things from the school in terms of learnings and curriculum, and I always gave back to the school. I volunteered a lot, for instance. I organized tons of activities and even coordinated the building of a new playground—from fundraising, designing, and overseeing the entire project. Very satisfying and creative work.

Chloe: Reciprocity is definitely part of it, but big picture—where does it come from? How do you think you were able to access that through all the complications of colonization and oppression of our systems?

Brenda: I think it came from having almost no pressure on me; conventional types of successes were not celebrated and conversely, failures were not harped on. Here's an example: if one of us had a report or a recognition that was glowing and the other had one that was mediocre—no biggy, for either. With that kind of reaction or non-reaction from parents, one learns that your successes and failures are your own. I think that is one of the seeds for intrinsic motivation.

Chloe: Yes, there's no pressure but how did Setsuné (my grandmother) know to not put pressure on you? How did you know not to put pressure on me?

Brenda: I believe that this way of being is simply an inheritance. I have always had confidence and understanding for how to move forward. I don't have a big ego that needs to be fed and that's really important—to be humble and satisfied in your ways. I wasn't doing it for anyone or to prove anything. I don't know how you give that to people, but I appreciate that it is inside me. I know that and I always held deep love and empathy for others.

I think a lot of people think they are reflected in their children, or students, or what's on the walls of their classrooms. You have to have empathy and love to separate yourself from outcomes and results. Taking too much pride in what happens breeds insecurity because you are never good enough, and then it becomes a cycle of unfulfillment.

I know that I can make people feel better about themselves simply by not taking their space. By loving, having empathy and compassion. Kids—everyone—need to have people who love them and accept them for who they are. We need parents to parent their kids and to love them. We need teachers to love their students. We need everyone to see the good in young people. You need peace for the kid.

Chloe: Reflecting on our conversation, I feel like I'm pushing for rather big systemic answers. Lately, I see the world in terms of these big systems (like Indigenous and Euro-Western) and am always curious about what is affecting what. As I push for these answers, you keep going back to personal attributes. And maybe that is part of the answer?

Perhaps what you are telling me is that we have to do some mindful relational work and spend some more time building relationships, self-actualizing, learning, and practising how to love and connect.

Brenda: Yes. That ability to sit with yourself. Love yourself and then you will have love for others. Love for yourself has to come first. And that comes through freedom and using your brain to think through it. Never underestimate the power of love.

Chloe: Do you think there needs to be education for parents too, not just teachers?

Brenda: Absolutely. There has to be opportunity to learn and grow for everyone. And I think humanity and the effect of love and kindness needs to be talked about and yes, taught. Love for animals, people, the land. Things like how to relax and just be—that cannot be understated. Being able to share beyond yourself and bring acceptance—for children, into the classroom and into homes, all this, Chloe, takes great love.

Afterbirth

Lianne Marie Leda Charlie

This is a story of intention.

Motherhood.

Ancestral desire.

Overcoming disconnection.

This is a story about the intimacies of resurgence.

Micro-moments. Micro-movements.

A multiplicity of fragments struggling to form some kind of recognizable whole.

I am sitting here trying to remember everything about that morning out at Little Salmon Lake. I have recalled the story a number of times to friends and family. I have told it in a number of different ways. Sometimes I share all the details. All the fear and anxieties. Other times I gloss over those parts. Hide it. I am just not sure my listener will understand. And I do not want to have to explain.

The river. I am in the boat with my family. The river water is clear. The kind of clear that is only understood when seen, not written about. What words can I use to describe the water's cool, silky embrace around my hand as I reach out to it from the boat? From where I sit at the bow, I can see bright-green reeds dancing in the current as we float along. The reeds are hypnotic in their vibrancy. Swirling. They so easily give in to the movement of the water. Seeing the river up close—intimately—makes me think about resurgence differently.

Jeff Corntassel and Sarah Hunt have written about the "everydayness" of resurgence. But out here I see that it is more than the everyday. The river is showing us that, here, resurgence is every pulsing moment. Every stillness. Every sway. Every current. Every rustle. This is our land creating and recreating itself right in front of our eyes. Today from the bow of my cousin's boat, I am lucky to be able to witness it. I have to remind myself that this re/creation is happening even when I am not physically here to humbly observe. This seems obvious, but it is such a powerful reminder to myself when I am feeling disconnected, city-bound, and far away. The reeds are swaying, the whiskey jacks are darting from tree to tree, the trout are resting in eddies, and the river water—so clear—is ever flowing along its journey to the sea.

It is my son's first birthday. We have organized a big family and friend gathering at Little Salmon Lake, which is part of our People's traditional territories in south central Yukon.

Since pregnancy, I knew I wanted to do an afterbirth ceremony for Luka. I just did not know what it was going to look like. I do not know our ancestral practices when it comes to afterbirth. (I do not know our ancestral practices when it comes to a lot of things.) I had never heard any of the women in my family speak about afterbirth. Even a couple of my closer cousins who had babies before me did not speak of an afterbirth ceremony, although one mentioned she took her placenta home from the hospital—it is still in her freezer. I figured that if I were to do an afterbirth ceremony, I would have to ask around my family to find out what to do.

I finally get the courage to call up an Elder who gave me her number at a community gathering a while back. Her name is Gertie. She is very well known in the Yukon. She is one of the few fluent Northern Tutchone language speakers remaining in our community. She started the Yukon Native Language Centre. She also grew up in the same village as my grandfather. Since returning to the Yukon, I have been wanting to meet with her. She published a collection of stories in the 1970s about life at Big Salmon Village. Her book connected me to home when I was far, far away.

I call her up and arrange a time to visit. I get up early. I pack up Luka. I stop at the grocery store for some snacks to bring over. I am worried about being late. I drive to where I think she lives, call her to confirm her address, realize I am at the wrong place, and drive back across town in the other direction. I am nervous. I do not know what I am going to say to her. I am worried Luka is going to cry or be a nuisance and we will have to leave early because of him or something like that.

I arrive at Gertie's little house. Her driveway is icy. I walk slowly as I carry Luka to her door. I knock. I hear her voice on the other side. "Come in," she yells from her couch. I open the door. Her living room and kitchen are sparsely decorated. There is only a clock on the living room wall. She has a huge TV at the centre of the room and one couch across from it. I put the bag of oranges and the lemon loaf I bought on her kitchen table, unpack Luka, and sit on the floor. "So," she says, "what do you want?" I am caught off guard by her direct question. *What do I want?*

"I want to know what life was like at Big Salmon," I say somewhat hesitantly. *I want to know what it's like to feel comfortable on the land and the water*, I think but do not say. "I want to know what women did with the placenta after birth."

"They would hang it in a tree," she tells me, "at the place where the baby was born." My baby was born in a hospital. I had imagined myself placing the placenta in the river at the place where we saw the flash of red from a salmon breaking through the surface of the water just after my cousin shared a story of my Dad.

I recall wanting to ask one of my aunties the same question: What did women do with the placenta after birth? But I was hesitant about asking. I felt guilty for not already knowing and by asking I was going to reveal to my auntie that I did not know. I also felt a bit awkward about imposing my wants on her. I did not know how she was going to react. My question also seemed intimate, and I have never really spoken about intimate or personal things with my auntie. I finally got the courage to ask when I was over at her house one day. I also shared what I had learned from Gertie. She said she had heard that, too. She said she would ask the Elders for me and did not share any more on the topic.

One of my older, distant cousins knows a lot about Northern Tutchone cultural practices and language. We stopped by her house this past summer and I asked her what she knew of our afterbirth practices. She said we would hang the placenta in a tree at the birthplace. She added that it was understood that whatever animal ate the placenta would be connected to the baby. We might never know what animal ate the placenta, but we believe that the baby would know, and they would be guided by and in relationship with this animal throughout their life.

Just a few weeks before Luka's first birthday, one of my other aunties stopped by my house for a visit. As she was leaving, I confirmed with her that she was still coming to Little Salmon Lake for Luka's party, and I mentioned that we will be doing an afterbirth ceremony. I told her I wanted to hang the placenta in a tree near the spot that I saw that salmon. She turned and asked: "Did we even do that?" I could not tell if she was questioning me or questioning the practice. Either way, for a moment I doubted what I had learned. I doubted what I was about to do. I doubted if I was doing the right thing by moving forward with something that I do not know much about. Did we even do that?

It is the morning after Luka's birthday. We are at Little Salmon Lake. Most of my friends left the campground yesterday. It is mostly family left. I realize that if I want to make this afterbirth ceremony happen, it has to happen this morning. There was already talk among the family of packing up early and beginning the long drive home. I go to my auntie's camper. I can hear her grandkids chatting inside, so I know at least a few people are awake in there. I knock on the door. My auntie answers. "Auntie," I say, "we are going to take Luka's placenta down the river in a bit. I was wondering if you could come and send us off in a good way." "Oh," she says, somewhat surprised. "Yes, I can do that."

I walk a couple campsites over to where my other auntie's camper is parked. Her husband is sitting outside by the fire. I ask if auntie is awake. He says, "Yes, she's inside making bacon." I knock on the door, open it myself, and go inside. I'm so nervous. I go to ask her to join us, but I start to cry. She looks at me and waits. Finally, I say, "We are going to take Luka's placenta out to the river. I was hoping you would come join us as we gather on the shore." She says, "Yes." I am not entirely sure, but it looked as if she had tears in her eyes, too.

My aunties: Residential School survivors.

My aunties: strong, stern, private women.

I have been away for thirty years.

We are connected by blood and familial values that instruct us to care for each other, but we are just getting to know one another.

My Dad, their brother, passed away in 1988.

My Dad, my aunties, and my Mom have a past I know little about, only that it was tainted by too much alcohol.

And here I am. Newly back to the Yukon after spending most of my life away.

We are all learning how to be with one another again.

We stand together on the shore of Little Salmon Lake. The morning air is cool. The sun is still low. The sky is clear and bright. I am standing in front of everyone. I have asked everyone to gather here for a reason. A reason I cannot articulate just now. The words are stuck in my throat. Tears flow freely. I am anxious and a little embarrassed that I am showing this much emotion.

Finally, I say, I am crying because I do not know what I am doing.

I do not know what I'm doing.

But I am going to try this anyway.

Because we have to.

Because deep inside, I know what I am doing.

We know what we are doing.

I tell my family how difficult my first year as a Mother has been. Harder than anything I have ever imagined. I struggled. My partner and I struggled. And I felt incredibly alone for a lot of the first year. Motherhood is hard for so many reasons. Many I did not even anticipate. I did not know some of the experiences or feelings I had were even possible until they were happening. I can remember a few times in the middle of ups and downs thinking to myself that no one told me about this. This being, well, everything. Nothing was familiar. I did not recognize my body. I did not recognize myself: sleep-deprived, depressed, and struggling to figure out how to make things better. Sometimes I did not recognize my partner. Where was the joy? Where was the love? Where was the deep appreciation for each other and this little, tiny life we brought into this world together intentionally?

I share a story with my family about an experience I had here at Little Salmon River a couple of years ago. I was with three of my older cousins. We went out one evening to look for moose. We came to this spot where this creek connects with the river. My eldest cousin in the boat, who grew up with my Dad, pointed to the shore and said, "I used to fish here with your Dad." Just as he said that, a king salmon broke through the surface of the water and we all saw the flash of its red body. I tell my family that I learned that we put the placenta in the tree at the birthplace, but part of me wants to put it in the water at that spot. I look at my auntie and say, "Maybe you could help me decide."

When she speaks, she starts by saying that she is not the oldest one in the family, but she is the oldest one here today, so it is okay that she speaks on behalf of the family. She tells me she is proud of me and of what we are doing. She says, "Our people would place the placenta in a tree, but if I wanted to put it in the river, I could put it in the river."

As I sit here writing this, I can see an image from that day so clearly in my mind. We're on the boat, driving away from shore. There is my family standing on the shoreline. The water at their feet. The trees at their backs. They are waving. We wave back.

We are all witnessing.

We step out of the boat. Michael, my partner, is holding Luka. I am holding the placenta. It is double wrapped in the plastic baggies it was put in at the hospital. I am carrying it in a little lunch bag my sister gave Luka; it has robots on it. My Mom, sisters, and cousin wait in the boat.

We walk toward this little spindly spruce tree that we spotted from the river. It is the tree we want to hang the placenta in. From the water, it seemed closer. Now standing on the bank, it seems kind of far away. The ground is very uneven. There are these big wells hidden below long grass. I step into one and my foot gets soaked from the water collecting at the bottom. It crosses my mind that a moose would have no trouble traversing this riverbank. I struggle while taking a couple of unbalanced and cautious steps. I suggest we pick another tree, a closer one. But Michael says, "It is okay. We can get to the one we want. It is not far."

The three of us stand beside our little tree. Up close, I can see the details of the lichen collecting on its twiggy branches. So many shades of white and green. It is so quiet. No one is talking in the boat. And Michael and I do not speak as I open the lunch bag to get the placenta. I pull out the plastic bag. Michael opens one of the blades of his Leatherman and hands it to me. The bag is full, squishy, and surprisingly heavy. It was frozen for a year. But now, after two days in a cooler, it has definitely thawed. I slice off the knot. Blood pours out on to the ground. I hand the knife back to Michael and use the bag and both my hands to pour the placenta out over a branch on the tree.

Now outside of the bag and on the tree, I see the umbilical cord. I am surprised to see it. For some reason, I was expecting just the placenta. Seeing the umbilical cord brings me right back to the hospital and to the moment of Luka's birth. It had been a year since I had last seen the

Author photo of her family.

umbilical cord. Everything that has happened since then comes rushing back to me. Overcomes me. A huge wave of emotions, memories,
anxieties, fears, pains—everything—wells up inside of me, and I sob.

I miss my Dad. I see the clear river water in front of me and I long
with my entire body that this land will be like this for Luka's life and
his children's lives and his children's children's lives. At the same time,
I fear that it will not be like this for him or them. I re-feel the loneliness
and isolation I felt for the first year of Luka's life and I cry because it
is over now, and I do not have to feel it anymore. For years, I longed
for connection to our homelands. I had written about it. I had studied
it. I had been schooled in the language and theories of the importance
of it. But this was the first time that I actually felt it.

It is hard to describe what it is like to see a part of my body and
Luka's body in a tree, beside a river, surrounded by thousands of acres
of beautiful, pristine land. Mountains. Lakes. Dense bush. And not a
sound. Just unwavering, silent presence. I lean into Michael, who wraps
his free arm around me. He holds me. He holds Luka. This land holds us.

When I finish crying, I open my eyes and look up. Luka is looking
right at me, smiling. I smile back at him. We walk back to the boat.
Everyone hugs and holds one another. We begin the slow journey upriver

and back to the campground. I nurse Luka along the way. He falls asleep in my arms. I make eye contact with my little sister, Faith, and I tell her how happy I am that she is here with us. She smiles. Michael points out the huge schools of lake trout gliding in the water. I glance back at the spot where Luka and I tethered ourselves to our homelands. I have never felt this grounded in who I am—in who we are—in all my life.

The sun is warm. Our wake ripples out behind us toward the shore and down river.

Tl'àkú hūch'i | That is all.

Bet'á ʔeghálada[34]

Kyle Napier

As a Dené/nêhiyaw Métis media-maker, I am often found at the conflu-ence of two currents: creatively using digital media and reconnecting to my ancestral roots.

Like many Indigenous Peoples today, I am walking slowly in my own language learning journey. Each time I learn a Dene Dedlıne Yatı or nêhiyawêwin word, I can feel them flowing off the tip of my tongue, back into my ears, guiding my pulse, and recirculating back into my bloodstream.

At the time of writing, I am completing my Master of Arts in Communication and Technology with the University of Alberta. I have dedicated nearly every assignment in my time in this program to Indigenous language revitalization in Tu Nedhé. Unfortunately, I am down south for the duration of my program, meaning I am away from my own homelands I am writing about.

My thesis will be titled "Tháydene Yatı Hóneneltën—Teaching the Ancestral Dene Language," and it's written through a collaborative process with Dëne Dédlıné Elders, speakers, and learners.

In their collective and independent wisdoms, the Elders of Denendeh remind us time and time again—our languages come from the land.

Each sound, word, and concept in our language is interconnected in relationality with our environment, and with the living and spiritual beings which have enriched our lands, our languages, and our worldview.

Our concepts and languages come from anywhere between the bot-tom of the waters of Tu Nedhé, then washing nutrients onto shore, and in the clouds to hydrate the soil under our feet, in turn sustaining the

---

34   The multifaceted histories and roles of decolonizing digital tools in Dene language
     revitalization, reclamation, and acquisition. The title is the word for computer and means
     "we use this to get work done".

ecosystems which feed the winged, who themselves find their freedom above the clouds and in the open horizon, then in turn dancing our eyes along up to our ancestors in the cosmos above.

Where most Indigenous Peoples from these lands communicated and thought fluently in several Indigenous languages only just a few generations ago, there are now fewer and fewer Indigenous language speakers each year. Familiarity with the statistics can be draining.

That said, this short essay you're reading now could easily focus on the drastic and compounding effects of colonization, capitalism, and religious imperialism on us as peoples, and the subsequent effects from each on our languages. However, you have likely already talked about these issues, and you may have already deeply considered how those issues have affected you, your relations, and your community.

Instead, this article looks to the history of Indigenous representation in the media, the potential and capacity in Indigenous-owned media production.

A short history of colonial appropriation of Indigenous languages and identities

Ever since the dawn of colonial documentation technologies, Indigenous Peoples have been sought for the inevitably remarkable footage or knowledges we provide. As you would know—we make for excellent footage and social media fodder when we're all dressed up in the kitchen wearing our finest caribou hide.

By the time capitalists, colonizers, fur traders, and missionaries arrived in Denendeh, we had already had our own communications systems for many thousands and thousands of years. We communicate through our drums, long-distance travel, our dreams, our ceremonies, the clothes we make and wear, our country foods and how we prepare it. We hold interspecies communication, particularly in our land-based languages and respectful and ceremonial conduct while hunting.

Because of European fascination with us, we Indigenous Peoples have been appropriated for our languages, ceremonies, medicines, imagery, and identities for centuries. This appropriation began ever since Europeans first saw the survivability in our knowledges, or a way to attempt to convert or assimilate us, particularly so they may claim ownership of Indigenous lands.

Consider one of the first citable examples of appropriation of Indigenous languages. The first bible produced on this continent, published in 1663, wasn't published in English or French. In fact, it was published entirely in Wôpanâak. Even then, 350 years ago, Indigenous languages were appropriated for the purposes of converting us into a different way of thinking.

Missionaries of the early 1600s would learn Indigenous languages, while Indian agents would learn the languages nearly two hundred years after. Each was guided through federal funding to convert, assimilate, or control us Indigenous Peoples into their religious or societal structures.

Consider another example of Indigenous language appropriation, this one even closer to our own ancestral homelands. Linguists often incorrectly classify Dene languages as *Athabaskan*. The language of my lineage is often defined as *Chipewyan*. However, both *Athabaskan* and *Chipewyan* are Anglicized terms from nêhiyawêwin—or the "Cree language," which is itself not a Dene language. Ironically, even the word "Cree" is itself a bastardization of a French word, itself not a word in nêhiyawêwin.

The concept of Athabaskan is a nêhiyawêwin word meaning "open, rolling hills." This word, Athabaskan, was appropriated by Europeans to categorize Dene languages by a linguist named Albert Gallatin in 1826, wherein he admits in his own writing that the word Athabaskan is used as an arbitrary reference. Similarly, Chipewyan is another nêhiyawêwin word used to describe Dene, where Chipewyan means "pointed skins."

Imagine classifying twenty languages into a single category, and the word used to describe them, like the word *Athabaskan*, isn't even a word in any of the languages it's describing; similarly, consider teaching *Chipewyan* language classes when the word *Chipewyan* isn't even a word in the language you are teaching.

In 1915, Edward Sapir would take credit for using the word Na-Dene, further categorizing our languages—and with willful use of the word *Athabaskan*. Well, it's debatable as to whether or not the work done by these early linguists to categorize and appropriate our languages has been helping, but the work has continually excluded the Dene involvement in credit, acknowledgement, and community support.

Even moments which were once revolutionary for us are now outdated. The Government of the Northwest Territories published the Dene

Kede in 1993, and they began plastering every classroom with George Blondin's Dene Laws in the late 1990s. By comparison, there were still two Residential Schools in operation at the time in the Northwest Territories—one in Yellowknife, which closed in 1994, and one in Aklavik, which closed in 1996.

Indigenous resurgence in media, and the questions to ask

Many Elders alive today were born before the first computer was mass produced for tangible profit. This was more than seventy years ago, when IBM sold two thousand of the same model of computer between 1954 and 1962. At the time, computers cost somewhere between $150,000 to half a million dollars each. That was in 1954 US dollars—so with inflation and difference in currencies, those computers would cost between $1.4 million and $4.8 million in Canadian currency today.

These ridiculously expensive computers could only hold up to twenty-five kilobytes of information each—the exact amount of digital space required for this article you're reading right now.

For perspective, you now have as much processing power as two-and-a-half million of those very expensive computers, which is all condensed neatly together into your compact cellphone.

A typical cellphone with sixty-four gigabytes of memory has exactly one million times as much memory as the computer used by NASA to send the first person onto the moon in 1960.

Granted, we have more capacity in our own minds than a computer, and a computer could never fully replicate the reliability or behaviour of even just one person's memory. But consider how we as Indigenous Peoples have already used media.

Indigenous media-makers have been developing our own media since the birth of media. We have developed our own all-Indigenous language newspapers since the mid-1800s. Newspapers throughout the 1600s to today have maintained heavy bias in favour of colonization and an exoticized romanticism of Indigenous Peoples. Even at the initial outset of the steam press, the first Indigenous-owned newspaper would print their first paper in 1828. ᏣᎳᎩ ᏓᏓᎾᏩᏟᏍᎩ, or the *Cherokee Phoenix*, published their newspaper half in Cherokee and half in English.

Indigenous Peoples have been featured in photography since film could be developed. Within the first few decades of the invention of the camera, Antonio Calderón Sándoval would be the first Indigenous person to own a photography studio.

The first documentary ever made, *Nanook of the North*, was produced in 1922. The movie followed Inuit in the Arctic in a reductive capture of appropriative exhibitionism of Inuit, and is criticized often for forcing scenes and displaying Inuit in a way they were not. In the early '80s, Inuit would begin making their own movies and broadcasting channels, such as through Channel 51: Igloolik and ISUMA TV, once Zacharias Kunuk sold enough of his soapstone carvings to buy a camera in Montreal and bring it with him to Igloolik, Nunavut.

We've also been developing our own all-Indigenous language radio programs since the mid-1950s. Even the first music video ever filmed in the northern half of this continent was Willie Dunn's "The Ballad of Crowfoot" in 1968—Willie Dunn himself had Mi'kmaq, Scottish, and Irish blood.

We, as Indigenous Peoples, now produce our own television channels, radio broadcasts, websites, books, universities, newspapers, movies, platforms, apps, games, and virtual worlds—and we have been for a while.

That is, we have the opportunity to speak for and represent ourselves through digital worlds, in a medium previously dominated by non-Indigenous people. Industrial revolution 4.0—or social media, apps, and the Internet—have allowed us to mobilize, to find community and culture, and to create digital and literacy media on our own terms.

Challenges and concerns when using digital media

The opportunities presented to us by using digital media for Indigenous language revitalization must also be considered with what those tools cannot do.

The benefits of digital technologies include being able to build, operate, and maintain sovereignty over your own networks and databases with your own protocols; create resources and recordings, which can be held in community digital or analog archives; and, ultimately, share our own voice and represent ourselves, as opposed to being spoken for.

However, we must always remember that we've had our own ways to communicate for thousands and thousands of years, and these digital technologies are new to the whole world. Digital technologies come with their opportunities for community empowerment, along with the challenges of digital dependence and global mining of Indigenous lands to sustain digital resource and technology development.

You are likely also already aware of limitations, such as with the issues around Internet connectivity, access to digital tools and appropriate training to make these tools work for you. Because of issues around digital decay, digital latency, access to technologies, network connectivity, and global dependence on extraction and technological production, these new digital technologies are not as reliable as our own collective memory.

Every single byte of information and digital data is at risk of loss if there's ever water damage, magnet interaction, overheating, impact damage, or malware. Even recently, at the end of 2019, every digital file held by the Government of Nunavut was compromised due to a malware attack. This shut down access to all digital files, including legal and health records, education records, access to birth certificates, and any other digital document connected to the government's network. The Government of Nunavut spent months and more than $5 million repairing those damages.

These digital knowledge systems are powerful, and simultaneously fragile.

Through classic Dene adaptability to technologies, we can use the devices which had once been used against us to reclaim our space, as long as we also consider their potential along with their limits.

As you can tell, this essay is neither in favour nor against using digital technologies for language revitalization.

What's most important is that we work with individual and independent Indigenous communities to determine how they would each, on their own, like to develop their Indigenous language programming which they feel is appropriate for them in their own situations.

Dene languages, for instance, are mostly made up of verbs—more than two-thirds of the words in our languages are verbs. These verbs are hard to communicate through an app, where you're sitting down and more likely to learn noun identification. You may hear the same nouns you've heard before, as each app generally has an introductory level to learning, and you won't likely learn to communicate in your own complete sentences. This might be beneficial for an early learner, or a learner distant from their language. You may, alternately, choose to learn through Zoom if you had enough internet bandwidth, and if you needed to learn from a distance.

However, when you're learning your language out on the land, you're able to talk about what you're doing—such as hide tanning, fishing, hunting, and berry picking. You're able to actually talk in a dialogue with a fluent speaker and progress your learning along. You're able to connect with the land, and the environment which your language is born from. After all, a computer would still not be able to pass a Dene language test with a fluent speaker, yet.

Ultimately, how you choose to use technologies is up to you and your community, but don't forget what our Elders always remind us of:

Our languages come from the land.

Buffalo bones and hope

Two Dene stories

Christina Gray

*So, I always remember that and I want to thank him for that.
That's about all.*[35]

Connection/Disconnection

My Father Joey was born in Yellowknife and raised by my great-grandparents who were fluent speakers of the Chipewyan language. When he was nine, the Canadian government forcibly removed Joey from the loving care of our family. He went to La Pointe Hall Residential School in the Northwest Territories. Then, in 1970, at the age of eleven he was transferred to Breynat Hall. As a result of attending these two Residential Schools, there were long-lasting detrimental effects on both Joey's life and my own too.

I had a lot of difficulty in trying to connect with Joey and learn more about his early experiences in life. He rarely talked about his experiences attending residential schools, unless I prompted him and asked him about it. For me, it's been a life-long process of trying to understand that history that so vastly impacted both of our lives. These are hard words for me to write, our two Dene stories are overlapping, intersecting and there's an inexplicable tension that exists between them. I am offering vignettes of narratives relating to my own experience, parts of his experience at Residential School, state assimilationist policies, reconciliation, and the collective reclaiming and revitalization that is happening.

35 Indian Residential School History and Dialogue Centre, Archival Item, "Joseph Desjarlais—Breynat Hall and LaPointe Hall, Northwest Territories", Legacy of Hope Foudantion 23, https://collections.irshdc.ubc.ca/index.php/Detail/objects/9721.

In 2013, I moved to Ontario to train to become a lawyer. I missed the Walk for Reconciliation that happened in Vancouver. I missed hearing my Father speak at the Walk where he shared his experience in attending Residential School. I was proud of him for doing that, but for years, I could not bring myself to search for the video that he provided because it was too painful. But after Joey's death, I watched his interview that is now part of the Indian Residential School History & Dialogue Centre. Joey spoke about his experience at Breynat Hall and had this to say:

> The second time, when I was in Fort Smith, Chief Dan George came up. This was when I was about eleven. He went up there and shot a buffalo. He shared it with all the students in the Residential School. All the Junior boys were at the front, and then the Intermediates and Seniors would be in the back because they could look over the shorter kids in the front. Chief Dan George looked at me. He could tell I didn't want to be there, eh. But he looked me right in the eye. He said something to me. It was kind of telepathic. It was just like he said, "Don't worry about it, you won't be here forever." "Stick with it and you'll be out sooner or later."
>
> So, I always remember that and I want to thank him for that. That's about all.[36]

There is such a strong and profound sense of sadness and desperation captured in his story. I can feel the tangible sense of isolation as his words impart a sense of dislocation and despair. But in that small moment, I also felt hope; a gift given by Chief Dan George in his compassionate words. Words that also ultimately rang true, as eventually Joey did leave residential school. But he didn't leave without the specter of colonialism looming over him; the traumatic experiences from his early life at residential school haunted him to the end.

Joey died in a palliative care centre after many years of battling addiction and complicated health issues. It was really the last ten years of his life that signaled his demise, but I know that he lived with the

---

36   Indian Residential School History and Dialogue Centre: Archival Item: "Joseph Desjarlais—Breynat Hall and LaPointe Hall, Northwest Territories", Legacy of Hope Foundation 23, https://collections.irshdc.ubc.ca/index.php/Detail/objects/9721.

pain from his childhood trauma from residential school for much longer. I know that he also had hopes and dreams too—he had an insatiable intellect and dreamed of becoming a helicopter pilot. It is unbearable that Joey, like so many other Indigenous Peoples, had dreams that never materialized because of residential schools and other similar child welfare policies like the Sixties Scoop. It is also unbearable in realizing that I really did not get to know Joey.

I was raised by my Mom in East Vancouver, far away from my Dene and Ts'msyen homelands. As a child, I often would dream of living in the North. In the middle of 2020, I moved to Prince Rupert, British Columbia, a small coastal town on the unceded Ts'msyen territories.[37] I made this move to connect to the land, peoples, and learn the Ts'msyen language of Sm'álgyax. My lived experience is quite different from past generations before me. But in some ways, our stories intersect as a result of our perseverance to connect to the land and 'acting otherwise' against oppressive forces.

And in this place, with my own specters, I, myself, and trying to learn more and tell Joey's story; a story inextricably linked to the history and legacy of Residential Schools in the North.

A Snapshot of Residential Schools in the NWT

The aim of settler colonialism and its project was the elimination of Indigenous Peoples. The settler-colonial logic of elimination is orchestrated in a variety of ways, such as through residential schools and other policies of dispossession.[38] At the core was the assimilation of Indigenous children into Canadian society.

The federal government and churches were integral to this tragic legacy of assimilationist policy. Their will was done through legislating compulsory attendance of Indigenous children to attend residential schools throughout Canada.[39] The first Residential School in the NWT opened in 1867, at Fort Providence, which is located on South Slave Lake.[40] By the 1950s, when in the rest of Canada many residential schools

---

37   Prince Rupert is part of the territories of the Ts'msyen Gitwilgyoots tribe.

38   Patrick Wolfe, "Settler Colonialism and the Elimination of the Native," *Journal of Genocide Research*, 8:4 (2006), 387.

39   The Truth and Reconciliation Commission of Canada, *Honouring the Truth, Reconciling for the Future: Summary of the Final Report of the Truth and Reconciliation Commission of Canada* (2015), 54.

40   Ibid 51.

were declining in numbers, the opposite was occurring in the NWT as the federal government continued to open more residential schools. Amongst other enduring harms, placing generations of Indigenous children into residential schools also cleared a pathway for the Canadian state to increase natural resource extraction in the North; evidenced by the many diamond, uranium and gold mines of today.[41]

The Truth and Reconciliation Commission's Final Report notes that the government expanded the residential school system and their policy of assimilation through building residences across the North. They did this, despite reports that children would not acquire the "skills necessary to live in the north, skills they would otherwise would have acquired in their home communities."[42] The specialized Indigenous Knowledge and skills necessary to thrive in the North, such as hunting or trapping are evident in other parts of the interview with Joey. In the interview, he speaks about the harsh treatment of children that ran away, and the bullying that ensued after children returned to residential school:

> Q. So you said that some of the kids used to run away. But it was an island so you had to be a good swimmer if you succeeded. What happened to them when they got caught?

> A. When they got caught some of them used to get roughed up. They knew who to pick on and who not to pick on. Like myself, they never really bothered me because I got a phone call every Sunday. I was always in touch with my family. I always had money in my account for canteen. But there were other children there that their parents were trappers and they would go on the trap line in the fall and they wouldn't come out until the spring. So basically, they were the ones that got picked on the most because they knew there was no one there to defend them.

> But all those kids were really good in the bush. They could take off and survive out there if they had to. But after it got dark, especially when it's forty or fifty below weather, and even in the fall time it's inclement weather when it's raining and gusting."[43]

41   Ibid 63.
42   Ibid.
43   Joseph Desjarlais, Legacy of Hope (2013), available online: <http://wherearethechildren.ca/en/watc_story/joseph-desjarlais/>.

This story is difficult to fully comprehend, but they also help to explain why some Indigenous peoples have difficulty with the language of forgiveness that is part of reconciliation.[44]

Reconciliation

In the era of reconciliation, the language of forgiveness replaced the past language of political recognition.[45] Dene political science scholar Glen Sean Coulthard asks in *Red Skin, White Masks*: "What are we to make of those who refuse and/or reconcile in these situations? They are typically cast as being saddled by the damaging psychological residue of this legacy, of which anger and resentment are frequently highlighted".[46] In delving into this question, Coulthard draws upon Frantz Fanon's theories of internalized colonialism and decolonization as negative response to the settler-colonial rule in Canada and the reconciliation discourse.[47] Was Joey one such person who was cast aside because of the damaging psychological residue?

The 'damaging psychological residue' that Coulthard speaks of relates to anger and resentment. But it could also relate to loss of connection of Indigenous peoples to their land and territories. In the *First Nations Child and Family Caring Society* case it was held that Indigenous children were discriminated against through the underfunding of child welfare of Indigenous children living on-reserve. The Canadian Human Rights Tribunal found, through expert evidence, that the impacts on Indigenous children who attended residential schools are vast and include loss of culture, loss of language, loss of cultural translation, depression, other mental health issues, and the loss of traditional parenting practices.[48] But, the work that lies behind these judgments, the work of the First

---

44   Desmond Tutu & Mpho Tutu, *The Book of Forgiving: The Fourfold Path for Healing Ourselves and Our World* (New York: HarperCollins, 2014).

45   "Politics of recognition" is a political theory that is used to describe when state governments provide for the recognition of Indigenous Peoples insofar as to serve their own interests. It is not the main focus of my article, but explored in great detail in Glen Sean Coulthard, *Red Skin White Masks: Rejecting the Colonial Politics of Recognition* (Minneapolis: University of Minnesota Press, 2014), 25–50, 107, 109.

46   Glen Sean Coulthard, *Red Skin White Masks: Rejecting the Colonial Politics of Recognition* (Minneapolis: University of Minnesota Press, 2014), 109.

47   Ibid.

48   First Nations Child and Family Caring Society of Canada et al. v. Attorney General of Canada (for the Minister of Indian and Northern Affairs Canada), 2016 CHRT 2 (CanLII), http://canlii.ca/t/gn2vg, para. 412.

Nations Caring Society and many others shows that alongside identifying the losses, there is also room for growth, compassion, kindness in the way we discuss such matters that show our love to ourselves, relations, and ancestors.

Choosing to Act Otherwise

So, I always remember that and I want to thank him for that. That's about all.[49]

In a world without certainties, I have learned that one thing is for certain. That is that the complexities of Indigenous people's lives cannot be accounted for in the language of forgiveness or measured in the words of reconciliation. I am learning that it is in the elevation of Indigenous voices that we are able to tell our own stories, the stories of people that came before us, and the stories of people yet to come, to counter such narratives.

There are many ways to choose to act otherwise, such as Joey did in sharing part of his story about attending residential school in the NWT; finding hope in his brief encounter with Chief Dan George. These are courageous acts that exercise Dene citizenship and autonomy through the practice of connecting to other Indigenous peoples, the land and animals. The other Dene story here is my own. I too have exercised my personal autonomy in returning to my maternal Ts'msyen homelands. These humble acts and experiences combined together create a much more solidified way of voicing our stories of continued connections to territory, ancestors, and relatives.

---

49   Indian Residential School History and Dialogue Centre: Archival Item: "Joseph Desjarlais—Breynat Hall and LaPointe Hall, Northwest Territories", Legacy of Hope Foundation 23, https://collections.irshdc.ubc.ca/index.php/Detail/objects/9721.

cîmân

Rachel Cluderay

A Dakelh Elder from Nak'azdii, Donald Prince, told me a story about when he was a young man. Having recently reconnected with his father, the two spent a year together on the Land along with Elders learning about their culture and ways of being. At the end of the year, his father asked, "Son, what are you doing with all the teachings you have learned over the past year?" Pointing his finger to his right temple, the young man replied, "It's all up here, Dad. It's all up here." His dad responded, "It's useless then." The young man was confused.[50]

Just as his father had bestowed the teaching onto him, the Elder shared this story with me: knowledge is only valuable and meaningful when you share it with others. If you keep it inside your head, if you keep it to yourself, it will no longer exist when you pass on. This is why it is important to pass down our knowledge from generation to generation, so it does not get lost. Indigenous Peoples share knowledge orally. However, now we are encapsulating our knowledge in writing as well. Books like this one provide a way for those torn from their culture and people to learn from other Indigenous Peoples, carry that knowledge with them, and pass it on to future generations.

I have struggled and continue to struggle with my identity and the feeling that I don't belong. My mum was part of the Sixties Scoop, which means she was apprehended from her nêhiyaw mother and handed over to a white adoptive family. Even as her adoptive family was caring and loving, she was nevertheless separated from her culture, language, and ways of being before she had a chance to learn any of them. My mum only learned she was nêhiyaw because her adoption paperwork had

50   Donald Prince, personal communication, September 8, 2020.

the word "Cree" written on it; there was no mention of which nêhiyaw nation she belonged to. When my mum was eighteen, she went searching for her mother and discovered that her birth mother was also part of Sixties Scoop. She too had been adopted out to a white family and assimilated into white culture. Two generations in my family have lost the knowledge of who they belong to and their nêhiyaw ways of being. I live with these losses.

When I am paddling on nîpîy (water), I feel a deep sense of belonging. I feel most safe and secure when I am in a cîmân (canoe) on nîpîy. nîpîy is strong and resilient. It moves across the land as streams and rivers, pushing soil and breaking down pieces of rock to create new pathways and land formations. nîpîy connects us. Rivers, streams, and creeks link lakes to ponds to oceans and seas, where nîpîy is evaporated back into the air and poured down on us again from the sky as rain. nîpîy is life. All living beings need nîpîy to survive and thrive.

I learned to canoe at seventeen, during a difficult time in my life. I spent many days guiding groups of youth up Wîlîıdeh/Yellowknife River, crying in the back of the canoe, but by the end of the day I would feel lighter. Canoeing has been critical for my reconnection with Land. This, in turn, has been the foundation of my healing journey. The Land heals. The Water heals. My relationship with nîpîy has shown me that I carry the same strength and resiliency. I too can carve out new pathways and shape the way I want to be in this world.

Shortly after learning how to canoe, I became a certified Paddle Canada canoe instructor. I travelled to communities across the Northwest Territories, Nunavut, and Yukon to teach canoeing and guide canoe trips. My discomfort with being a Paddle Canada instructor started during a big canoe course in Behchokǫ̀. The participants were leaders for the Whaèhdǫǫ̀ Etǫ K'è, the annual Tłı̨chǫ Trails of Our Ancestors trip. One of the Elders in the course was a phenomenal paddler—he knew all the strokes and maneuvers, and he was excellent at teaching the others in the group. I thought to myself, why isn't this knowledge and skill and learning valid? Why are we only learning and teaching non-Indigenous ways to canoe?

When I learned to paddle, I knew the canoe was integral to the Dene People whose land I grew up on; however, I didn't know that it was also an important tool of transportation for my own ancestors.

Indigenous nations across this Land we now call Canada, including nêhiyaw nations, designed and built beautiful, architecturally ingenious canoes adapted to the diverse environments they thrived in prior to contact from the coastal waters to prairie rivers to boreal watersheds. The canoe was essential to each nation's way of life as they traversed their lands and waterways in search of sustenance, people, and trade. Colonization changed this.

In the sixteenth century, Europeans came to the coasts of what is now called Canada, and flourished when they made use of Indigenous technologies, including the canoe. Traders and settlers adopted the canoe as a practical, necessary tool for exploring Indigenous lands and peoples further and further into the interior. The canoe enabled the expansion of the fur trade and assisted settlers in displacing and harming Indigenous Peoples.[51] The fur trade was dominated by the Hudson's Bay Company, which, with the support of the British Crown, was charged with governing the territory deemed Rupert's Land.[52]

The canoe remained vital to settlers as they surveyed and mapped the territory that became the Dominion of Canada in 1867—facilitating European settlement, resource extraction, and industrial development. As Jessica Dunkin has demonstrated, recreational canoeing developed in tandem with a broad suite of state policies meant to assimilate Indigenous Peoples:

> It is no coincidence that at the same time that Euro-Canadian canoeists were taking to the water in boats appropriated from Indigenous nations, the Canadian state was implementing the *Indian Act*, a comprehensive set of laws introduced in 1876 to destroy Indigenous cultures and assimilate the continent's First Peoples into mainstream settler society. Residential schools, forced settlement on reserves, the outlawing of cultural practices such as the potlatch, and the destruction of traditional economies,

51   "Is the canoe a symbol of Canada, or of colonialism?" *CBC News*, March 4, 2016, https://www.hbcheritage.ca/things/artifacts/the-royal-charter, https://www.cbc.ca/radio/the180/electric-cars-aren-t-green-pot-is-still-a-drug-and-we-need-to-rethink-the-canoe-1.3475291/is-the-canoe-a-symbol-of-canada-or-of-colonialism-1.3475381 and M. Dean, *Inheriting A Canoe Paddle: The Canoe In Discourses of English-Canadian Nationalism* (Toronto: University of Toronto Press, 2013).

52   Hudson Bay Company. n.d., "The Royal Charter", https://www.hbcheritage.ca/things/artifacts/the-royal-charter.

all profoundly affected Indigenous lifeways, including the construction and use of canoes.[53]

Little has changed in recreational canoeing since the nineteenth century. Most "wilderness" canoeists continue to come from privileged backgrounds—the majority are well-educated, upper middle class, white men.[54] Like their nineteenth-century predecessors, they are looking to escape their urban lives and "explore" Canada. Channelling early explorers, these enthusiasts produce films and write books about "conquering the North." They claim to have been the first people to paddle waterways or hike landscapes that Indigenous Peoples have lived in relation with since time immemorial. Canoeing continues to be practised and represented by non-Indigenous recreational canoeists in appropriative and exclusionary ways.

This history is woven into the fabric of canoeing curriculum I used to deliver. The national and provincial certification organizations and their respective instructors are predominately white. The knowledge and skills of Indigenous Peoples are sidelined, if not completely ignored, in canoe courses. While certifications do incorporate "canoe history," these courses often include little to no guidelines for what should be taught, allowing instructors to repeat the same tired stories about the canoe as a Canadian icon that enabled the fur trade and led to the making of a nation. Being subject to these stories is not an option for Indigenous paddlers. Insurance companies often require these certifications for organizations leading paddling programs. In this way, certifications are a barrier for remote communities wishing to take advantage of funding programs to support Indigenous Peoples spending time on the Land.

As I reflect on the story Donald shared with me about the importance of passing on knowledge, I realize that teaching canoeing, especially to other Indigenous Peoples, is an act of revitalization, resurgence, and resiliency. It is a way for me to connect with my ancestors and culture. As I paddle down rivers and across lakes, I often find myself reflecting

53   J. Dunkin, *Canoe and Canvas: Life at the Encampments of the American Canoe Association, 1880-1910*, (Toronto: University of Toronto Press, 2019) and J. Dunkin, "Cultural Manoeuvres," *Canada's History*, https://www.canadashistory.ca/explore/books/cultural-manoeuvres.
54   Newberry, L. (2003). Will any/body carry that canoe? A geography of the body, ability, and gender. *Canadian Journal of Environmental Education*, 8(1), 204-216.

on the ones who have travelled these routes before me. The strength and resiliency it took to paddle many kilometres in search of moose, family, or trade goods. I imagine families, brought together by these waterways, reconnecting on the shore and having great feasts. I think about how they would have passed down the knowledge and skills of being safe on the Water to future generations as they dipped their paddles in these same Waters. I recognize that these waterways didn't just connect people to each other, but also to all other living beings who depend on Water for life. I can see past paddlers watching fish swim, moose drink, and chives grow on the edges of shore.

During a paddle this summer, I had an epiphany that I am doing what Donald talked about. It just looks a little bit different. I am sharing my knowledge on canoeing with other Indigenous Peoples when I come to their communities and deliver a canoe course or participate in their canoe programming. I am sharing the Indigenous lens on the history of the canoe and its purpose for our nations. I am learning from Elders and knowledge holders how Indigenous peoples have stayed safe on Water since time immemorial and giving space for those teachings in courses. I am empowering other Indigenous Peoples to learn strokes and manoeuvres, and feel connected with and empowered by the canoe as I did. By passing along my knowledge and skills, I am in turn connecting with my own culture and identity. This is an important part of ending the cycle of intergenerational identity loss and trauma within my family.

The story of the canoe in Canadian history is often told through a colonial lens. The canoe, in this telling, is framed as integral to the exploration of and trade within what is now called Canada. Unfortunately, this narrative hides the theft and genocide that Indigenous Peoples experienced through non-Indigenous people's use of the canoe, and obscures the fact that the canoe is symbol of colonialism, imperialism, and marginalization. It also ignores how the canoe is a symbol of resilience, resurgence, and nationhood for Indigenous Peoples.

To decolonize the canoe and canoeing, and nurture respectful relationships between Indigenous and non-Indigenous people, we all need to educate ourselves on the complicated history of the canoe and take action. For my part, I want to celebrate and support the acts of revitalization underway. Across the continent, Indigenous nations are reclaiming the canoe through canoe building and paddling their ancestral trails.[55] These reclamations, often only accessible through funded on the Land programs, are integral to strengthening Indigenous Peoples' connection with their waterways and ways of being. It is important for the revitalization of our cultures, languages, and knowledges that we reclaim these ways of being, including Indigenous canoeing practices, so we are able to share this knowledge with future generations.

55   Raymond Yakeleya, *The Last Mooseskin Boat*, 1982, National Film Board, https://www.nfb.ca/film/last_mooseskin_boat/ and *Nahanni: River of Forgiveness*, 2020, directed by Geoff Bowie, https://riverofforgiveness.com/prologue.

Starpath

Siku Allooloo

What if all you saw
was this expanse of dark space
Pitch black, distance
. . . and from the corner of your eye
a tiny, soaring light
drawing an erratic pathway / jagged line / silhouette
Like the steep trace of mountains
. . . or the precarious line of a heartbeat
marked by spikes and falls, in a rhythm that signifies life

Spikes, and falls
Like the elusive state of safety
people like us exist in

What if you knew that this view
took several years of climbing, to see it in full
All of the loss . . . and abuse
All of the u n f a t h o m a b l e
imbued within my line

From this 360 view, the pillars that have shaped me
and all the ones that broke me
held together in place
. . . A b a c k b o n e , they say
And my line—a starpath
across Nio Ne P'ene, where the ridges meet the sky

I feel in this view, within some timeless depth
the faint trace of inertia . . . My orbit, coming around
I cannot see it, but I have a knowing
about my shape
my base, my core

Like, I am a planet—f a r f r o m t h e s u n
A being in dark matter
that is sensing her weight

Gravitational force realigning
particles of l i f e t i m e s forgotten
An orbit knocked off kilter—stabilizing

. . . .

If I told you my story
you'd hear of loss after loss
Someone conditioned to tragedy
Not conditioned to trust

I grew up jumping between ice flows, wondering
when I'd slip and life would s w a l l o w m e w h o l e

When it did, it drew me
to the bottom of the sea
. . . across the cosmos

. . . . .

From above, you see my life
An endless spiral, unfolding in quantum places
Continuity interrupted
Spontaneous light

All my roots chopped and cast
into the abyss like Tutalik's fingers

One by one, they each find me
Each one a new formation, pulled back into my orbit
as my gravity grows in strength, and speed

. . . .

There is a place
I f e e l , and I d r e a m , and I k n o w
. . . though, it doesn't exist yet

There is a place I am building
that is building itself within me
A beautiful place
I have   n e v e r   known

Ni horelyan—how I learned to express
It's a beautiful day
in the language of the land that has healed me

Ni horelyan
a beauty that is held in both the earth
and frame of mind

Horelyan nide means
a beautiful day
in the language of the land that has healed me

Horelyan—a beauty that is sacred
Heavenly, says my elder
Happiness all over
Happiness felt with a l l o f t h e s e n s e s

Nide—knowing / hoping / praying

Nueba—for all of us

In Denesułine
to want / to need / to enjoy / and to love doing something
are all intertwined, she says
encompassed in the word *basthi*

As in, a need and a want
that when met—is a gift that makes me happy

I am orbiting along toward this vision
Encompassed by this word that's taken years
for me to find

To know that what I want
        and what I *need*
        the prayer that is always praying inside me
        the gift I hope to bring

                . . . is what also brings great joy

. . . .

N u e b a   H o r e l y a n   N i d e

Eyìıt'ıì Nǫts'ıde [56]

Katłįà Lafferty, translated by Mary Rose Sundberg

Dechįnıì nàts'ede edàgǫ̱ht'e wek'èts'ezhǫ,
Shèts'ezhe gha nàts'ezè eyıts'ǫ golà t'à eghàlats'eda,
Edàanì tıch'àadıı łàts'ehwhì wek'èts'ezhǫ,
Wet'à kǫ̀ ts'eèt'ı̱, goht'ǫ eyıts'ǫ wet'à gokǫ̀.
Edàanì ewò ts'ehwhe wek'èts'ezhǫ,
Tsàwò ts'ehgǫ̀ǫ̀ eyıts'ǫ ło wek'e ahts'eh?ı̱,
Asìı wetą̱t'e ts'ehwhį̀ wet'àts'eet'ı̱;
Ayìı ts'ı̱wǫ sìı goghàye?a gha mahsì ts'ı̱wǫ.
Kw'è eyıts'ǫ ekw'ǫ sìı wet'àts'et'ı̱,
Wet'à k'ı̱ eyıts'ǫ ı̱htı̱ ts'ehtsı̱,
Zha ka goı̱wa k'ets'edè,
Nahwhı̱ t'à ?ets'eè?ı̱-le.
Gokè mbehchı̱ı̱ yìı nàgèats'ahsò,
Chǫh yìı goshı̱t'a k'egets'ege,
Mǫht'aà edza hò tłı̱ k'ets'ezhoo,
Kwesǫ̀ǫ̀mba gha dzǫwò nèts'ele.
Ndè gonàdı wet'à nàdets'ejì,
Xah eyıts'ǫ k'amba ts'ehch'ı,
Goht'ǫ k'enàts'ehtse,
Łè eyıts'ǫ tłeh t'à dǫłèt'è ts'ehtsı̱.
Jìe ts'eèmbe,
Łıwejì wedę łıwe ts'ehchı,
Tamı̱ wek'ats'ehta,
Kwe k'e łıwe ts'eèht'ìı.

56 A previous English version of this piece appeared in *Up Here Magazine* and is reprinted
    with permission.

Kw'ah k'e ts'etı̨,
K'omǫǫ̀dǫǫ̀ gok'ò ts'eèjì.
Ịda gots'ǫ edàaht'e chı nıìde ha wek'èts'ezhǫ,
Edàaht'e nǫdı dıh ghǫ nàzè wek'èts'ezhǫ,
Edàaht'e dą̀ą̀nı̨hts'ıı ts'ǫhk'e sa nà?à wek'ets'ezhǫ,
Gohłı̀a det'oo yehtsı̨ dè wek'èts'ezhǫ.
Nàanı̨hts'ı ts'ǫhk'e tǫ akwełǫ̀ nayų̨ wek'èts'ezhǫ.
Edàaht'e detı̨ wek'èts'ezhǫ.
Goxı̨ whacho ts'ejı̨ xè dats'etłoo,
Gowhàedǫ nàowo wexòedı,
Yak'e tł'a whǫ̀ wegaht'ı̨,
Goneè sa nà?a-le,
Ǫhdaà gınàowo t'à goxè gogedo,
Edàanì ndè eyıts'ǫ donę ełexè nàdè,
Eyıı nàowo goghàge?à.
Goyatı k'è gots'ede nı̨dè edàanì ne wek'èts'ezhǫ,
Adı̨ gots'ǫ ats'ı̨t'e weghǫ axòts'edì.
Whacho edets'enda ayıı ne wek'èts'ezhǫ,
Eyıts'ǫ gowhàedǫ gıgondı ats'ǫ̀ wenàts'edì.
K'ıìtì ats'ı̨t'e,
Ts'ı ts'ǫ et'e;
Tł'oh ndè k'e wek'eweèts'ı lanì ats'ı̨t'e;
Tatsǫ̀ ats'ı̨t'e,
Netı̨ndà eze;
Sah ats'ı̨t'e,
Asıı deè?ǫ̀ ts'ı̨wǫ;
Nàdets'eèh?à,
Hòezı k'e,
Go?ǫhdaà lanì teè goıwa lanì nàts'eh?ı̨,
Shìh gombaà ts'eèjı̨ t'à ts'eèjì ha dìı;
Ndè gotł'a ts'ǫ̀ asıı deèdì,
Esagodı-le wets'ehkw'ǫ;
Goxı̨ got'ǫ̀ nàhòe?ı̨;
Goxı̨ got'ǫ̀ asıı wexòedı ha;
Dìı nèk'e donę sǫłı̨ hazhǫ nàgèdè lats'ı̨t'e,
Gòet'ı̨ı̨ achı̨ nàgetso ade ha.

Contributors

Siku Allooloo is an Inuk/Haitian/Taíno writer, artist, and community builder from Denendeh (Somba K'e and Tthebatthi) and Mittimatalik, Nunavut. She is a Dechinta alumni and often joins the staff team as a land-based coordinator, facilitator, and educator. She has been leading Indigenous resurgence and decolonial work since 2012 through her artistic practice, advocacy, and cultural programming on the land. Her writing and multimedia work have been featured in *Canadian Art* magazine, *The Capilano Review*, *The Malahat Review*, *Briarpatch Magazine*, *The Guardian*, and Graphic History Collective's *Remember | Resist | Redraw* series (along with Dechinta faculty and artist Lianne Marie Leda Charlie).

Asinnajaq is an Inuk visual artist, filmmaker, writer, and curator based in Montreal, Quebec, and from Inukjuak, Nunavik. Asinnajaq's practice is grounded in research and collaboration, which includes working with other artists, friends, and family. In 2016 she worked with the National Film Board of Canada's archive to source historical and contemporary Inuit films and colonial representations of Inuit in film. The footage she pulled is included in her short film *Three Thousand* (2017). The film was nominated for Best Short Documentary at the 2018 Canadian Screen Awards by the Academy of Canadian Cinema & Television. Asinnajaq was a part of the curatorial team for the Canadian Pavilion at the 2019 Venice Biennale and was long listed for the prestigious Sobey Art Award in April 2020.

Tiffany Ayalik and Insuksuk Mackay, sisters, come together to creat the Inuit style throat singing duo PIQSIQ with a style galvanized by darkness and haunting northern beauty. Performing ancient traditional songs and eerie new compositions, they leave their listeners enthralled with the infinity of possible answers to the question "What is the meaning of life?"

With roots in Nunavut's Kitikmeot and Kivalliq Regions, the sisters grew up in Yellowknife, Northwest Territories. Their love of katajjaq, Inuit throat singing, began in childhood and has bonded them together throughout their lives. After years of forging the hard won skill, they developed their own form blended with their love of haunting melodies and otherworldly sounds.

As PIQSIQ, they perform improvisational looping live, creating a dynamic audience experience that changes with every show. PIQSIQ incorporates their dark and ethereal style into their recordings and have produced three studio albums to date.

Inuksuk and Tiffany continue to blend magic with sound to further develop their entrancing style for both national and international audiences.

Randy Baillargeon is a member of the Yellowknives Dene First Nation and is the land-based coordinator and community mentor at the Dechinta Centre for Research and Learning. He loves teaching Dechinta students and youth in his community how to hunt, trap, set and check fish nets, and how to drum and sing. As much as he loves teaching, he is also always learning from others, which is why he loves to help the Dechinta Elders with various building project on the land. Randy is a talented drummer and singer; you may recognize him from community drum dances or opening prayer songs. In addition to drumming and singing, Randy loves making drums, which he learned from his family.

Josh Barichello is a kuskāni dena (white person) who grew up in the territories of the Kaska Dena, Shúhtaot'ine, and Kwanlin Dun. For the past fourteen years Josh has worked with the Ross River Dena Elders Council on various Dena knowledge projects and culture camps. He also works with the Dechinta Centre for Research and Learning in coordinating land-based education programs in Kaska Dena Territory.

Taylor Benh-Tsakoza is an Eh Cho Dene and Dene Tsaa woman from Fort Nelson First Nation, BC Treaty 8 Territory. Being a Dene handgames enthusiast, a beginner beader, and dry meat maker, as well as the first in her immediate family to obtain a university degree, Taylor encourages others to pursue contemporary and traditional forms of education. Her time at Dechinta in the Fall of 2020 is a prime example of incorporating both forms of learning. When Taylor is not out in community delivering programs and workshops to youth, you can find her traveling the world or out on her traditional territory with her family exercising their Treaty Rights.

Justina Black is a member of the Yellowknives Dene First Nation, born and raised in Yellowknife Northwest Territories. Her grandmother was Tłı̨chǫ Dene, and her grandfather was Tetsǫt'ıné Dene. They were raised in hide tents in the thick boreal forests that blanket over Denendeh. She has spent the majority of her life involved in land-based education having attended the community school of Ndilǫ. Justina is passionate about learning from Elders and knowledge holders to pass on the teaching to youth who she engages with in the Dechinta community.

Lianne Marie Leda Charlie is Wolf Clan and Tagé Cho Hudän | Big River People (Northern Tutchone speaking people of the Yukon). Her maternal grandparents are Donna Olsen (first generation Canadian of Danish ancestry) and Benjamin Larusson (first generation Canadian of Icelandic ancestry) and her paternal grandparents are Leda Jimmy of Tánintsę Chú Dachäk | Little Salmon River and Big Salmon Charlie of Gyò Cho Chú | Big Salmon River. She was born in Whitehorse to her Mother, Luanna Larusson, and late Father, Peter Andrew Charlie. Lianne grew up on the unceded Lekwungen territories in what is commonly referred to as Victoria, British Columbia, where she went to school and university. She is a recent graduate of the PhD program in Indigenous Politics in the Political Science Department at the University of Hawai`i at Mānoa. Her research focused on modern treaty politics in the Yukon. Lianne is a multimedia artist and Mom to Luka Gyo. She has created community murals in Whitehorse, Łu Ghą, and Mayo and co-created four pieces for *To Talk With Others* (Valerie Salez), including a life-size, hot pink papîer maché bull moose made out of the Umbrella Final Agreement. Lianne is a faculty member at the Dechinta Centre for Research and Learning.

Rachel Cluderay was born and raised in Sǫǫ̀mbak'è (Yellowknife), Denendeh where she still lives today. She is a nêhiyaw-English paddler and land-based program advocate. In 2019, she completed a Bachelor of Commerce specializing in entrepreneurship at the University of Victoria. Rachel also has a certificate in Land-Based Research from Dechinta/ UBC. Currently, Rachel is studying a Masters of Indigenous Land-Based Education at the University of Saskatchewan where her work focuses on developing a canoe training from an Indigenous paradigm. Being on the Land makes Rachel feel whole. This is why she is passionate about strengthening peoples connection to Land as she believes it is the foundation for the resurgence of Indigenous cultures, languages, and ways of being.

Noel-Leigh Cockney is from Tuktoyaktuk and Inuvik, Northwest Territories. His whole life he has grown up along the coast of the Arctic Ocean hunting and fishing. Once he graduated from high school in Inuvik he went to college in Wisconsin, at Northland College, for four years and graduated with a major in Outdoor Education and minor in Native American Studies. After graduating, he worked for six years for NOLS, instructing backpacking, rock climbing, and whitewater canoeing courses all over the United States. He moved back home in the winter of 2018, working in tourism for over two years, before finding his current position at the Dechinta Centre for Research and Learning as their safety coordinator and regional programmer.

ᐊᗺ ᐎ ᑕ ᒡᵒ ‾ ᖬ ᕐ ᒡ ᑌ ᴠ | Angela Code, Sayısı Dene
Hello.
Watsiye.
My name is Angela Code.
Angela Code husyé.
I am a member of the Sayisi Dene First Nation.
Sayisi Dene hes lį.
I was born in Churchill, Manitoba.
Tthé'ye ni yą.
My parents are Allan and Mary Code.
Setikwi Allan chu Mary Code chu.

I have two older brothers named Robert and Michael.

Nadene suna Robert chu Michael chu dahulye.

I spent my childhood in Tadoule Lake, Manitoba.

Tes'he'uli twe niyą.

There, I was surrounded by my Denesųline language, culture, land, and people.

Denesųline yatiye chu, denechániye chu, ni' chu, dene chu, heł.

When I was ten,

Honena seghai'u,

my family and I moved to the Kwanlin Dün and Ta'an Kwäch'än Territory of Whitehorse, Yukon, to pursue more education, recreation, and work opportunities.

Kwanlin Dün chu, Ta'an Kwäch'än chu benene ke, Whitehorse, Yukon ninidel. T'ant'u huno'henełt'en hilısı ho ha…dene honelteni'kwę́hu, są dą́'lu aládai dą́'lu.

In 2012, I graduated from the University of British Columbia with a Bachelor of Arts degree—major in First Nation Studies and minor in First Nation Languages and Linguistics.

2012, 'University of British Columbia' hotsı̨, 'Bachelor of Arts' ediklis sąchuth, 'First Nation Studies chu, First Nation Languages and Linguistics' chu hasunełtą.

In 2011, I also attended Dechinta Centre for Research and Learning, a community led initiative that delivers land-based, university-credited experiences rooted in northern Indigenous knowledge and skill.

2011, 'Dechinta' honeltenı'kwę́ː naıthed, dene chaniye hasunełtą, ałnethi dene honelteni.

I am currently working as an archivist for Library and Archives Canada as a part of the Listen, Hear Our Voices project—an initiative focused on Indigenous language revitalization through the digitization of Indigenous language recordings.

'Library and Archives Canada' ha'eghá'lasna. 'Listen, Hear Our Voices' project hulyé. Deneyatiye naiłchu'hą. Yanisi ta beyatiye hı̨łchu ne'lénisi éyita.

I am also engaged in an informal master-apprentice Denesųline language-learning process with my Mother.

Ené Denesųline yatiye hasunełten.

We work together to translate audio and video of our people that my Father recorded and digitized.

Ą́łá éghlaidahu - seta deneyatiye ediklis dadaki chu, beyati t'a chu, deneyatıye hı̜łchu nis'ı̜ banlai yatiye ta di'klis.

Some of my hobbies include hunting, fishing, tanning hides, competing in Dene handgame tournaments and travelling.

Naszé'u, jetthé thidow, tenthed hes'tthıu, udzi senasthedu, hodelyu neneke zédes'sow kuntu hesna.

I am an advocate for social justice, healthy lands and waters, and Indigenous language and cultural revitalization.

Ą̨n'tu álainá hilisi k'osté seyatiye t'a. Ą̨n'tu dene tsen suwai'li chu, ni' chu, tu chu, deneyatiye chu, dene chaniye chu bebazi.

I hope to continue using my skills as a researcher, writer, film-maker, archivist, and artist to further promote Indigenous health and empowerment.

Dene tsosni nesthen ta'losi ta t'a huzu tahota hode'ai'li Dene ha nanéstow edisklisu honi hes'tsiu deneyatiye hes chu denehéyestiyu asihes'tsi'u kuntida.

Thank you. **Masi cho.**

Glen Coulthard is Yellowknives Dene and an associate professor in the First Nations and Indigenous Studies Program and the Departments of Political Science at the University of British Columbia. He is the author of *Red Skin, White Masks: Rejecting the Colonial Politics of* Recognition (Minneapolis: University of Minnesota Press, 2014) and winner of the 2016 Caribbean Philosophical Association's Frantz Fanon Award for Outstanding Book; the Canadian Political Science Association's CB Macpherson Award for Best Book in Political Theory, published in English or French, in 2014/2015; and the Rik Davidson Studies in Political Economy Award for Best Book in 2016. He is also a board member and faculty member at the Dechinta Centre for Research and Learning, a decolonial, Indigenous land-based post-secondary program operating on his traditional territories in Denendeh.

Beatrice Deer is a Canadian Aboriginal Music Award-winning singer-songwriter from Nunavik. Half-Inuk and half-Mohawk, Deer left her small hometown of Quaqtaq, Quebec, in 2007 for three life-changing reasons:

1) She moved to Montreal to get serious about making music—and it worked. Deer has now released five albums, each deepening her trademark blend of traditional Inuit throat singing with contemporary indie rock. *My All to You*, her fifth record, marks a significant milestone in the history of Inuindie music (a genre Deer pioneered), as this is the first time she composed all the songs' instrumentation as well as the lyrics. Her themes range from classical Inuit folk tales and legends to the importance of finding understanding and the search for meaning within personal growth. Her songs are especially beloved in Arctic Canada, where she tours frequently and where audiences sing along to her songs during concerts. She sings in three languages: Inuktitut, English, and French. Her collaborators include luminaries from the likes of Land of Talk, The Barr Brothers, Stars, Timber Timbre, Bell Orchestre, Suuns, and executive producer Michael Felber.

2) The second reason Deer left the North was to pursue higher education—and to ensure that her two daughters (now aged sixteen and eighteen) also had access to proper schooling as well. Deer's artistic experience manifests itself in countless ways: she has been everything from a book designer, to an actor, to a model. A highly regarded seamstress, she's also the voice of safety briefings on First Air and can be heard on children's TV shows. But above all, her primary medium is music, both as a singer, and now, with *My All to You*, as a songwriter as well. The education she sought in Montreal manifests itself in this latest release. It's an album of maturity, of hard-fought wisdom, and of spiritual depth.

3) The final reason Deer came to Montreal was to get therapy. "*My All to You* is all about owning up," she explains. "It's about reconciliation with yourself—which is the hardest thing to do. And I mean that on a personal level as well as on a national level." At this moment in the country's history, when reconciliation between Canadians and First Peoples has finally become a central issue, Deer has an important message to share: she believes that reconciliation begins with each of us. "You can't be a change maker if you haven't gone through it yourself,"

she says. "You can't help if you haven't gone through healing yourself. It's a lot easier to forgive other people than it is to forgive yourself. To get to where I am today, I had to forgive myself many, many times. I still work on it."

As a role model for her community and an advocate for healthy living, Deer is often asked to do speaking engagements. Her primary message is that each of us must take control of our own life. "Nobody else can do it for you," she insists. "You can't change what happened. You can only change how you deal with it." The starting point for her latest album was a desire to relive the moment in her own life when she decided to transform her outlook. "I'd struggled for many years, in many ways—until I realized the change had to come from me," Deer says. "I know that now that I'm not in constant pain anymore. I can finally perceive things properly. And I want to use that to help others. Music is such an effective way to help. It can be such a positive tool for empowerment."

Brenda Dragon was born in 1962 in Fort Smith. She is the second child of six, born to Jane Dragon nee Mercredi and the late David Dragon. Brenda grew up in Fort Smith and was raised with acceptance and a great love for land and Indigenous culture. She graduated in Fort Smith and moved to Yellowknife where she began a career in health care. Brenda is a natural caregiver and travelled as an eye care technician to all the communities in the Northwest Territories and what is now Nunavut. When she had her first child, Chloe, at the age of twenty-seven, she quickly made a choice to be home full time. Another early decision was to homeschool and brought Brenda down a path of learning about education and she involved herself in the public schooling system. Over the course of years, her expertise expanded to both the development of Indigenous cultural education and then onto university at the age of forty-eight for another career in Indigenous tourism development. Currently, Brenda is the president and founder of Aurora Heat, Inc. Her passion and mission with her business is to provide sustainable fur for warmth and health while strengthening both her community and the tradition of wild fur harvesting. She remains ever committed to her family and to living a positive and productive life.

Chloe Dragon Smith was born and raised in Somba K'é (Yellowknife), Denendeh (Northwest Territories). Of Métis, German, Dënesųłiné, and French heritage, her Mother is Brenda Dragon and her Father is Leonard Smith. She is passionate about relationships between lands and peoples. Her work varies from education and on-the-land learning to Indigenous-led conservation to climate change. As a mixed-blood person, she feels a sense of responsibility to help create balance and build bridges and relationships in all she does.

Thumlee Drybones-Foliot is the daughter of Aileen Drybones and Anthony Foliot. As a child, she lived on a houseboat, played on Great Slave Lake, and walked up the hill to school. Thumlee's Mother grew up living on the land with her grandparents Madeline and Noel Drybones at Fort Reliance and she was very lucky to see them live a traditional Dene life. Her Mother took her hunting, and she would watch her grandmother tan hides, bead and sew. After finishing high school, Thumlee worked at a number of little jobs, travelled and then went to Dechinta Centre for Research and Learning where she had a place to hone her skills. At present, Thumlee works part time at Dechinta and full time as a Mother. In July 2019, she had a daughter named Katche Alexandra, who at the present time is the centre of her universe.

Jamesie Fournier is an Inuk in Denendeh. Jamesie works in alternative education in Tthebacha/Fort Smith between Salt River First Nation, Smith's Landing First Nation, and the South Slave Metis Nation. He was a guest author at the 2018 and 2020 Northwords Writers Festival and a runner up for *Up Here Magazine*'s 2018 Sally Manning Award for Indigenous Creative Non-Fiction. His work has been in the *Inuit Art Quarterly*, *Red Rising Magazine*, and *Northern Public Affairs*. The piece in this book will be his second contribution to a compilation publication. His first was the Northwords' 2012 release *Coming Home: Stories from the Northwest Territories*. In his time off he enjoys walking the dog, drinking coffee, and looking for fallen trees.

Jeneen Frei Njootli is a 2SQ Vuntut Gwitchin, Czech, and Dutch artist working in performance, sound, textiles, images, collaboration, workshops, and feral scholarship. They are now living in the ancestral, unceded territories of the Musqueam, Squamish, and Tsleil-Waututh Peoples and teaching at the University of British Columbia. If you are interested in learning more about Jeneen's work, please check out *my auntie bought all her skidoos with bead money*, available through the Contemporary Art Gallery bookstore in Vancouver, British Columbia.

Camille Georgeson-Usher is a Coast Salish/ Sahtu Dene/Scottish scholar, artist, and writer from Galiano Island, British Columbia, which is the land of the Pune'laxutth' (Penelakut) Nation. Usher completed her MA in Art History at Concordia University. Her thesis, "more than just flesh: the arts as resistance and sexual empowerment," focused on how the arts may be used as a tool to engage Indigenous youth in discussions of health and sexuality. She is a PhD candidate in the Cultural Studies Department at Queen's University and has been awarded the Joseph-Armand Bombardier Canada Graduate Scholarship for her research-creation work looking at ontologies of gathering in urban centres. She was awarded the 2018 Canadian Art Writing Prize and recently has had work exhibited in *Soundings: an exhibition in five parts*. Usher is the executive director of the Indigenous Curatorial Collective, board member of Artspace in Peterborough, board member of the Toronto Biennial of Art, and is part of the curatorial team for MOMENTA 2021.

Leela Gilday is a celebrated musician-songwriter, singer, guitarist, composer, and creator from Denendeh. Her family is from the Sahtú region and she was born and raised in Yellowknife on Treaty 8 Territory. If you're from the North, her music is home. If you've never been, it will take you there. She writes about the people and the land that created her—of love and life and a rugged environment and vibrant culture. She believes music has an inexplicable effect on people. It is a place where she can share light and dark and the most vulnerable moments. Her music has been recognized with many awards including a Juno, and she has toured nationally and internationally for the better part of twenty-five years. Leela has also embarked upon a career as an artistic director, with projects such as the Circumpolar Soundscape, Muskoskwew Quartet, Tsekwi Huya Gala celebration, National Aboriginal Achievement Foundation Finale, Gho-Bah/Gombaa collective concert and recording, and most recently as the musical director for the Arctic Inspiration Prize

Ceremony. She presents workshops on vocal and personal empowerment, most often to Indigenous communities.

Robert Grandjambe is a member of Mikisew Cree First Nation. He spent his childhood in Fort Chipewyan, Alberta, and later lived in Tthebacha (Fort Smith). His Mother is Barbara Grandjambe (nee Schaefer) and his Father is Robert Grandjambe. He has been an active trapper since he was six years old, and he is proud to thrive as a full-time trapper and harvester. He shares with people as much as possible, introducing culture and knowledge though camps, universities, boards, and film.

Christina Gray is a Ts'msyen and Dene citizen. She is an associate at JFK Law Corporation where she practices in the area of Aboriginal law. She is currently completing her Master of Law at the University of Victoria. Her research focuses on issues of gender within the Ts'msyen legal tradition. She has a law and art history degree from the University of British Columbia.

Coleen Hardisty is of mixed Dehcho Dene descent originally from Líídlįį Kúę, Denendeh (Fort Simpson, NWT). She has lived in Sǫǫ̀mbak'è (Yellowknife) for the last fourteen years. Coleen is an aspiring Indigiqueer musician, a beginner speaker of Dene Zhatié, and the youth literacy coordinator at the NWT Literacy Council. Outside of office hours, she can often be found volunteering for the Rainbow Coalition of Yellowknife, where she currently facilitates a biweekly social group for Two-Spirit and Indigiqueer youth. Coleen hopes to learn her Dene language and the skills to be self-sustainable on the land. Her greatest realizations have been on the Dehcho (Mackenzie River) during the 2018 Dehcho First Nations Yundaa Gogha canoe excursion, and on Horseshoe (Mackenzie) Island with the Dechinta Centre for Research and Learning in October 2020. Coleen has been alcohol-free since June 9, 2019, and is learning more on her healing journey every day. She is an advocate for women, Two-Spirit, Indigiqueer, and LGBTQ+ Indigenous people in ceremony, music, art, harvesting, and leadership. In her spare time, she loves to read, write, craft, chop wood, and pay the land.

Niillas Holmberg is a Sámi poet, novelist, scriptwriter, and musician. He has published one novel and six books of poetry. His works have been translated into more than ten languages. In the field of music he works as a vocalist, composer, and lyricist. Besides working solo he has performed with several bands, currently with Guorga. Niillas is known as an upfront spokesman for Sámi and Indigenous rights to self-determination. He has been involved in several movements against extractivism in Sámi areas. Niillas lives in Ohcejohka, Sámiland.

ᐃᓴᐱ **Elisapie (also known as Elisapie Isaac)** is an impressive musician, filmmaker, and writer from Salluit, Nunavik, Quebec. Based out of Montreal, Quebec, she has been performing as a musician since 2002, first in the band Taima and then as a solo artist. Elisapie's first solo album *There Will Be Stars* (2009) was an ode to the North and lead to a 150-date North American tour. Isaac mixes English, French, and Inuktitut into her work. Recently, Elisapie was a 2019 Polaris Music Prize shortlist artist and Juno nominee for her album *The Ballad of the Runaway Girl* (2019). Along with her band, Taima, Elisapie won the Juno Award for Aboriginal Recording of the Year in 2005. Additionally, Isaac has worked on the soundtracks as a writer, singer, and composer for many films and television shows and was nominated by the Canadian Screen Award for Best Original Song for her song "Far Away" from the film *The Legend of Sarila* (2013) as well as the Eval-Manigat prize from the SPACQ Foundation, in the Multicultural Song category in 2012. Elisapie won the Ambassador Prize at the 2011 Teweikan Awards for her activism, film, and music work throughout Canada. An accomplished filmmaker as well as a musician, Elisapie released her documentary *If the Weather Permits* in 2003 with the support of the National Film Board, which looked at the changes in lifestyle of Inuit in Nunavik, Quebec. *If the Weather Permits* received many awards such as the Claude Jutra Award for Best New Director at the Rendez-vous du Cinéma Québécois and the Rigoberta Menchu Prize at the First People's Festival.

Katłįà (Catherine) Lafferty is a writer and aspiring lawyer specializing in intellectual property with a focus on literary copyright to mitigate ongoing colonial cultural appropriation and Indigenous victimization in storytelling narratives. Her memoir *Northern Wildflower* (Fernwood/ Roseway Publishing) published in 2018 was the top selling book in the Northwest Territories upon release and is used as a teaching tool in both secondary and post-secondary Indigenous studies across Turtle Island. Her recently released novel *Land-Water-Sky/Ndè-Tı-Yat'a* (Fernwood/ Roseway Publishing) was added to the CBC's Fall 2020 Reading List along with being placed on the Scotia Bank Giller Prize Craving Canlit list. Katłįà is a member of the Yellowknives Dene First Nation from Sǫǫ̀mbak'è (Yellowknife), Northwest Territories, to which she previously served as a councillor for her community of Ndı̨lǫ. Having grown up in Sǫǫ̀mbak'è, she currently splits her time between her northern homeland and the traditional territories of the Coast Salish Peoples in Esquimalt, British Columbia, where she is completing her Juris Doctor in Common Law and Indigenous Legal Orders with the University of Victoria.

Kyla LeSage is Vuntut Gwitchin from Old Crow, Yukon, and Anishinaabe from Garden River, Ontario. She grew up on Chief Drygeese Territory in Yellowknife, Northwest Territories. Kyla is a Dechinta Alumni where she received credits toward her UBC Degree in Political Science and Indigenous Studies. She now works full time for Dechinta as the land based academic and regional outreach coordinator.

Tanya Lukin Linklater is an artist and writer. Her recent exhibitions of performances, installations, and works for camera include San Francisco Museum of Modern Art (2020), Chicago Architecture Biennial (2019), Crystal Bridges Museum of American Art (2018), Art Gallery of Ontario (2017), Winnipeg Art Gallery (2017), and elsewhere. Her Alutiiq homelands are in southwestern Alaska where much of her family continues to live. She is a member of the Native Villages of Afognak and Port Lions and has lived and worked in Nbisiing Anishnabek Territory in Northern Ontario for over a decade. *Slow Scrape*, her first book of poetry, was published by The Centre for Expanded Poetics and Anteism in fall 2020. *Slow Scrape* is, in the words of Layli Long Soldier, "an expansive and undulating meditation on time, relations, origin and colonization." Lukin Linklater draws upon documentary poetics, concrete-based installations, event scores, and other texts composed in relation to performances written between 2011 and 2018.

The book cites memory, Cree and Alutiiq languages, and embodiment as modes of relational being and knowledge. The book unfolds a poetics of relation and action to counter the settler colonial violences of erasure, extraction, and dispossession. Lukin Linklater is a doctoral candidate at Queen's University.

Dian Million is Lower Tanana, or Tanana Athabascan from central Alaska. Her Mother was from Nenana, Alaska. She was born in 1950. Her extended family is still located there, and in Oregon where her Dad is from, and now in Washington State where she lives and works. Through the 1970s she worked as a community poet and organizer for United Indian Women, a group affiliated with Women of All Red Nations in Portland, Oregon. She also organized for the Big Mountain Support Group and the Leonard Peltier Defense Group. She went back to school when her kids were grown. She has a PhD from Berkeley in Ethnic Studies and she is currently Chair of American Indian Studies at the University of Washington. Dian is a Mom, a grandmother, and a great-grandmother. She currently lives near Bellingham, Washington.

Tyra Moses is a Dene woman from Pehdzeh Ki and Liidlii Kue. Her Dene ancestral roots place her in the Shehtah mountains and in the Dehcho region of Denendeh. Tyra is the founder and CEO of Dene Media, which is committed to Dene and Indigenous representation in media and education. She is a red seal electrician by trade and a graduate of the Dechinta Centre for Research and Learning Fall 2020 program and is currently an undergrad at the University of Lethbridge pursuing a combined degree in Business Management and Anthropology. Tyra pursues her passions in Dene paradigms and ways of knowing, entrepreneurship, and education in both worlds while passing on all the teachings to her four-year-old daughter.

Antione Mountain is Dene originally from Radelie Koe/Fort Good Hope. He is a painter and a writer. He holds a Bachelor of Fine Arts from OCAD University, as well as a Master of Environmental Studies from York University and he is currently a PhD student at Trent University in Peterborough, Ontario.

Kyle Napier is a Dene/nêhiyaw Métis media-maker and academic from Tthebacha in Tu Nedhé in Denendeh. He is often found at the confluence of the world of digital tools and technologies and language revitalization for both Dene Dedlıne Yatı and sakâw nêhiyawêwin. Kyle has now completed his MA in Communication and Technology at the University of Alberta. He also currently works as an instructor, a researcher, an audiovisual technician, and a consultant around communications and curriculum development. He applies this work and these roles to further the development of Indigenous sovereignty over use and applications of digital tools and technologies by addressing the specific challenges faced by Indigenous communities in Denendeh and beyond. His goal is to support skill and capacity development for Indigenous media-makers through conscious application, cautious optimism, and a critical Indigenous framework for decolonizing digital and non-digital media. Kyle has presented to numerous regional and global conferences addressing Indigenous and marginalized language revitalization, reclamation, and acquisition; decolonial processes in digital media-making; and intellectual property and story sovereignty among and from Indigenous communities and content creators.

Juniper Redvers is a member of the Deninu K'ue First Nation, an academic, auntie, counsellor, and land-based leader. With Dene and Métis roots on her maternal side and English, Italian, and Irish roots on her paternal side, she was born and raised in Treaty 8 Territory, Northwest Territories. After wandering many natural spaces around the world, she now lives on Kwanlin Dün First Nation and Ta'an Kwäch'än Territory in the Yukon, where she works as a counsellor supporting mental wellness in children, youth, and families. She also supports curriculum development, training and research for mental health, trauma-informed practice, and land-based healing throughout Turtle Island. She can often be found wandering the forests, valleys, or hills in search of deeper connection and grounding.

T'áncháy Redvers (she/they) is a Dene/Métis, Two-Spirit social justice warrior, writer, creator, performer, and facilitator from Treaty 8 Territory, Northwest Territories. With a BA Honours in International Development, Certificate in Civic Engagement & Global Citizenship, and a Master of Indigenous Social Work, she has been nationally and internationally recognized for her work and advocacy. In 2016, T'áncháy and her brother founded We Matter, a national campaign and organization dedicated to Indigenous youth hope and life promotion. Her debut collection of poetry, *Fireweed*, was published in 2019 with Kegedonce Press. With a passion for exploring and unpacking topics such as intergenerational trauma, philanthropy, gender and sexuality, youth and queer empowerment, and positive representation, her approach is one that aims to decolonize and Indigenize identity, mental health, and healing. She has spent considerable time living, travelling, speaking, and working with Indigenous communities internationally and across Canada, and considers herself a nomad just like her ancestors.

Megan Samms is the L'nu and Nlaka'pamux daughter of Renee Samms and Gerry Samms. She is a weaver, natural dyer, bee-keeper and farmer in her home territory in Ktaqmkuk. She has had her writing published in various small scale publications. In Katalisk, Ktaqmkuk/ Codroy Valley, Newfoundland she makes makes cloth, grows food, makes medicines and is deeply involved in community work focused on food sovereignty, community building and craftwork with desires to decolonize rural food systems, care and craft. Megan was part of the Dechinta student cohort in 2018.

Sı̨ **Jessica Sangris** sìyeh, T'èʔehdaà gots'ǫ aht'e. Semǫ Alice Liske wìyeh, Setà Allen DeLeary wìyeh. My Mother is a Yellowknives Dene First Nation member from T'èʔehdaà and my Father is from Bkejwanong First Nation. My parents met in Ottawa, where both my sister and I were born and raised. I moved to Yellowknife in 2009. Once I moved to Yellowknife, I began learning about my Dene traditions and culture. Over the last five years, I have taken a lot of steps to be more involved in the Dene way of life and learning the Wıìlıìdeh language. I am currently serving as a Yellowknives Dene First Nation councillor representing T'èʔehdaà and I also have a spot on the Dettah District Education Authority. My family currently lives in T'èʔehdaà, my husband works as a cultural resource worker in TéʔehdaÀ, Ndı̨lǫ, and Yellowknife and our three older children go to school at the community school—Kaw Tay Whee K'àtehwhìì and my youngest son stay home with me. Our family tries to get out on the land as much as we can, and we try to pass down as much of our traditional knowledge to our children as we go.

Leanne Betasamosake Simpson is a Michi Saagiig Nishnaabeg scholar, writer, musician, and member of Alderville First Nation. She is the author of seven previous books, including *A Short History of the Blockade*, and the novel *Noopiming: A Cure for White Ladies* which was released in the United States in 2021 by the University of Minnesota Press. Leanne has released four albums including *f(l)ight* and *Noopiming Sessions*, and the Polaris short-listed *Theory of Ice*. Her latest book is co-authored with Robyn Maynard and entitled *Rehearsals for Living*. Leanne is a board member and a Faculty member at the Dechinta Centre for Research and Learning. She served as a mentor and editor on this project.

Mary Rose (Maro) Sundberg is the great-granddaughter of Chief Jean Baptiste Madzii Drygeese, Chief Drygeese, who signed the treaty of 1921 (Treaty 8). Her parents moved to Yellowknife in order for her father to work with DPW and helped build St. Patrick School. She has dedicated her life to the transmission of her language and traditions to other generations. Maro is the executive director of the Goyatıkǫ̀ Language Society in T'èʔehdaà (Dettah). An interpreter/translator since 1982, a community leader, and instructor at Dechinta, Maro teaches language and history to various organizations and schools.

Kristen Tanche is Łıı́dlı̜ Kų́ę́ First Nation, Dehcho Dene from Łıı́dlı̜ Kų́ę́/Fort Simpson, Northwest Territories. She was raised in Southern Canada and the Northwest Territories. As a young adult, she returned to her Mother's home community of Łıı́dlı̜ Kų́ę́/Fort Simpson, Northwest Territories, to re-connect with her family, community, and Dene culture. Kristen is an alumni of Dechinta, the Aurora College Social Work Program, and the Jane Glassco Northern fellowship. Kristen currently works in health and wellness for her regional Indigenous Government Organization, Dehcho First Nations. Kristen is passionate about the North's well-being and people in her community and region.

Jennie Vandermeer is Sahtúgot'ı̨nę and grew up in Délı̨nę, Northwest Territories, Canada. She currently resides in Norman Wells, Northwest Territories, and works in Indigenous health and research. A recovering alcoholic and survivor of domestic violence, she credits her recovery to having a strong tie to her Dene culture and people. She believes that although many Indigenous Peoples are challenged by intergenerational trauma and addictions, we are incredibly strong and resilient. She spends her time creating and leading wellness and leadership projects that benefit Indigenous Peoples. Jennie does presentations and workshops throughout the Northwest Territories on nutrition, exercise, yoga, mental health, addictions, intergenerational trauma, domestic violence, and most importantly, resiliency.

Jasmine Vogt is Tetlit Gwich'in and Sahtú Dene from Tetlit Zheh (Fort McPherson). She was raised in Somba' Ke on Chief Drygeese Territory. Jasmine has completed two semesters with Dechinta on Indigenous Self-Determination with the University of Alberta and Community and Land-Based Research with the University of British Columbia. Since Dechinta, she has been studying and working toward her bachelor's degree in Indigenous Studies with the University of Alberta while also working full time with Environment and Natural Resources. Jasmine loves to bead and sew, travel, and spend time on the land with her son, Kurtis. As a young Indigenous woman and Mother, Jasmine has faced many obstacles and continues to overcome hardships by connecting to culture and having a strong relationship with the land. She continues to persevere with resilience and hopes to one day use her hardships as a way to help and give back to the community in a traditional, cultural, and healthy way.